THE END OF AN EARRING

headline

First published in 2015 by
HEADLINE PUBLISHING GROUP

First published in paperback in 2016 by
HEADLINE PUBLISHING GROUP

1

Cataloguing in Publication Data is available from the British Library

ISBN 978 1 4722 2215 2

Typeset in Baskerville by Avon DataSet Ltd, Bidford-on-Avon, Warwickshire

Printed and bound in the UK by Clays Ltd, St Ives plc

Headline's policy is to use papers that are natural, renewable and recyclable products and made from wood grown in well-managed forests and other controlled sources. The logging and manufacturing processes are expected to conform to the environmental regulations of the country of origin.

HEADLINE PUBLISHING GROUP
An Hachette UK Company
Carmelite House
50 Victoria Embankment
London EC4Y 0DZ

www.headline.co.uk
www.hachette.co.uk

To Lif

Without whose collaboration and bullying this book
would never have seen the light of day!

A Note from the Author

Readers will notice that occasionally I have included a photograph of those people who were so important in my early life, and the early life of my 'aunt' Sylvia, within the text of the book. This is because when I read a memoir I like to put an image to the name as soon as I encounter that person in the story. I hope that you will feel the same way.

Contents

'In Defence of Actors'

This extract from an essay by William Hazlitt was written in 1817. It is as relevant today, nearly two centuries later, as it was then.

Actors have been accused, as a profession, of being extravagant and dissipated. While they are said to be so as a piece of common cant, they are likely to continue so . . . With respect to the extravagance of actors, as a traditional character, it is not to be wondered at. They live from hand to mouth: they plunge from want into luxury; they have no means of making money breed, and all professions that do not live by turning money into money, or have not a certainty of accumulating it in the end by parsimony, spend it. Uncertain of the future, they make sure of the present moment. This is not unwise. Chilled with poverty, steeped in contempt, they sometimes pass into the sunshine of fortune, and are lifted to the very pinnacle of public favour; yet even there cannot calculate on the continuance of success . . . With respect to the habit of convivial indulgence, an actor, to be a good one, must have a great spirit of enjoyment in himself – strong impulses, strong passions, and a strong sense of pleasure: for it is his business to imitate the passions, to communicate pleasure to others. A man of genius is not a machine. The neglected actor may be excused if he drinks oblivion of his disappointments; the successful one if he quaffs the applause of the world . . . in draughts of nectar. There is no path so steep as that of fame: no labour so hard as the pursuit of excellence. If there is any tendency to dissipation beyond this in the profession of the player, it is owing to the prejudices entertained against them . . . Players are only not so respectable as a profession as they might be, because their profession is not respected as it ought to be.

We Have Our Entrances and Our Exits

All changes, even the most longed for, have their melancholy; for what we leave behind us is a part of ourselves; we must die to one life before we can enter another.

Anatole France

I died on New Year's Day 2012. Over ten and a half million people witnessed my passing.

It feels like a brief moment, certainly not twenty-five-and-a-half years, since a brash, brazen bleached-blonde sashays into Walford; a touch of colour in The Square; her air of confidence belying the chaos of her own life. The only control she seems capable of harnessing is her appearance. She wears sexy slingbacks, bright blue eyeshadow, her lips are neon pink, her earrings outrageous. That look is her mask. She's a force to be reckoned with. She's in Walford to cause trouble and she'll take no prisoners.

The viewers were saying goodbye to Pat and so was I. It was a momentous time for me. I had created Pat and played her in *EastEnders* for over a quarter of a century. I had lived with her, laughed with her, suffered with her and, although there was still life in the old girl, I felt the time had come to hang up her earrings for a while and take a break from The Square. I wanted to recapture a freedom I had lost. The routine of an ongoing series is unremitting, relentless. I think, somewhere along the way, I had lost sight of me. I was giving out, but never recharging my own batteries.

Initially, I took Bryan Kirkwood, then executive producer, out for dinner to Colette's at the Grove Hotel in Hertfordshire. During the course of our meal I found what seemed to be an appropriate moment to broach the subject about my leaving. He appeared shocked by this and suggested that I had a sabbatical of three months, a year, or a time frame I could suggest. At that stage, I didn't feel able to make a hard and fast commitment to a return date. After all, several of the regular cast had 'left' in the past: June Brown, Patsy Palmer, Sid Owen, Barbara Windsor and Mike Reid. During Mike's absences from *'Enders* people were always coming up to me and saying, 'Where's Frank? When is he coming back?' There is always a sense of a well-established character's presence, even when they are not on screen, and their return is awaited with great anticipation.

2

One crucial thing I asked for was that Pat shouldn't be killed off. I felt that with her connection to so many characters in The Square, her presence in the wings and the possibility of her return would be useful to the ongoing story. Also there was a danger that losing a matriarchal figure with this much history would leave a void in the structure of the community. This is not something that can be created overnight by bringing in another character's 'aunt' to plug the gap. I felt, and still do, that the show is very dependent on its history and the mix of different generations. Bryan's response was unequivocal. He assured me that Pat wouldn't be axed but, in fairness to him, I gave no commitment about a return at that stage.

Not long after that, John Yorke, then BBC head of series, took me out for dinner at the Ivy. As ever, he was most warm and respectful towards my character and me. Once again I requested that Pat should not be killed off and was reassured by John's response. But things change. Some months later I was called to see Brian Kirkwood, who said they had a story about Pat's death that they would like to run for my exit. As far as I was concerned it seemed a fait accompli rather than a choice, given that I had already asked that Pat shouldn't end up as 'brown bread'. So, I suppose, I demurred rather than contested it; I always try to be dignified in the face of adversity. I went away feeling empty and bewildered about why the goalposts had moved. But we all know that a story-line is a collaboration of many people, and with hindsight I can understand. Fate deals the hand; how you cope with it is the vital part. Upon reflection, from an actor's point of view, it gave me a cracking storyline and a memorable exit. I embraced the script totally.

Strangely, bringing the curtain down on the life I was playing on screen as Pat has enabled me to know who I am again. It is not just the day-to-day freedoms that I have recaptured, but those interests which nourish the spirit. It has allowed me to reflect on my life; a life which has been fulfilling despite its adverse beginnings. If my story gives hope to those who feel that their beginnings cannot be overcome, good. If it entertains, good.

To quote Robert Graves, 'Let me tell you the story of how I began.'

Aged eight months.

Chapter One

Pass the Parcel

There is a day of sunny rest
For every dark and troubled night:
And grief may hide an evening guest
But joy shall come with early light.

W. C. Bryant, 'Blessed Are They That Mourn'

'Monday's child is fair of face'. I am not sure about that, but the one thing I am sure of is that I was born on Monday 11 May 1942 at The Pines Nursing Home in Middlesex, around eight in the evening. My father always said that I was a 'lady', because I arrived just in time for dinner. My birth certificate states that my name is Pamela Ann Clements, my father was Reginald Arthur Clements, a company director (whatever that is supposed to mean), and my mother was named Irene Ann Clements (née Tribe). Some details of my early life, as well as those of my father, come from what little he told me himself. A larger part of it, however, comes from people closely involved with him.

My maternal grandparents' family was called Moore and came from Ireland; they proved to be upwardly mobile tinkers, graduating from a caravan to a shop where pheasants and hares hung for the delectation of the gentry. They were successful traders. My mother also decided to be upwardly mobile. Spurning the butchery trade, she took a secretarial course to improve her chances of employment. In the early 1940s, she not only worked as a secretary for my father who, by this time, was

My father.

a successful businessman with offices in Mayfair, she married him as well. For some reason he had been exempted from military service during the Second World War. I was led to believe that it was not on health or age grounds, but to do with what he was manufacturing for the war effort. Apparently, he had fancied my mother like crazy, adored her; she took his breath away and he wooed her relentlessly, as with all his women. But, with him, it was all physical and my mother needed more. She needed him to love her, to show his feelings for her rather than being an object of his lust and desire. Perhaps this desire for my mother made him feel guilty and so a part of him didn't quite like her for the way she made him feel. Despite this, he was gutted when she became ill and died, but although he was bereft, his eyes had already strayed elsewhere. In other words she was replaceable, as all the women in his life had been and would continue to be. My mother was aware of this in the latter stages of her illness, and I often wonder if she gave in to the inevitability of death more easily because of it.

I close my eyes and try to visualise my mother, but I can't. I have no memory of her at all. She died when I was very young, about eighteen months old, leaving me with her green Irish eyes and a faded photograph of herself. A brunette, happy and carefree, looked out at me. Little did she know when that photograph was taken then that she would die of tuberculosis before she was thirty. It was the early days of streptomycin and, had we not been at war, there might have been sufficient medication to cure her. Once that picture was given to me it was my most treasured possession, and stayed with me through thick and thin, until it was destroyed in a flood when I was in my twenties. So my mother, like the photograph, gradually faded from my life. Possibly, this would not have happened had I been brought up by my maternal grandparents as planned.

My father found it difficult to cope with me after my mother's death. He was often away on business and always distracted by a variety of women. The drinking, dining and expensive nightclub culture that arose from financial success became the breath of life to him – done, as with most things my father did, to excess. In order to have the freedom to follow this lifestyle, the obvious solution was to make an agreement with my maternal grandparents for me to be brought up by them. I have no memory of what was to be a very brief spell with them because, the moment it suited him, he took me back to live with him and his current amour. Ostensibly kidnapping me, on the basis that the environment my grandparents were providing was not suitable for his young lady. Despite being reasonably well-off, they would not have given me the sort of upbringing and education my father had in mind for me. Their aspirations were less sophisticated than my father's. It seems strange he had not considered that before conveniently off-loading me in the first place. My grandparents were devastated. After all, I was the only living memory of their daughter after she died.

Some years were to pass before my maternal grandmother saw me again, my grandfather having died in the intervening period. I was about eleven or twelve when I met up with her; she was by then a widow in poor health. Our reunion came about because I was often looked after by friends of my father, 'Uncle' Rudi, an Austrian dental surgeon, and his wife Connie. One day while I was with them I was introduced to a man called Ted who, apparently, had known my mother. On reflection, I wonder if he may even have been related to her. He told me that my grandmother was still alive, living in south-east London, and that she would like to see me. With that, he scrawled her address on a torn-off piece of bright yellow 'Sweet Afton' cigarette packet, so that I could write to her. Perhaps it was no coincidence that these cigarettes were Irish and made by P. J. Carroll and Co. in Dundalk.

With 'Uncle' Rudi.

The knowledge that my grandmother was still alive and wanted to see me created a huge emotional turmoil within me. It was obvious that I couldn't discuss this with my father because he had shared almost nothing of my mother's past with me, but I knew I needed to have contact with someone who could tell me who my mother was and what she was like.

Even at ten, I knew I needed some sort of resolution, but another year was to pass before I met her. We communicated by post in the meantime but I learnt little more about my mother from her letters. What eventually caused me to hasten to see my grandmother was a letter she sent to me at my boarding school, just before the end of term, in which she told me she was very ill. I was staying in London with my father and the woman who'd become my stepmother for the first few days of the holiday.

Seizing my opportunity on a day when they were out, I decided to visit her. The journey was a daunting experience for a youngster. On a winter's afternoon I set out, taking three different buses to reach her part of London. It was dark by the time I arrived and I still had to find where she lived.

I wish I could say that this one and only meeting had been a pleasant one. I found an elderly and frail woman eaten up by vitriol and vindictiveness, which should have been directed at my father, not at me. It was an extremely upsetting experience and a lost opportunity to find out more about my mother and her family. The one redeeming feature of the visit was that she gave me that photograph of my mother. I left clutching the precious photo as if it were the Crown Jewels, but feeling emotionally battered. I never heard from her again. I have often thought of this meeting and wonder if she saw me as my father's daughter and not her daughter's daughter.

It was my father who had originally created the breach all those years before, so you would think that snatching me away from my grandparents, without giving them any say in the matter, would mean he intended to keep his beloved daughter close to him from then on. You would be wrong. I was once again to be foisted on to someone else. This was to be a pattern that would recur throughout my childhood. So who was my father and what happened in his life that made him behave as he did?

Reginald Arthur Clements was the son of a railway worker for one of the major railway companies. The family lived in a tied cottage close to the Stratford marshalling yards in the East End of London. His father died, while still employed by the railway, in circumstances unknown to me. The impact of his death upon his wife and children was like something out of Dickens. It was cataclysmic. It meant eviction without notice. My bereaved paternal grandmother appealed to the rail authorities to be allowed to remain in the house on the strength of my grandfather's loyal service. She was told that they needed to replace her husband as soon as they could and, because the cottage went with the job, it had to be vacated without further ado. Desperate, and decades before women's lib, my grandmother suggested that she took over her husband's duties. With an eye to business the Railways Board, probably due to the loss of a generation of men in the First World War, agreed to this extraordinary proposal. She was given the job, but with a fraction of her husband's wages.

The devastating consequences of this menial salary did not escape her: she could not earn enough to support all five of her children. There were few choices in those days; one of the children would have to go, and that one was my father. The need to give away one of her children broke her heart and the job broke her physically. She didn't make old bones. Getting up before dawn, day after day, donning a pair of her husband's dungarees, she wielded the heavy jack-hammer necessary for repairing and realigning track. She used all her strength to maintain and manually change points; hard, heavy and thankless work that helped to keep the wheels of commerce turning. Comfortable society, going glibly on its way, was not aware,

13

and maybe never is, of the invisible hard toil that goes on 'below stairs' to maintain their lifestyle.

My father, still a young child, was sent to an orphanage in Suffolk, leaving behind the security of family life and a close East End community for ever. One can only imagine the sense of loss and abandonment he suffered, and I am sure this dislocation affected him for the rest of his life. It was almost as though his constant pursuit of women was a quest to find the mother he had lost. Whatever the reason, he was incapable of engaging emotionally with anyone; this probably helped him to cope with the continuing chaos of his life, preventing him from being hurt further. Certainly he was incapable of making and sustaining long-lasting relationships, particularly with women. I'm not even sure he really liked women; he could lust after them and woo them but he was incapable of the kind of deep love which binds people together for ever. To my surprise, I found out later that my mother wasn't his first wife; there had been one before her. Whether this lack of constancy was rooted in his abandonment by his mother, the first woman in his life, one will never know, but it would make sense. In other words, he was never going to be beholden to another woman; the control was always going to be his.

Women adored my father. He promised them the earth because, at that time, he was a successful and wealthy business-man, thanks to the start given him by the orphanage. It appears that, by cauterising his emotions, he had the ability to accept the status quo and make the most of the opportunities that arose in the institution, without being stultified by resentment. As a result, he left with training in basic accountancy and office skills. Maybe a deep fear of the poverty that my father had experienced as a child, and an overwhelming desire to be in control of his own choices in life, were the two factors that made him the driven man he became. His drive was not just for the satisfaction of the work itself, but for the rewards that money could buy; the fruits that he could consume.

Father was a Freemason, a sign of his success and business status. Another one of the badges of his success was to have a beautiful woman on his arm. This was not difficult. He was a snappy dresser and a charmer – a combination of Anthony Eden and Errol Flynn – but it was all superficial. Throughout my childhood I watched a series of wives come and go, all of whom were dressed to kill. They wore furs, high-heeled shoes, had bright red lipstick and long red manicured nails. They arrived like bombshells, smelling of expensive perfume and radiating a *joie de vivre* that goes with the expectation of a lifestyle that would last for ever. Every night my father and his current woman went out; dining at the Savoy, or dancing and clubbing at many well-known nightclubs. Their lives had a brittle gaiety that snapped all too easily when adversity took hold.

My stepmothers stayed for varying lengths of time but eventually, with all glamour and expectation gone, they left tired, lonely and disillusioned. All the confidence and hope with which they arrived had been destroyed by their abusive husband, my father. He was a drinker, and drink made him vicious. He became verbally abusive and physically violent. Strangely, my father never hit me, nor was he unkind to me, and for that I shall always be grateful. In fact he was always considering my welfare, but he had no parental role model and his lifestyle didn't embrace being a parent.

Having been snatched away from my maternal grandparents, the clearest memory I have is of entering an enormous apartment in Regent's Park and being told to remove my shoes before entering the drawing room. It was the size of a ballroom, or so it seemed to a little girl. It was magnificent. What little I could see of the floor was highly polished wood, but it was almost completely covered in rugs with a pile so dense that my toes disappeared from sight. Dazzling chandeliers hung from the ceiling, and the draught from the open door had set the crystal drops tinkling, throwing prisms of light across the walls, as though a hundred Tinkerbells were dancing there. It was like fairyland – I'd never seen anything like it. I was so entranced that I hadn't noticed a blonde and very beautiful woman, dressed to the nines, moving towards me in a miasma of expensive fragrance; it could only be my Fairy Godmother.

As in so many fairy stories my fairy godmother was, in reality, my stepmother – though not a wicked one. Mary was my father's third wife. Looked after by a nanny, I didn't share their lives at all, neither eating with them nor having outings of any sort. I became a dark silent observer sharing only Mary's perfume, mingling with the smell of my father's Cuban cigars, which pervaded the atmosphere. Everything they did spelled money. I would watch my father putting pearl studs into his

My father with his third wife, Mary.

dress shirt and Mary tying his bow tie. She would dress her long blonde hair in 'victory rolls', slip on a Schiaparelli creation, put on her diamond and emerald jewellery and finally clip together the two snarling fox heads that made up her stole – the stuff of nightmares for a child. Then they were gone, leaving Nanny and me behind in the cavernous apartment while they danced the night away, their presence lingering only in the smoke-scented haze. All too soon it became apparent that I was an inconvenience, because it was not long before I was once more off-loaded. I was three years old.

My father asked his closest friend, Tom, if he and his wife Violet would consider bringing me up with their own family.

Tom, who managed a bookstall at the Dorchester Hotel in London, agreed to this bizarre request. It was thus that my next move was to Station Approach in Sudbury, Middlesex, to be brought up with their children: Jean, who was my age, and her younger brother Michael. I remember very little about my time with this family, but do know it was a time of security and comradeship, having other children to play with. Many years later, after I appeared on *This Is Your Life*, I received a letter from Jean, which she'd sent to the BBC. She had been watching the last five minutes of the programme and wanted to know if I was the child who had lived with her family all those years ago. She told me I was brought up as part of the family and that I was with them for about two years.

Apparently my father and Mary visited every Saturday. I don't remember that, but I do remember the day my father came to reclaim me. It was 1947 and, once again, my father was taking me away with no warning. Whilst he was trying to hurry me out of the house, I remembered that I had left my teddy bear, Snuggles, in the bedroom. Wrenching myself from his grip, I rushed up the stairs to get my bear, the one constant thing in my life. Snuggles had seen it all, he had shared my travels. His frayed paws and threadbare chest were testament to the love I bestowed upon him. For some reason, which I don't fully understand, the family was told not to contact me again. I got the impression from Jean that my father wanted something more for me. His lack of finesse or gratitude towards the family, who were kind enough to take me in, was astounding.

With Michael and Jean.

I was taken back to my father's home to find Jackie, stepmother number two. My father's story was that Mary had gone off with another man who could afford to lavish her with larger diamonds than he could. Perhaps inventing this excuse was easier than addressing his own shortcomings. I remember Mary as a gentle, glamorous but distant figure. Extraordinarily, I met her again after many years, but this time as an adult. She had realised that I was her stepdaughter, Pamela, when she saw me in various programmes on television. During my early years in *EastEnders*, there was an advertisement in her local paper saying that I would be making a personal appearance one Saturday, close to where she lived. On that day I was being escorted by a bouncer when a woman approached, somewhat hesitantly. She came closer and asked to speak to me privately. The burly escort said, 'She'll be signing autographs in a minute,' and brushed her away as she blurted out, 'I'm her mother.' Now, to overhear that in a public place means either you have been unfortunate enough to encounter a complete loony, or it is something that has to be taken seriously. She looked harmless and I am incurably curious so, with instinct overriding any hesitation, I asked the escort to step aside whilst I spoke to her. After all those years, I hadn't the slightest recognition of the smartly dressed, neatly coiffured woman in her seventies standing in front of me. 'I saw it advertised that you would be here and had to see my Pamela again,' she said as she held out two black-and-white photographs. One was of me as a baby and the other a photo of her and Reggie. We talked and arranged to meet.

I went to visit her and her beloved cat several times before her death. She enquired after my father, her generosity of spirit showing in that she never made any derogatory comment about him. When I asked her if she wanted me to tell him I had seen her, she said, 'Given the passage of time, what is the point?' Both the responsibility of the secret, and being confronted with that forgotten history, unsettled me initially but, with my usual ability for emotional recovery, this was relatively short-lived.

Mary's replacement, Jackie, was a raven-haired Jewess who, on reflection, looked very much like Maria Callas. She brought with her an extremely domineering mother, a ghastly woman who soon became the bane of my father's life. Her father was also in tow. He hardly said a word, but had adopted diplomatic hearing . . . deaf to everything his wife said. To say that tensions were high would be an understatement.

Once again I was incarcerated, temporarily, in the vast apartment, but this time with the addition of a governess. She didn't last long, nor did the next two governesses. I can't blame this entirely on my father's new wife and in-laws because, by this time, I was becoming disturbed and unruly, presumably due to the lack of stability in my life.

The tension in the house was not helped when I nearly killed the final governess, a Brunhilde-like German. Maybe I thought I was fighting the Second World War single-handedly. I opened the schoolroom door a fraction and put a plank above it piled with textbooks, so that the whole lot would come crashing down when she came in to give me a lesson. However, with a typical child's thoughtlessness, I had not considered the consequences of my actions. The poor woman was slightly injured and badly shocked and, as a result, left. She did not deserve it; she had never done anything to hurt me. I should have been thrashed within an inch of my life.

No more governesses for me. I was immediately sent off to a private preparatory school which kept me out of the apartment during the day. I don't remember being very happy there but, as with all things in my life, this arrangement only lasted for a short time. It was not long before I was shipped off to a boarding preparatory school called the Red House in Worthing, the junior school of the Warren where I was to go later.

The Red House was to be my home during term, and at other times I would live in a holiday home, of which there were many during that period. My father decided on Foxmead in Little Bookham, run by two elderly sisters, the Misses Eleanor and

Dora Joce. Life in these two structured establishments suited me. I was having fun being with children of my own age, whom the sisters also had under their wing. It was a place where accepted boundaries did not change, providing a stability which my parental home would never have been able to give me. I loved it and never looked back. It was in this childhood idyll of freedom and blue summer skies that we played pirates under tall elms. In solemn ceremonies we buried the shrews that the cat killed. We paraded in cloaks and pantaloons, sported swords and crowns. We were queens and pirates, knights and damsels in distress. It was forever summer.

Back home, if one can call it that, Jackie, with her parents in tow, and probably with their encouragement, departed for good. The divorce proceedings took place while I was away, both at school and at Foxmead, and they were messy.

During the time of the divorce, and the subsequent court case brought against my father, I hardly ever saw him. I know there was a jury, so one can only assume that Jackie had charged him with assault. He told me many years later that he thought the only reason he didn't go to prison was because there was a woman on the jury who fancied him – ever the optimist as far as women were concerned! How ironic, because by this time the case had reduced my father to a haggard and unshaven shadow of the man he once was, and he was drinking even more heavily. Having always been immaculately dressed in tailored Savile Row suits, the trousers of which were held up with smart braces of varying colours, he now wore a shabby jacket, and trousers held up with a belt. It was the belt that held such poignancy for me, there was something so pathetic about it. What a curious observation for one so young.

As time went on, I settled happily into my Red House and Foxmead routine, only to have my life disrupted yet again. I must have been about nine years old. My father telephoned Miss Eleanor to notify her that he wished to take me out that weekend. Little did I know that it wasn't to see me but to introduce me on neutral territory to his new woman, shortly to be his fifth wife and my third stepmother. He drove down from London with Sally in his Frazer Nash, a magnificent chestnut-coloured car in which a dicky seat had been created in the boot. These were often referred to as 'mother-in-law' seats. Such a pity he didn't have that car when Jackie's mother was around – she'd have been well out of earshot. How I longed to ride in that seat, but I suspect safety precluded it, because I was never allowed to.

We all went out to Polesden Lacey, a National Trust Edwardian house with a broad expanse of parkland and gardens. Without realising it, I was being checked out as a potential daughter, a pawn in this new relationship. Sally had never been able to have children of her own; Chico, her beloved chihuahua, was her child-substitute.

My father, with an eye to the main chance as always, saw himself and his daughter as the ideal package. For Sally, the idea of a ready-made daughter was a wish come true. With so much hope in her heart and so much love to give, she must have

My father's fifth wife, Sally.

been devastated by my lack of response. She had brought gifts and pretty dresses for me. I may have been thrilled but I doubt I was very gracious. After all, I was an old hand at this game; I wasn't going to make it easy for her. Children have instincts and I suspect I knew, deep down, that she was to be the next stepmother. This situation was made worse by the fact that I trod on Chico's tail, which forever after had a kink in it. This was certainly not deliberate, I loved animals. It was more a manifestation of my awkwardness and the fact that Chico was so small you could hardly see him. Added to which he was not at home at floor level, living almost permanently in Sally's arms; he was only put on the ground when he needed to relieve himself. Maybe that's why he didn't see me coming and get out of the way.

My father moved almost exclusively in Jewish circles, probably for business reasons, which led to socialising in that milieu. So it was not surprising that Sally, like Jackie, was also Jewish. She was a brunette, chic and rather Continental-looking. Her forebears had come from Holland originally and most of her family were in the rag trade. I remember her sister Tilly and husband Nat particularly well; we would often celebrate the start of *Shabbat* with them. If anyone mentioned the word Gentile, Sally would softly point out that she was married to one, although no one really believed my father was not Jewish, because he lapsed so easily into Yiddish. Maybe as an outsider, and one with little acquired identity of self, he felt comfortable with a group of non-judgemental people whose history had been as rootless as his own. I had a sneaking admiration for Sally's brother Jack, who I understood was the black sheep of the family. He didn't conform to a well-heeled, hard-working Jewish business family's idea of a man. Firstly, he wasn't married, and there was a dark cloud over his sexuality. What with that, and the odd incarceration at His Majesty's pleasure, it is hardly surprising that he wasn't embraced by his conventional family. When I was older, I was aware that he contacted Sally when he was in trouble, rather than his other sisters Tilly and Gracie. I'm sure it was a streak of idealism as much as rebellion that led him to be involved in the Battle of Cable Street. This occurred in October 1936, in an area of East London with a large Jewish population. It was a confrontation between the Metropolitan Police, who were supposed to be overseeing a march by Mosley's Blackshirts, and a disparate group of anti-fascists. I only met Jack a couple of times, but took a shine to him – he was a bit of a renegade. Maybe he got this daredevil streak from his mother, because I remember Sally telling me that their mum cooked bacon on a Sunday morning in their East End home. Local children would run over to ask her what the wonderful smell of cooking was, to which she replied, 'Delicious smoked beef!'

It soon became clear that the plan was for me to live *en famille* with my father and Sally at her small apartment. My father's circumstances had been somewhat reduced by the court case, so he could no longer keep his large glamorous apartment in Regent's Park, let alone shower Sally with as much munificence as he had showered upon his previous amours. Sally's flat would have fitted into the living room of his erstwhile apartment. At any rate, the initial idea was that I would live with them. Her dining room (part of the hallway) was to be my bedroom with a put-you-up bed, and I was to be sent to the nearest private day school which, ironically, was High Anglican. Sending me there was extraordinary, because we lived in a block of Jewish-owned flats, every flat having a *mezuzah*, a sign of faith, on its front doorpost. Leading up to the start of *Shabbat* every Friday night, the whole building was redolent with the smell of fried or *gefilte* fish, chicken soup and warming *challah* bread. My somewhat varied life has certainly left me with an interest in comparative religion.

It quickly became clear that this arrangement was not going to work 365 days a year. It was bad enough for me after twenty-four hours, an active child cooped up in a very restricted environment and longing to escape, to go back to boarding school, my friends and fun. I think they realised pretty quickly that it wasn't working for them either. The situation worsened when I contracted measles. It must have been as awful for them as it was for me. Having a very sick contagious child, confined and nursed in the dining room by a couple who were not endowed with either parental instincts or experience, pointed up the futility of the plan. This misguided concept of a happy family life came to a head a little later when I saw my father, in a state of aggressive drunkenness, hit my stepmother, knocking her to the ground. Then, taking a lighted cigarette, he burnt her arm with it several times. I remember throwing myself at him, to prevent him from hurting Sally any further, but he knocked me away. I ran to their bedroom to get the heavy silver-backed hairbrush that sat on their dressing table and hit him with it. That had about as much effect on him as swatting a fly, but the effect on me was that I lost the last vestiges of respect I ever had for him, if any.

I was completely unable to cope with this adult situation, one that was way beyond my comprehension and experience. For a child who had been let down almost constantly by adults, I did a rather strange thing: I turned to an adult for help. I went downstairs to the hall porter who allowed me to telephone Uncle Rudi. I was hoping he would come over and make everything right. Instead, he asked the hall porter to write down his address and to get me a taxi over to his house, which he would pay for when I arrived. Looking back, I remember the apprehension I felt. I was a child, it was night-time, I had been very frightened and, although I wanted to escape from the situation, the last thing I felt like doing was getting into a taxi with a stranger and driving to north London. I think the porter must have realised this because he settled me into the taxi. I wasn't old enough, at that time, to understand grown-ups' rules. Consequently I didn't anticipate that Uncle Rudi would tell my father where I was. I felt completely betrayed by this because I had seen him as an ally. Now, as an adult, I appreciate that he behaved in a completely responsible way. When my father came to collect me the next morning I was bewildered, resentful and ill at ease.

It won't surprise you to know that not long after, my father went back to his original plan of sending me to boarding school again, and to a holiday home during the school vacation. I was too old to go back to Foxmead, so he decided to farm me out to another holiday home – and little was I to know the consequences of that for me.

My first real home.

Chapter Two

Red Earth, Red Apples and Red Cows

The rosy-fingered Morn appears
And from her mantle shakes her tears
In promise of a glorious day.

John Dryden, *Albion and Albanius*

That enduring periodical, *The Lady*, was Reggie's first port of call. From my perspective now, it seems a highly unlikely source for my father to turn to, but I imagine the suggestion came from Sally. My father eventually found an advertisement from a Miss Chaffey, who took in paying guests at her house in Devonshire. After a long telephone conversation, it transpired that she had neither the room nor the facility to take on a child under teenage years. However, she had some friends who not only took in paying guests, but welcomed youngsters. They had a farm on Dartmoor.

It is not often in life that circumstances lead one down a path that opens up into a place where one's soul is fed and feels at home; a place of heart's-ease. This serendipitous move was such for me.

I was just eleven when my father escorted me through the austere nineteenth-century portals of Paddington Station, the home of the Great Western Railway. The noise of clanking engines and the smell of the smoke billowing from the steam engines were almost overpowering. There was frenzied activity everywhere. Porters, in uniforms and caps, trundled trolleys bearing heavy monogrammed leather suitcases. Trains moved off when guards waved flags and blew whistles. In hindsight it must have seemed like Dante's *Inferno* to a child embarking, once again, on a journey into the unknown.

My father and I followed a porter down the platform until we located the appropriate carriage in which he had reserved a window seat for me, close to the guard's van. Minors in those days travelled under the protection of the guard. No Criminal Records Bureau checks then. We were brought up to believe that adults, known and unknown, were trustworthy and to be turned to if we were in trouble, just as I'd appealed to Uncle Rudi. Having made sure that my suitcase was firmly stowed in the netted rack above the seats, and the guard made aware of my existence, my father said, 'See you at the end of the holidays,' and made a hasty exit. I was alone and starting a journey that could have lasted two hours or six hours. No one had thought to give me any details. All I had was a small piece of paper tucked into my blazer pocket with the address of where I was being sent. More like a parcel than a person.

There was a big gap between my skirt and my socks and the velvet-flocked seat tickled the back of my legs. All the wriggling in the world didn't solve the problem but, by about Reading, having read my copy of *School Friend* from cover to cover, I worked out that it would provide a wonderful barrier against the flock!

The longer the journey went on, the more engaged I became with the countryside through which we chugged. Maybe the rhythmic swaying motion of the steam train helped to soothe any anxiety and consequent introversion. I was still strangely lacking in curiosity regarding the next place I would lay my head, presumably because uncertainty had become such a frequent occurrence in my life, it was almost commonplace. Fellow passengers broke my solitude only between Reading and Exeter. I was not an open, smiley, sweet child who would encourage a concerned approach from an adult. I had a brooding watchfulness born of the need to make judgements about situations that were way beyond my years. When the train plunged into tunnels from time to time, smoke billowed through the carriage windows and formed a welcome cocoon around me, until we emerged into the daylight once more and the wind sucked it away. Oh, the joy of seeing that we were almost running along the sea's edge, with the odd wave breaking over the railway line! What is it that draws us to the sea? All I know is that it pulls us, as the moon pulls the tides, even though at its fiercest the ocean is both terrifying and magnificent at the same time; a paradox of nature, I suppose.

An added wonderment, as we turned inland, was that the earth was russet red and so were the cows. I couldn't believe my eyes. It was as if I had entered a storybook. I was still thinking about this when, a short while later, the guard came along to my carriage to tell me that I would be getting off at the next station. As we pulled into Newton Abbot, then a bustling market town, he took my case down from the rack and carried it on to the platform, where I was immediately spotted by an elderly lady who introduced herself as Mrs Molly Court. She looked ancient, but then anyone over the age of thirty looks old to a child. In fact she would have been in her early fifties. I had no qualms about being handed over to this gentle-looking woman, who was wearing a smart tweed costume with a stylish matching felt hat. This was worn at a jaunty angle, and sported a cluster of feathers out of which thrust a handsome pheasant tail. I was to learn later just how much she loved that hat. Her face was not only kindly, but had that skin that only country-women of a certain age have, soft and powdery; revealing that the kitchen and the household were her domain. She would never have the beaten, ruddy look of those who farmed the land in all weathers.

The journey from the town on to the moor, in a stately Morris saloon used as the local taxi, was a progress of sheer joy. Nose pressed tight against a half-opened window, I gazed in wonder at the sight of moorland scattered with grazing sheep, ponies and cattle and topped with granite tors. I drank in the sweet scent of bright yellow gorse and purple heather. Sections of the moor had been tamed into patchwork fields, their patterns created by hedgerow and dry-stone walling. I was in the first flush of love but didn't yet know it.

Our final destination was a thatched farmhouse, about a mile outside a small hamlet on Dartmoor, built with a hill at its back and sloping meadows at the front. We drove into the cobbled farmyard to a welcoming committee of chickens, quickly dispersed by two collie dogs, soon to be introduced to me as Fly and her daughter Moss.

Mrs Court, inviting me to call her Courty, carried my little brown leather suitcase in through the porch. The front door opened into the parlour, a beamed room with an open fireplace, which I never remember anyone using. She told me to take the case up to my bedroom but, try as I might, I could see no sign of a staircase. As I was to discover, many farmhouses had staircases leading from the main rooms that were often hidden behind doors. This was an inexplicable delight to me, the thrill of the semi-secret; the illogicality of what I perceived to be the ordered world of adults. Once Courty had shown me the secret door, I went upstairs and opened the latched door to my bedroom. There was a bed under the window with a floral counterpane, upon which was a thick, faded, peach-coloured satin eiderdown. An elderly stripy rug lay on the wooden oak floor next to the bed. On the dressing table the glass of the mirror, speckled with age and the vagaries of damp, reflected an arrangement of ling and bell heather in a pottery vase. On the side of the vase was a picture of an old horse with seven bearded men (not dwarves) on the poor nag and the words 'Widecombe Fair'; it eluded me, I was still a newcomer to the fables of Dartmoor. A brand-new wax candle in a slightly chipped enamel candleholder, white with a blue rim around the edge, stood on the bedside table with a small box of Bryant and May matches next to it. I felt completely at home. It was my space and it welcomed me. I was left there to unpack before being summoned down for tea.

As I entered the kitchen, two cats blinked at me from their warm perch on top of the Aga: Mo, a black cat with a white bow tie (always the perfect gentleman), and Sukie, a pretty little black female with white face markings and matching paws. Not to be outdone, and probably curious about a newcomer, a ginger tom came through from the scullery. Mr Wong was a big boy who arrived one day and stayed for ever. He was a bruiser, a yard-cat and a thief, as I was soon to learn. Not many weeks after my arrival, he purloined a string of Courty's home-made sausages which were hanging in the dairy. It was somewhat foolhardy for Courty and me to take off up the yard after a demented and determined feline carrying its prey but it was, after all, our supper! We were joined in our chase by Sid, the cowman and ploughman. Fortunately for us, in his haste to get away fast, the cat lost most of the sausages en route, probably due to Sid's yells, 'Yew contr'y devil, yew!' The abandoned bangers were duly picked up by us, washed and fried. Many a time we wished Mr Wong would rehouse himself, or become prey to some marauding fox, which was unlikely because he was one vicious cat!

Just before I was invited to sit at the wide-planked oak farmhouse table, Courty asked me to ring a large school handbell kept outside in the front porch. I was to ring it long and loud. This seemed very strange to me outside school, but she explained that it was always used as a summons for meals. We waited for a very long time but, in the absence of anyone answering the call to tea, we both tucked in. That teatime was a never-to-be-forgotten introduction to Courty's excellent cooking: home-made flapjacks, home-made scones with home-made jam, all washed down with a cup of tea poured from a large and ancient chipped teapot. The crowning glory was a glass bowl filled with light-yellow honeycombed-crusted cream from the farm's cows.

To make this, Courty used to pour the milk into a vast enamel bowl, gently bring it up to simmering point and then leave it to cool in the dairy. Once a crust had formed she gently scooped it off and popped it into jam jars. This cream was also used to make the butter, a little salt added to preserve it. In time I was often asked to help her churn it by hand, a time-consuming and arduous job, but I failed to be as deft as her at forming the large rolled butter pat, the equivalent of today's half pound. Somehow the serrated butter bats she used to form this roll defeated me. When you cut through the roll of salty butter little droplets of dew-like water made the cut surfaces of the butter glisten. There was never any wastage because the whey was used to make scones and cream cheese. Bread-making was a weekly event, using stone-ground flour that was emptied from its sack in the larder and poured into a large stone crock to keep it safe from mice. I seem to remember her making about six loaves at a time, but we weren't allowed to eat the new loaves on the day they were baked for fear that the batch would be devoured within the day. These precious loaves were stored in another stone pot in the dairy. Her bread and cakes were the envy of the Women's Institute. The sadness there was that she was never allowed to join the WI because she was a divorcée. How things have changed since then. No humanity was shown for the fact that she had had a violent husband – added to which one did not undertake divorce lightly in those days.

⁂

Long after Courty and I had finished tea that first day, there was a loud crash as the outer door was flung open and the sound of gumboots being tossed on to the flagstoned floor was accompanied by, 'Blasted sheep!' The kitchen door burst open and in strode a tall, manly woman. It was Sylvia, the owner of the farm. My first thoughts about this handsome and impressive figure were that she might be stern and unapproach-able, a person who might judge me and find me wanting. I wasn't yet acquainted with the spirit that dwelt within. Little did I know, innocent child, that this would be the beginning of a relationship that would form, and inform, my entire life. My mentor, my guide; the parent I never had and one who remained steadfast, despite my sometimes rebellious behaviour, until the day she died.

When Sylvia spoke, far from being intimidated, I was taken aback by the soft and cultured timbre of her voice. Another pot of tea was brewed by the ever-patient Courty as Sylvia plonked herself down, blaming the errant sheep for making her late. I learnt over the years that Sylvia was late for everything. It was not a conscious lack of consideration but more that she got herself totally absorbed in the moment. It could legitimately be

Sylvia with Fly and Moss.

the day-to-day chores on the farm, or simply hailing a passing farmer, neighbour or, come to think of it, anyone, with whom she could chat. There was never a brief exchange of essential words with Sylvia, she just loved to talk . . . and talk . . . and talk! I have to admit as the years went on that it was I, more often than not, who kept her chatting, particularly during my teenage years. This lack of attention to punctuality was the one trait in Sylvia's personality that drove Courty to distraction. Who could blame her when it happened nearly every mealtime? After all, she made the most wonderful food, which was very often eaten by Sylvia an hour or so after it was ready and well past its prime. Courty learnt various strategies, one of which was to say the meal would be ready at, say, one o'clock but not get it ready until two, having rung the bell half an hour before. Even that did not always save the food from being over the hill.

As an adult, I became much more aware of the difficulties this inconsiderate and shoddy timekeeping caused Courty and would go in search of the wayward agrarian myself. Courty and I were to become very close as time went on. In the latter years I spent as much time in the kitchen with her, as in the cowshed with Sylvia. We were often partners in crime, even having a surreptitious nip on the side. Sylvia did not drink alcohol, only pushing the boat out with half a glass of sherry on Christmas Eve.

⁂

My first morning on the farm, I woke at dawn. I gazed out over the meadow as the mist rose from the dewy grass to reveal, in the glimmer of early sun, the veiled outlines of the red cattle. In wonderment I stared at this enchanted new world. 'Hoey! Hoey!' accompanied by the occasional bark of a dog pulled me out of my reverie. It was Sylvia calling the cattle in for milking, with Moss and Fly in tow. Suddenly, I too wanted to be in tow, to run free. A gentle tapping at the door, and there was Courty with a cup of sweet tea and a slice of home-made buttered bread. Downed in a trice! Clothes thrown on, all thoughts of washing and cleaning teeth abandoned, I flew downstairs and rushed outside.

The perfume of the morning was so different from that of the previous afternoon, when it had been warm, hay-filled, and honeyed. Now, it was earthy and damp with an all-pervading smell of animal. Following the gentle lowing and the rhythmic squirting sound of milk hitting the inside of a galvanised pail, I soon found the cowshed, with Moss and Fly waiting outside, the ever-attentive guardians of their mistress. Peering into the gloom I could see Sylvia, seated on a three-legged milking stool, with her forehead on the cow's flank, squeezing the milk from a warm udder and quite unaware of my presence. Apart from the odd fidgeting of a cow, there was a stillness and an overwhelming sense of peace. A happiness and feeling of belonging, such as I had never known before, engulfed me. Since that time, I have always loved the serenity of a cowshed with the pungent aroma of cattle and the cows' breath, the smell of fresh grass. During the holidays, that shippon became my schoolroom, a place of learning and discussion, a sanctuary for tutor and pupil alike. Sylvia had a first-class mind, she was stimulating and thought-provoking and, in a different age, might well have gone to Oxford as her father had done.

That holiday was happy and carefree, but the long and glorious hours were stalked by the spectre of my father. All too soon it would be time to return to him, to start a new school. I started to have nightmares. The grown-ups thought it was because we often had cheese for supper but I knew, with increasing certainty, that it was due to a deep-seated distress that my idyll was coming to an end. I'd never had any control over my destiny but, in a moment of sheer desperation, I found myself asking if I could come back for the next holidays. It was the first time I had ever attempted to take control of my life. I think I surprised myself as much as the adults. They seemed content with my request but, as Sylvia pointed out, it could only be with my father's consent. I knelt by my bed each night and entreated God to make my father acquiese and allow me to return. Would my prayers be answered though?

Summer uniform: despite the heat I am still wearing my beloved blazer.

Chapter Three

Not Built for Speed on Land

One gift the Fairies gave me . . .
The love of Books, the Golden Key
That opens the Enchanted Door . . .

Andrew Lang, 'Ballads of the Bookworm'

I arrived at the Warren in 1953 at the age of eleven and, somewhat reminiscent of Daphne du Maurier's nameless heroine
gazing at Manderley, stood by the gate leading to the drive and
had my first glimpse of the school. It was an imposing Victorian
Gothic house with mock Tudor chimneys; an architect's
nightmare. I was suddenly overwhelmed by these first steps to
adulthood. There was nothing to worry about, I told myself. I
was used to moving from establishment to establishment, being
self-sufficient and finding new friends.

My father had considered sending me to Roedean rather
than on to the Warren, the senior school of the Red House, but
said that, in his opinion, Roedean turned out little snobs and the
Warren turned out young ladies. There are people who may
question whether that were so in my case.

As with the Red House, I took to the school's structure, the learning, the sport, everything, like a duck to water. Just like the moor, I was destined to be happy there – though not all the time. There were many moments of despair and darkness, even moments of a desire for death, hampering my metamorphosis. It was as though my emergence from the chrysalis was too obstructed by the pain of what had gone before. Not surprising, really, when you consider a background with no mother, a maverick, somewhat unstable father and numerous stepmothers, along with a multiplicity of different holiday homes and different schools. That was the way it was. There was nothing I could do about it, nor was there any point in blaming my father; he was what he was. I learnt quite early on that if one wants to make the best of life there is no point in spending time on past misfortunes. I am not sure when I realised that acceptance of the status quo was the only way forward. One can't go through life wishing things had been otherwise because it stunts and damages one for ever. These gifts of a new life which were being offered to me were impossible to ignore: I had just found happiness and stability with Sylvia and Courty on Dartmoor and I continued to pray that I would be allowed to spend all my holidays with them.

The school building had originally been known as Warren House, which had been built in 1867 by one Thomas Wisden, on his estate in Broadwater, just north of Worthing. After his death part of the estate was leased to Worthing Golf Club. From 1930 Warren House was used as a girls' school, simply named the Warren. The Warren would become my term-time home for the next seven years. It felt right. Every establishment to which I had so far been sent had offered me structure and stability. Each institution, to a greater or lesser extent, had something individual to offer and, perhaps, I was fortunate enough to have within me the ability to take a small piece from each that would fit the jigsaw of life.

I was well equipped for my new school. Sally, my stepmother, armed with a long list of school uniform requirements, had taken me to the specialist outfitters, Kinch and Lack, in London's Victoria, where I was fitted and kitted out. The entire purchase was delivered by them soon after. It was thrilling to have several huge boxes addressed to me and it wasn't even Christmas. We knelt on the floor unwrapping each item before carefully putting the folded tissue paper aside with the string, unknotted, for reuse. In those days nothing that could be reused was ever thrown away – a very efficient way of recycling.

Some of the many items included white cotton knickers, which were known as linings and only changed twice a week! Over these were worn navy-blue bloomers. Oh Lordie, bloomers dated back to the 1850s and were popularised by Amelia Bloomer. They were worn at ankle length by fashionable aristocracy in those days. Fortunately, our 'modern' bloomers were a sort of short bloomer-cum-directoire knicker, elasticated at the knee. Not things of beauty, despite us tucking them up high to make them look alluring. Quite who was supposed to be allured by these pathetic attempts at sexing up the knicker, I know not. The uniform for gymnastics was a vest worn with these same ghastly bloomers, which were only changed once a week. They, and the knicker linings, almost took themselves off to the laundry. Daily wear was a navy blue jibber, the kind of garment other schools called a tunic. The name jibber may well be a derivation of the Arabic *djellaba*; a heritage, like so many of the words we use, from the then British Empire. The jibber was worn over a white blouse with red spots and one's house colours were attached to the left shoulder. The *pièce de resistance* was the blazer. I loved it. It was navy blue and its breast pocket was emblazoned with the school badge. I was wedded to it – a surgical procedure would have been required to remove it from me. The final flourish was a tie of blue, red and white stripes.

Sunday meant church; it also meant wearing your Sunday best. Thus we were adorned with green jibbers, cream blouses and a brown herringbone Sunday coat with a brown velvet collar and brown felt bowler hat (thrown from the train window on the day we left school for ever). The quality of the clothes was reflected in the price. This was an ongoing expense, because the growth between the ages of eleven and eighteen meant numerous replacements. There were no second-hand facilities as far as I know. This may have been due to the fact that no parent at such an elite school would ever have countenanced their child wearing second-hand clothes; but what a missed business opportunity.

Every garment had to be labelled, and that label stitched on by hand. Not a job for the fainthearted. I have no recollection who that brave person was, but I suspect it may have been Sally. The name tapes were manufactured by a company called Cash and beautifully made. The one thing I had been allowed to choose was the style of script and the colour in which my name was to be machine-embroidered on to the tape. The tape duly arrived neatly folded in a box. It had a continuous repetition of my name, with little marks in between, where the strip had to be cut to form a single label.

Everything for the term was packed into a large school trunk, reminiscent of the steamer trunks in the days of long sea voyages. My father would send the trunk with his driver to Victoria Station to be sent ahead. We girls, clutching our lacrosse sticks and latest Elvis or Little Richard LPs, would catch the school train the next day. That was always such a fun journey, chattering nineteen to the dozen and finding out what all your friends had been up to during the school hols. My biggest dread was that if my father insisted on taking me to the school train, he would turn up the worse for wear. Since the divorce case he was drinking even more heavily, starting early in the day. Most teenagers have an irrational fear of being embarrassed by any parental behaviour that would set them apart from their peers, often to do with what their mother is wearing. My fear was real; my father behaved atrociously when drunk. The same dread would occur time and again, particularly with such events as Speech Day, Sports Day and exeats (days out) or, worse, my Confirmation. Fortunately, my anxiety was increasingly unfounded because he came up with more and more excuses to be absent. On the few occasions when my father did take me out, it was fairly joyless: formal dinners in hotels, where the cocktail bar held more interest for him than I did. In fairness to him, how could he possibly relate to me, a child he hardly knew, and one who was being educated out of his sphere? He came to visit me less and less but I was fortunate that this inadequacy was compensated for by the many happy exeats I had with some of my friends and their parents.

Elaine's family lived in Brighton. She had a great sense of humour and so we got on well. Her father, a retired army officer, was a small man with a bombastic personality that more than made up for his size. I learnt very early on in our acquaintance never to mention Edward VIII or Mrs Wallis Simpson to him. Neither Elaine nor myself ever quite knew whether it was because he perceived the ex-king to have been a traitor by abdicating or whether he had the hots for his wife Wallis. This was never resolved, particularly because we could never discuss the subject.

My friend June's family were landowners and must have foreseen the changing economy of the countryside because they had diversified into successful leisure parks that were a great attraction to us visiting youngsters. The added allure was her very good-looking stepbrother, some eight years older than us. Much to our chagrin, he never looked twice at any of us even though we tried to attract his attention. The only thing he was interested in was fast cars. I believe he eventually became a racing driver, no doubt having glamour on his arm.

A sweet and gentle girl called Sue was another friend who invited me out for exeats. Her mother was a delightful, classically attractive woman, beautifully attired in the inevitable twinset and pearls. Her father worked in the City and was very charming and hospitable. He went up to London on the same train each day clad in his morning suit and bowler hat. He always carried a briefcase and furled silk umbrella with a curved wooden handle which, despite its age and frequent use, always looked new. The image brings to mind the story of the city gents, dressed identically, who used to catch the same train and get into the same carriage each morning. After tossing their bowler hats, briefcases and umbrellas on to the rack over their heads they all settled down to do *The Times* crossword. One morning the gentleman sitting in his usual seat by the window finished his crossword puzzle well ahead of the others. As he tossed the newspaper up on to the rack with a satisfied flourish, the man opposite said, 'Great Scott, old chap, you made short work of the crossword today. I've almost finished myself, apart from one clue.' The successful crossworder enquired which one he was missing. 'Well, it's eight across, four letters and reads "pertaining to the female". I've got UNT but I'm completely stumped.' To which the crossworder replied, 'That was easy, it's "AUNT".' At which point a vicar in the far corner peered over his half-moon glasses and said, 'Oh Lord, has anyone here got a rubber?'

Back to real life, those three friends all left in the fifth form and only a handful of us went on into the upper sixth. I didn't lose touch with them immediately but, when lives take off in different directions, it is inevitable that distance develops. This was not so with another Sue, who was doing the same subjects as me and was also a keen member of the Dramatic Society. She became senior prefect when I was vice-head girl. We stayed in touch during her university years, after which she married and had a large house in Southampton which was not only occupied by her family, but bursting with student life. She was a bright, intelligent, life-affirming person so it was a shock when she died a couple of years ago.

It was not unusual in girls' public schools at that time for teachers, as well as parents, to take out on an exeat a girl who might otherwise have been left in school. One outing in particular springs to mind, when Miss Hawes the French teacher took me to Bignor to visit the remains of a Roman villa. We picnicked on the South Downs. Curiously, I was not bored, I had a fertile imagination and a budding interest in history. Her kindness was particularly surprising since I was not a very receptive French pupil. Perhaps my greatest regret, during my time at school, was that I could never return the many kindnesses I received by inviting my friends out. My father's unpredictable behaviour put paid to that.

However, it was not always his behaviour that was questionable; so was mine at times. I clearly remember him taking me to the Horse of the Year Show at Olympia, because my idol Pat Moss was competing. At the jump-off, my father in his excitement shouted, 'Go on, girl!', at which point I turned to him and said, 'You're not at the races now.' It showed the widening gulf between us but it was, nevertheless, a thoughtless, rude and very cruel thing to say. In my defence it was born of embarrassment. Not only was I a self-conscious teenager, but I didn't want to draw people's attention to my father behaving in a way that wasn't acceptable at a showjumping event. To add to what was rapidly becoming a disastrous day, the showjumper Pat Moss waved me away in a rather dismissive fashion when I asked for her autograph, leaving me feeling embarrassed and rejected. I took this example to heart and hope that I have never left anyone feeling the same way. After all, fans are the ones who support and follow your career, sometimes for years, and one should be grateful to them. Time permitting, it doesn't take long to give someone an autograph, most especially when they have had the courtesy to ask. The one thing I do not like is when someone tries to take a sneaky photo of me without asking. Once asked, if I have time, I will happily pose with them and, if possible, get someone else to take the shot – it seems to make it much more personal. Apart from anything else it gives me a chance to engage with people I don't know but who, in a certain capacity, know me.

❦

How strange it is that some of one's vivid memories are often auditory and olfactory, taking one back down the years to schooldays. Even now, hearing oratorio, I am reminded of school choir practice and the reward each individual contribution makes to creating a whole, producing an overwhelmingly powerful sound. Even now lines of poetry, learned by rote, can pop into my head involuntarily and the words of hymns are carved in my memory in a way that recent events can never be. I don't remember ever seeing our School Song written down but I can sing it to this day. It is very much of its time, exalting valour, achievement, honour and loyalty. Not bad precepts to have been taught.

Our School Song

Oh may the school we love forever flourish
And be the better for our passing through,
For we upholders of an old tradition
Are builders of a new.

So in our school we crave a healthy outlook
A quickened interest in all we find,
That we may never know the sin of boredom
Or listlessness of mind.

But look on living as a great adventure,
The challenge of a quest which never ends;
Along whose paths we find the lilt of laughter,
The faithfulness of friends.

Oh may the school we love forever flourish
And be the better for our passing through,
For we upholders of an old tradition
Are builders of a new.

I can still smell the school's boot-room, which had a particular odour of its own. This was due no doubt to our sweaty lacrosse boots and the grease with which we lovingly softened the cradle of the lax stick. This encouraged 'give' when you were catching and cradling the ball, slipping and sliding over a frosty pitch in the winter. How extraordinary that the game of lacrosse was adopted by English girls' schools, just over a hundred years ago, from a game that had hitherto been played for centuries by native North American warriors in what is now Canada. From plains to playing fields!

How I hated being turfed out for sports on a grey afternoon. Donning sports jumpers, short divided skirts and studded canvas ankle boots laced tightly, off we went. Once out there, we loved it. We returned in time for tea in the Junior Common Room (known as the JCR) and homework, our bodies and brains tingling, our cheeks and thighs glowing lobster-pink from the cold and exertion. Tea comprised two slices of bread and a mug of tea. If you forgot which day of the week it was, you were soon reminded by the topping on the bread: jam (Monday), Marmite (Tuesday), sandwich spread (ugh! Wednesday), chocolate spread (Thursday), Shippam's bloater paste (double ugh! Friday). Same spread, same day, each weekday. There's a lot to be said for routine.

My sports mistress once said to me, 'Pamela, you weren't built for speed on land, more for speed in water.' It was to be some years before I could show her any sort of prowess in water because the school pool was only put in towards the end of my time at the Warren. Disproving her theory, I only reached the less than dizzy heights of style swimming for the house team.

Apart from playing tennis, netball and rounders for the house, I did manage to represent the school in the lacrosse team playing in goal, probably because I filled more space than anyone else. Come to think of it, all my sports positions were defensive. We were given the opportunity to play cricket; I soon discovered it was a boring game but certainly better played than watched, although cricket enthusiasts will disagree. We also learnt archery, which was very innovative for a girls' school. It tapped perfectly into my role-playing aspirations. I could imagine myself as Robin Hood (far more interesting than Maid Marian who, I'm sure, was probably hard at it stitching a tapestry). We were also taught the basics of golf, which made sense, since the other half of the original estate had an eighteen-hole golf course. This game didn't seem much more fun than cricket.

As if this was not enough to choose from, the school had its own stables, surrounded as it was by plenty of countryside over which to hack. Now that really interested me. I was desperately in love with an Irish pony, a Palamino-cross called Connaught of Connemara, a pretty animal who gave one a spirited ride. He would do anything to slough off an inexperienced rider whom he didn't want on his back but, as he was Irish, it was doubtless humour rather than malice. The stables were run by the very eccentric, bandy-legged Captain Willy, who was far from comfortable with teenage girls. Perhaps that was why he hid behind a pall of smoke emanating from a Woodbine permanently hanging from his lower lip. He'd allocate the mount he felt appropriate for each girl and accompany about six of us on a ride, never conversing with any of us, just barking out the odd instruction from time to time. The one thing that always coloured our feelings about riding on the Downs during the fifties was seeing rabbits dying of myxomatosis, the result of the illegal importation of two infected rabbits. These had been brought into the country to control the rabbit population on an East Sussex estate in 1953. Two years later about 95 per cent of rabbits in this country were dead, or dying. It was very distressing to see blind bulging-eyed rabbits stumbling around. They were quickly dispatched by Captain Willy, who would dismount and put them out of their misery by hitting them on the head with his crop. Even at that age, however hard it was emotionally, I instinctively understood why he did it.

Our school held two major annual events. Sports Day in the summer was an impressive occasion. Before the day, we knelt in front of Matron who measured all of us, so that each skirt length could be altered to finish exactly four inches from the floor, neither one inch higher, nor one inch lower. For most of us, this meant alterations on an annual basis. This tedious procedure was paid off by the spectacle of the entire school, led by the head girl, marching in height order (highest to lowest) past the long terrace, across the bridge, over the ha-ha, and down the length of the sports field accompanied by the strains of the RAF march past, 'Boys in Blue', blaring through loud-speakers. The only fly in the ointment was that on many occasions, the head girl was considerably shorter than some of the rangy sixth-formers she led!

Parents came dressed as though for a garden party, to see us compete in athletics. I don't remember it ever raining on that day and the event always went well, except on one occasion. A stray dog from the village, chasing after the slowest girl in the 100-yard race, attached itself firmly to one of her legs and proceeded to hump up and down. It was bewildering for us all, especially the girl concerned. Various fathers rushed forward to save the maiden from a fate worse than death. What the dog was up to was firmly pushed under the carpet by the adults but, thereafter, we instinctively felt safer competing in the sack race!

The second event was Speech Day and Prize-Giving, always held in the autumn term in the Town Hall in Worthing. Pupils displayed their talents in music, literature and drama, and those of distinction were awarded prizes for academic excellence. A well-known luminary, not necessarily known to us, would be wheeled in to give a speech, present the prizes and exhort us to greater things and usually bored us stiff. The one exception to this was when the Duke of Norfolk's daughter was invited to do the honours. She was much closer to our age and spoke in a way we understood; consequently we listened with greater attention. I seem to recollect the only prizes I received in my school career were for poetry speaking, singing and drama.

Acting had always been a passion at school and I was student president of the Drama Society run by Miss Millicent Mather, our drama and English mistress. Under her frivolous exterior lay a sharp wit. She was exotic. Sporting the most luxuriant head of hair, bound in a chignon, wearing a shawl tossed around her shoulders, she adorned herself with rings and jangling bracelets. I was fascinated by her and once asked her what she would like to have been if she hadn't chosen the teaching profession. In her broad north-country accent, she said, 'Ooh Pam, I would have been a nun if only I could have worn jewels and make-up.'

I was often co-opted to play the part of a man. My physicality, coupled with the gravitas that was an inherent part of my personality, made me the obvious candidate to take a male role. How I longed at times to play the *ingénue*, to feel silk and lace next to my skin, but I never did, even in my early career. I was never the stuff of a pretty innocent. Under Miss Mather's direction we put on a production each term. I gave my all in two of my male performances as Mr Bennet in *Pride and Prejudice* and Joss Sedley in *Vanity Fair*.

There was a flourishing school magazine called *Steyne*, named, for some strange reason, after an area in Worthing. I contributed to it in my first term and here are two examples of my somewhat pretentious childish ramblings. It might be embarrassing but at least I can say I was published.

Solitude

It isn't in the mind,
Or in books of any kind
That I can ever find . . .
Solitude

While walking in the rain
Or hay-soaked on a wain,
That is when I gain . . .
Solitude

The End of an Earring

Then the thoughts sail free
Above our life's cold sea
And then returns to me . . .
Solitude

On the Untamed

My heart pounds to see
The foam-ridden sea
Lapping over a desolate quay
A brook tumbling free
By Ambrosial haunts of a bee;
The wind whistling in ecstasy
Through leaveless boughs of a tree,
Is this God's promised land?
It is to me.

I wouldn't have missed my schooldays; I loved the rigid, almost military, routine. There were hardships, but it was a good lesson in life. We had to survive as a group and to think of others before ourselves. We learnt quickly that one should own up to one's own misdemeanours to prevent the entire class from being punished. One never split on an individual member of the group; that was the most heinous crime of all. We were all equals, our uniforms made sure of that. We didn't have anything that set us apart from each other, no jewellery, no pocket money, even our shoes were identical. The only adornments were our house colours, prefect sashes and badges. The only privileges we had were those that were earned. Thus, we knew nothing of each other's backgrounds, barring the occasional secret shared in the dormitory at night. These usually covered far more exciting topics such as Radio Luxembourg, listened to under the bedclothes. Radio Lux was our only exposure to 'real life'. We listened to the emerging pop scene – Elvis, Guy Mitchell, Tommy Steele . . . and we even learnt about the football pools, thanks to Horace Batchelor of Keynsham – spelt: 'K-E-Y-N-S-H-A-M'!

A typical school day started with a loud early morning bell. We queued for one of the basins lining the walls, to strip-wash. In winter it was absolutely freezing. Each girl only had a longed-for bath once or twice a week. Then down to breakfast which always started with thin slimy porridge, the gruel of *Oliver Twist*, which I loathed and have done ever since. Then, after this less than delectable meal, we went back upstairs to the dormitories to make our beds. Woollen blankets and sheets were tucked under horsehair mattresses, finished off with hospital corners that had to be folded and tucked under perfectly. All our clothes were kept neatly folded in a sort of dog basket under the bed. Both the bed and the basket were inspected before one was allowed downstairs for the first lesson. No talking or running was ever allowed in the corridors. Lessons went on until lunchtime, with a break in the middle, when we queued for a bottle containing a third of a pint of milk. I loathed most dairy products at that time, particularly warm milk from crates that had been left in the sun for too long, and got shot of it, clandestinely, at the first opportunity. Fortunately, it wasn't difficult to find someone who would drink it on my behalf. These were post-war times and we needed building up, except that I didn't. We were given cod liver oil, which I also loathed with a passion, and Radio Malt, which I adored, but wasn't allowed to have because of my size. It didn't seem very fair.

Much of the afternoon, as I mentioned, was taken up with sporting activities, after which we came in for tea and maybe a quick look at one of the daily newspapers. Then back to our classrooms for prep, homework done at school, overseen by a member of staff or a prefect and conducted in complete silence until suppertime, when we were given a light meal. The main meal of the day was lunch, with such things as stew with gristly bits, boiled potatoes and overcooked greens, followed by blancmange, milky rice pudding with skin on top or stewed apples with bits of core in it, just like fingernails. After supper came welcome free time, which could be spent in the Junior Common Room either talking or reading, followed by bed . . . and no talking after lights out – except that we did, in whispers.

Dormitories varied in size and style. The first-year pupils were all bunged together into large dorms with beds in serried rows. The next progression was an enormous cubicled area where each curtained cubicle contained two beds, except at the far corners, where there were single cubicles housing a couple of sub-prefects. Each sub-prefect had to do a term's supervision in the large dormitory. We loathed it because it meant going to bed earlier than one's peer group, and being deprived of whatever fun we were having at the time. It was a pain in the neck having to tell the juniors off for various misdemeanours or making sure, if they got up in the night, that they were all right. It didn't make having a good night's sleep very easy, though things improved as one grew older. The dormitories grew smaller and increasingly pleasant, culminating in single rooms for the four senior prefects.

❧

Just because I liked the regime didn't mean I always conformed. I had a wicked sense of humour and an irresistible urge to push the boundaries of authority. I was an ace at breaking bounds and it didn't take me long to find some fellow rebels. Quite how we managed to be cycling around Broadwater Green in the dead of night, with just coats over our pyjamas, is a mystery. Our escape route was usually by window, doors being beyond our lock-picking ability. It was on one of our nocturnal expeditions that we were surprised to see a tall figure coming out of the gloom. It was a policeman on patrol wheeling his bicycle. His height had been exaggerated by his tall custodian helmet, reminiscent of Kaiser Bill's. As he got closer, we could see the silver buttons on his serge tunic and the crest on his helmet reflected in the light of the moon. We stopped dead in our tracks, terrified that we were in for real trouble, especially when he said that it was unwise for young ladies to be out in the middle of the night. Having ascertained pretty quickly that we were Warren girls, instead of being soundly berated as we anticipated, he suggested that we walk back to the school with him, via the bike shed, and re-enter the way we had got out. Now, as an adult, it amuses me to think how undignified a group we must have looked as we scrabbled over the windowsill back into school, still scared that he was going to split on us. To my knowledge, he never did, but being found out certainly put a stop to our nocturnal ramblings . . . though daylight was still an option.

Breaking bounds became even more exciting. Interest in cycling soon waned, becoming redundant – we discovered golf! Well, not the game, but the boys who played on the golf course. Now, access to the golf course was strictly forbidden. There was an avenue leading to it, adjacent to the netball courts and close to the vegetable garden. This gloomy avenue was made almost tunnel-like by the densely overhanging branches that blocked out the sunlight, making it dark and pretty spooky. It was supposed to be haunted and always known as the Ghost Walk. We were typical girls en masse, spooking each other with tales of gruesome happenings, and leaping out at each other with ghostly wails. The fears of a phantom were soon forgotten, however, as we made our numerous excursions up the forbidden avenue to the golf course in search of the opposite sex. We took our luminous socks, our prize possessions, in our pockets and put them on as soon as we broke bounds. Strolling nonchalantly on to the golf course, we not only felt hip but extremely daring. I daresay the lads we had in our sights, who were older than we were, thought we looked ridiculous but, nonetheless, they egged each other on to chat up the 'posh' girls. Probably more as a sport than with any genuine interest, but we were too naive to realise that. For all our front, we had the sense and instinct to stay in a pack, flirting from the sidelines and offering the promise of possibilities to come. The encounters never went beyond being chatted up until the day I spotted a really handsome boy. It was not long before I broke from the pack to get to know him a little better. Inexperience is not good for your first kiss. I just couldn't understand why he was trying to force my mouth open to get his tongue down my throat while I was endeavouring to keep my lips firmly closed. However, it didn't take me long to discover the art of kissing, but that was as far as it went. I got bored with it after a while and returned to the security of the pack. Those tentative kisses, however, foreshadowed a more scandalous relationship a few years later, while I was still at school.

We made up for our lack of sex education by being past masters at voyeurism, as the Downs and golf course were a hive of activity for courting couples. With regard to sex, what they got up to was far more interesting than my faltering explorations on the kissing front, or our biology lessons on the reproductive system of a rabbit; the nearest our spinster teacher exposed us to the facts of life. Talking of which, we were often exposed to more than was desirable for young maidens. An open area close to a girls' school was a magnet for every flasher in Sussex. Our eyes were out on stalks, with no understanding of the risks we were taking. I was about fourteen when we had our own resident flasher who took up his undesirable activities in the school copse. He became quite an attraction. Reading in the common room didn't have quite the same allure after that. Prefects, wondering where everyone was, would come across groups of girls giggling to the point of weeping. When, eventually, the police were called, I was one of the unfortunates whom they interviewed. A male police officer asked me to describe what I had seen. I was mortified. What could a teenage girl of that time say to any adult about such things, let alone a policeman? What had started off in childish ignorance as a laugh left us feeling ashamed and guilty.

Pashes, or crushes, at school were a given. It was probably a way of locking on to an older role model and focusing our free-floating hormonally charged emotions. I think I was a bit of a late starter; I had to invent my first crush as all my class had them. Being fairly indifferent to all of the sixth form on offer, I decided to choose a rather gentle, undynamic girl, because she had no devotees. However, a year or so later, she was quickly abandoned when I became deeply enamoured of a sixth-former who was tall, elegant and an enviable musician. I remember swooning over her playing a Chopin polonaise at a school Speech Day concert. For a single-sex school there was very little hanky-panky going on, or at least I was unaware of it. Rumour had it that in one dormitory a girl was quite notorious for kissing the pathetically burgeoning breasts of third-formers. I passed all that by somewhat shyly and indifferently.

Despite my notoriety as an inveterate renegade, imagine my surprise at the end of my upper-fifth year, being called in to see the head. She announced that from the beginning of the next term I was to be a sub-prefect. Seeing the fun of my rebellious days disappearing before me and not quite comprehending the logic of her reasoning, I queried this decision. She very calmly got up from her desk and looking directly at me said, 'My dear, you set a thief to catch a thief.' In fact this poacher turned into a very diligent gamekeeper, ultimately becoming vice-head girl. Joy of joys, this meant me joining the elevated band of four senior prefects who not only had their own rooms, but their own bathroom in which one could bathe at will. My room, however small, was still mine and was sandwiched between those of Penny, the head girl, and my close friend Sue, the senior prefect.

The one exception to this conversion from rebel to pillar of the establishment, and one I regret, was 'The Incident of the Missing Peaches from the Walled Garden'. The theft of these special peaches, tended lovingly and grown especially for the last dinner of the summer term, was worthy of Agatha Christie. Espaliered against the southern wall of the walled garden, they looked magnificent. So precious were they that, if they were ripening too fast, they would be carefully covered to ensure they were perfect for the special dinner. I had taken my A levels and the dinner would be the last evening meal I would ever have in the school. The night before would also be my last midnight feast. What a temptation for somebody who had been so responsible for the last few years and who thought that peaches would make an excellent dessert for the prefects' late-night feast. I, along with two fellow miscreants, crept out of a window in the dead of night, across a flat roof, quietly dropping down on to the lawn and across the dewy grass to the walled garden. I climbed the wall with one of the girls, who dropped down into the garden and slowly stripped the tree bare, passing the fruit to me as I sat on top of the wall, ready to hand them down to the girl holding a pillowcase below, on the other side of the wall. On our return the fruits of our labour were received rapturously by the rest of the prefects . . . guilty only by association. We feasted happily on those forbidden peaches with not a care in the world.

The following evening we all filed in for dinner where it was solemnly announced before grace that there had been a terrible calamity. The peaches had been stripped from the garden; a fruit salad would be served instead. The culprits had not been asked to own up, so I assumed suspicion had fallen on local youths. Breathing a sigh of relief, I felt a tap on the shoulder from my somewhat daunting Classics teacher, Miss Ashwin, who leaned over and said quietly, 'Isn't it a pity that someone stole the peaches from the walled garden?' I was completely taken aback; especially when she went on to say as she left, 'Remember, when you go out into the world, not to let your sense of fun get the better of you.' It was obvious that she knew but, instead of openly chastising me, it was her quiet aside that was far more powerful, and her words went home.

Irene Ashwin's personality can be summed up in her teaching, when she often exhorted us with the phrase: *per angusta ad augusta* (through difficulties to honours). She even owned a house in Bexhill called Res Angusta, which she interpreted as Small Place and always said that the name should not be confused with Res Augusta (Big Place), which showed a lovely self-deprecating sense of humour. She once visited the Holy Land and saw a man travelling on a horse and cart on the Sabbath Day with a bucket of water under his seat. When she asked someone for the reason why the water was so strategically placed, she was told that he was permitted to travel on water on the day of rest! Strangely enough, we stayed in touch until she died. I remember her taking me to see the remake of *Ben Hur* at the Empire Cinema in Leicester Square, a couple of years after I left school.

As well as my love of acting, I had developed an interest in veterinary science. One of my most treasured teenage birthday presents had been a copy of Black's *Veterinary Dictionary*. I carried it throughout the school; it went everywhere. I was wedded to it in the same way I was wedded to my school blazer. One of my greatest delights was making Mendelian charts to work out the genetic probabilities in sheep. I was beginning to know sheep and cows like other children know rabbits and guinea pigs. The seed had been sown in that first holiday on Dartmoor. However, it was not to be: fate had other plans. By the time I discovered one needed a good Latin A level to get in to veterinary college, it was too late. I had dropped the subject to pursue different A levels on the basis that *Infelix Dido verus mihi nuntius ergo venerate exstinctam, ferroque extrema secutam*, from Virgil's *Aeneid* (fondly known by us as 'Enid the old Roman harlot') bore no relevance to the anatomy of an animal!

I left the Warren at the age of eighteen, after seven fulfilling years. My time there gave me a love of books and was the golden key that opened an enchanted door to learning and enquiry; that quest for knowledge has remained with me ever since. As an only child with a chaotic parental background, I needed that stability. A stability that was complemented by the love and security I found in my holiday life on the farm; for, all those years ago, my fervent prayers had been answered.

George with Duchess and Violet.

Chapter Four

Blooming in the Heather

It was summer
On the lake hung a golden haze
It was summer
It was one of those endless days
So we walked
Through a field of clover
And over a sheep spun hill
And it seemed it would last forever
And it did . . .

Spike Milligan, 'Lyric'

Almost immediately after the start of my first term at the Warren, Sylvia had telephoned my father. She told him that I had been very happy on the farm and that they would welcome me back. My father agreed that, for as long as the two women were happy to have me, all my holidays would now be spent on the moor, a routine of visits that would last until the end of my schooldays and beyond; Dartmoor in the holidays, the Warren in term time. I was fortunate that my personality was such that I saw these two different structures as gifts; which enabled me to benefit so completely from them. My father paid for any new clothes I needed and made sure I was collected and taken to the train: Victoria for school, Paddington for Devon. Apart from change-over days, I hardly ever saw him. Neither he nor Sally ever visited the farm, for which I was grateful. The diverse worlds never collided.

From then on, this darkling child, this emotional orphan, was in the care of people who nurtured her soul as well as her body. It was to be an ideal passing of childhood and on into adulthood. I can never thank Sylvia and Courty enough for opening the door on my life and letting the light stream in.

The one exception to the moorland routine was a summer holiday when I was sent to France for six weeks, at the age of twelve or thirteen. Now, it was unusual for a mixed group of girls and boys, aged about nine to fifteen and unknown to each other, to fly to the Côte d'Azur alone without teachers who were known to them at one end, only to be met and supervised by unknown adults at the other end. It was a journey that seemed to take for ever – no easyJet in those days. The only time I had flown before this was as a very small child. Father, impressing one of his ladyloves, flew all of us, along with a nanny, on a Dakota to Switzerland. We stayed at the Grand Hotel Villa Castagnola overlooking Lake Lugano. The magnificence of the hotel pales into insignificance compared to my memory of the flight. I was utterly thrilled every time the plane hit an air pocket and suddenly dropped down, something most passengers dread. No doubt made worse by a tedious child trotting up and down the aisle shrieking with glee. I think I was about five years old.

On the Côte d'Azur trip I was with my own age group (and a proudly seasoned traveller to boot). The organisation with whom we went rented the entire west wing of an enormous monastery overlooking the Mediterranean. After a monk-like breakfast of dry baguette and black coffee served in a wooden bowl, we spent most days on the beach, swimming, snorkelling and running wild: feral children having fun. In those days, the predominant smell on the beaches in the Med was the glorious, heady scent of the original Ambre Solaire; not an ounce of protection, just designed to make you fry in the sun. We were all as bronzed as hazelnuts, except for one poor girl with very fair skin whose entire back was burnt. When it eventually peeled we were thrilled and, like little monkeys, helped to pull off the dead skin!

The days on the beach were interrupted by occasional outings. One of the more exciting adventures was taking a boat to the Île Sainte-Marguerite to see the fortress, one of the prisons in which the Man in the Iron Mask was incarcerated, inspiring Alexandre Dumas's book of the same name. I had read this book and was excited by the idea that the prisoner could have been Louis XIV's twin, imprisoned to maintain the Sun King's power (the more likely story that the masked man was a political prisoner, Eustache Dauger, didn't have the same appeal). Indeed Dumas's book set the tone for me in that I still love reading historical thrillers.

I was a little too young to appreciate some of the outings, particularly when, in St Paul de Vence, I gawped uncomprehendingly at pictures by Modigliani: paintings of miserable-looking people with bizarre and unrealistic elongated faces and necks. Maybe I would have greatly appreciated the trip to Grasse, the world centre of perfume, had I been in my late teens and old enough to use scent. We dipped in the freezing cold water of the Gorge du Loup and cooled the wine (permitted for the young, French-style, watered down). The gorge was steeply wooded and our imaginations ran riot with thoughts of wolves roaming those hillsides. This idea was somewhat tempered by being told later that, in the South of France, the name *loup* also meant bass (as in the fish), named after its wolf-like aggression, no doubt.

To our delight we were once taken to Antibes where we boarded a modest, elderly craft. Not one of those seagoing gin palaces. Once in the bay, we surfboarded on an old piece of wood tied to the stern of the boat. We were having such a good time that nobody noticed the darkening sky and a storm on the horizon. The moment the adults became aware, we were hauled back on board and the boat rapidly turned round, heading back to the harbour at full throttle. The engines spluttered in protest at being thrashed as we ploughed our way through rollers, whipped up by the increasing force of the wind. We got back to dry land, soaked through and pretty scared. Back at the monastery, after drying and being fortified with a bowl of hot soup, we stood at the open full-length windows of our dormitory. In awe, we watched the most majestic display of nature venting her anger over the sea. There was no rain, only jagged streaks of forked lightning splitting the sky, an electrical storm lighting up the entire ocean and the grounds of the monastery. There were moments of eerie quiet into which came the sound of chanting. A group of monks came slowly into view, carrying candles as they processed through the gardens, celebrating the festival of the Immaculate Heart of Mary. The scene struck us as Gothic, almost satanic in a way, which was quite unsettling for fertile teenage imaginations. It didn't make us feel any the less spooked seeing the statue of the Blessed Virgin being held aloft, with her heart displayed and glowing in the candlelight. It was theatre at its most potent.

It had been an exciting holiday, full of new experiences. I got back to school speaking reasonably good French, thanks to the adults looking after us; only to be told that it was not acceptable as I spoke it colloquially and with an accent! How foolish to give a child the impression that they were no good at languages. The die was cast and has stayed with me ever since.

⚜

I was in my fourteenth year in 1956 when Aunt Sylvia, as I now called her, needed a larger farm and one that could be worked more easily. I returned to what was now, ostensibly, home during the school holidays and the news was broken to me. 'Pamela, we may be moving to a bigger farm. We are going for a second look and would like you to come along to see what you think of it.' It should have come as no surprise to me as the farm was not only hilly and boulder-strewn, but was merely rented.

It was a cold frosty day when we set off. Fortunately, Sylvia's father had replaced the ancient army dispatch motorbike, which she used to have for getting about, with his old maroon Austin

Seven. Something for which I was incredibly grateful. Not only because it would make the journey possible in icy conditions, but because I didn't have fond memories of her motorcycle. I was once felled by a terrified ram that had been startled by the roar of the two-wheeled monster starting up. He had taken off across the field, burst into the yard and butted me behind the knees. I went down like a ninepin, only to see the departing Sylvia in the distance, quite oblivious. Sylvia's relationship with anything mechanical was never very good. She was an appalling driver and never improved over the years, probably because no one of that generation ever needed to take a test. None of her vehicles retained its entire body throughout its life. Each holiday I would return to find another bit missing, a door kept closed with baler twine or a new dent. To cap it all, I was amazed to see that the Persian runner from the hallway had been cut in half. It had seen better days but was still very valuable. One half had been placed in the back of the open truck to serve as a non-slip mat for lambs being ferried backwards and forwards and the other half placed in the scullery. The lambs' half lasted for years, far longer than any of the vehicles in which it was used. As each truck gave up the ghost and was towed to the scrapyard, the precious rug was lifted out to grace the old truck's successor. Despite the weather the rug still had value after Sylvia's death; even more so when it was cleaned and reunited with its better half.

We bumped across the moor, only just making it up an icy hill that was more like a bobsleigh track than a road; through a gate, along a private road about a quarter of a mile long, passing fields, cowsheds and yard, down to the farmhouse. Sylvia loved the place but she didn't let on. She turned to me and said, 'I have a feeling I know what you're thinking, Pam – it's written all over your face.'

I was as entranced as Sylvia and Courty were; it was the right home for them. The thatched house was tucked into the side of a hill in a sheltered wooded valley next to the Webburn River, a tributary of the Dart, flowing 'twixt house and trees. A pretty bridge over the river led one through a conifer wood, which we later discovered was carpeted with daffodils in spring, apparently planted in loving memory of a previous farmer's deceased wife. From this wood the path led on and upwards through fields, until one reached the boundary of the property on the high moor.

For me it was yet another change, a fresh start, but from a secure base this time. There was no dread, only excitement. However, to my disappointment, the day of moving occurred during term time and so I couldn't be there to help Aunt Syl and Courty out. Sylvia, with the ever-present Moss and Fly, drove the sheep and cattle across the moor in several stages, aided by a band of willing helpers under the watchful eye of Sid, her farm hand. Many times when Sid was having a cup of tea at the kitchen window he would try to tempt Courty into joining him in a cigarette, even offering to roll it for her. He knew she had been a smoker and liked a tipple or two, despite having signed The Pledge in a fit of teenage fervour. The cats were the only ones who had the luxury of a vehicle for the move. Last-minute clothes were bundled in with them and old Mo, one of the felines, made himself comfortable on one of Courty's skirts and so was for ever after known as Pleated Skirt.

I loved the place and found my own secret hideaways; the hayloft where I would lie on the warm bales in a nest of sweet-smelling hay, reading a book, out of reach of adult demands. The branch of a tree that jutted out over the river was often my bolt hole when I had been chastised and was feeling that teenage self-pitying sense of injustice. There I would brood. On warm sunny days, when all was well with my world, I would meander along the bank to the lower reaches of the river, where the gentle sandy edges sloped down, allowing the cattle to drink. The water was clear, sparkling and freezing cold, reflecting the myriad colours of the river's mineral deposits, and was my own personal swimming pool on summer days.

I was not alone; there were other children in the neighbourhood of my age. Lif became a lifelong friend. She would find particularly inopportune moments to set the pair of us off into uncontrollable mirth. In Widecombe Church the organ was hand-pumped with a handle to get the air in, by a willing volunteer. At one particular service, Miss Harvey, the ancient postmistress who also doubled as the organist and who frequently missed the odd note, was playing fortissimo when the organ suddenly gave a groan and, sighing, died. The poor old chap who, up to that point, had been pumping air in like mad, presumably having dislodged a considerable amount of dust, had gone into a paroxysm of sneezing. This was too much for us, we were weeping with the effort of controlling our laughter. For weeks after, Lif kept imitating Miss Harvey's remonstrations with the unfortunate old man in a broad Devon accent.

In those days the church, St Pancras, known as the Cathedral of the Moor, was lit by candles and oil lamps. It was an imposing late gothic edifice lying in the valley, a bowl formed by the surrounding hilly fields, moorland and tors. It is documented that in 1638 there was a violent thunderstorm in Widecombe

Lif on Dartmoor.

and lightning struck one of the pinnacles of the church, killing several people and injuring many others during a service. We had been brought up on the myth that this storm had been the work of the Devil, who had come to claim the souls of those who had sinned. This was grist to the mill of a child's imagination.

Sylvia had a godson, Peter, who with his sister Mary some-times came to stay during school holidays; they have also remained lifelong friends. Peter was the apple of Sylvia's eye. She adored boys and men and had almost no time for girls. How Mary and I giggled at the two of them as they walked ahead of us, earnestly engaged in a conversation of great import. Sylvia's basic perception of the female was very much like that of a Victorian husband: 'the little woman' whose advice, especially on practical matters, was less than that of a man. Even as an adult, when offering her my advice on, say, the need to service the malfunctioning Aga, it would be dismissed with a wave of the hand, 'It was working fine last week, it's the fault of the easterly down-draught,' even though it had been blowing a westerly at the time! However, it was only when some visiting male friend made the same suggestion that the idea of servicing the Aga would be heralded as a splendid notion. This trait was infuriating and got worse as she aged.

The farm was often busy during the summer months when paying guests would stay year after year. They were usually single, elderly, moorland enthusiasts and birdwatchers. The one I remember most clearly, probably because he scared me the most, was a retired army man, the mustachioed Major Mott. He wasn't fierce, but his somewhat military demeanour caused me to be uncharacteristically demure. It was a great relief when he left and I could revert to type.

Days were far from leisurely. On the home front, as well as on the farm, there was always some creature giving birth. It was a warm spring day when Sukie decided to have her kittens. She was very vocal all day, following us around the farm telling us the glad tidings that a kitten was about to be born. She may have chosen the wrong season and certainly had higher aspirations than a stable in which to give birth. She chose the comfort of the deepest drawer of a Victorian chest in Courty's bedroom, giving birth on her best hat, the favourite one. The one that sported the exotic cockade of feathers and which she had worn on the day she collected me for the first time from the station in Newton Abbot. Sukie presented Courty with a great dilemma: there she was, a proud and content mother, displaying her feathered kittens. How Courty loved that gorgeous hat, how she loved her little cat . . . Sukie won! Now, to know Courty was to know that hats were her passion, she never went anywhere without one, be it feather, fur, felt, bright yellow beret or straw. She didn't drive and so one of her greatest joys was to be taken in the motor car, duly cranked and driven by Sylvia at an alarming speed, on an annual hat-shopping expedition. The purchases were followed by tea at Madge Mellor's Cafe. This was the only part of the outing that Sylvia liked; she loathed shopping and had absolutely no interest in personal adornment.

Fly was a fantastic working dog. She was self-contained and utterly devoted to Sylvia and hated being fussed. However much people were warned to leave her alone, there would always be some dog lover who thought they had the skill to melt Fly's heart, but all they'd end up with was a warning nip. Fly did her own choosing. On one occasion, after she had given birth, a friend of Sylvia's called round to see the pups. Knowing her own dog, Sylvia was against this. However, when Fly went off with Sylvia and briefly left her babies, the friend foolishly seized her opportunity to stroke the pups. Sylvia returned with Fly who went to the scullery to check her litter, then came straight out and gave the silly woman a nip on the leg!

Work on the farm continued in earnest throughout the year. When I was at home I helped with calving, milking by hand, rearing calves, the hay harvest and sheep-dipping and, when the vet came to visit, which was rare, I was Santa's little helper. Veterinary help was needed in cases of summer mastitis and tuberculin testing. One year, the entire flock of sheep went down with heather blindness, a contagious condition akin to our pink eye, which can occur when the heather is in bloom. It meant putting ointment in their eyes twice a day. Before this could be done, we had to confine them to a smaller area of the field without further frightening the already blind, panicked sheep, making sure they were not too closely confined. A sheep with heather blindness cocks its head as though listening for sound clues to help them locate their whereabouts. Often, on moving, they stagger around in circles lifting their forelegs in a high-stepping dressage gait as though trying to feel their way out of danger. It is a pitiful sight and was an additional burden on us, in what was already a very full day, but it had to be done and they did recover.

Soon after we moved George took over as full-time farm hand as it was too far for Sid to travel. George was a little whippet of a man with prodigious energy and strength – he worked from milking time at 6 a.m. through to 6 p.m. We'd have been lost without him. In the winter there was kale to be cut and root vegetables to be pulled up as supplementary feed for those animals wintering outside. We had two working horses, Duchess and Violet, and feed would be loaded on to a cart pulled by one of them and distributed over the fields. We never had a tractor; the horses were used for ploughing, sowing and turning the hay, and this was George's province.

Thankfully, at haymaking time, a contractor would be employed for cutting and baling the hay, which would later be loaded by us into the barns. When rain was forecast, there would be a scramble to get the hay under cover fast and neighbouring farmers would turn up to clear each other's fields. In this way many harvests were saved from becoming silage. On hot humid days when distant thunder warned us of an approaching storm, we took every precaution to avoid being struck by lightning. Pockets were emptied of their change. Penknives, even belts with buckles were removed, lest the lightning be attracted to the metal. At least, in the middle of a field, there was no danger of being caught under a tree.

After finishing a backbreaking day's work in the heat, strangely the most refreshing drink one could have was a hot cup of tea to accompany the sandwiches, sausage rolls and cakes aplenty. There was always cider and home-made lemonade on offer but they never quite hit the spot. It was a scene somewhat reminiscent of Pieter Breughel's *The Harvesters*.

I loved working with the horses, despite the fact that Duchess was a demon to catch. After a long walk across the field holding the halter behind my back, I would almost reach her when she would kick up her heels and take off. She wasn't averse to aggressive behaviour if she felt particularly uncooperative; head snaking out unexpectedly, she'd give you a nip. Her workmate Violet, on the other hand, was a gentle black horse with one mood and one pace, ideal for work. I suppose the cattle were the animals with which I had the most contact, mainly because of the frequency of the milking routine and the relationship you have with each cow. In the early days we milked only by hand, each cow requiring a slightly different technique. It was not something you could learn overnight. The animal would soon let you know if she didn't like what you were doing – up would come the rear leg that could easily knock you off the milking stool. But, if you got it right, you were rewarded with a calm patient animal who let her milk flow. When we got a milking machine, the time was cut down, but there was still the odd animal that required hand milking.

We were part of the cycle of the land and, as such, knew that rearing and selling was our livelihood. The greatest number of creatures that went to market were Aunt Syl's beloved Whiteface Dartmoor Sheep, a hardy breed, fitted for life in high wet moorland conditions, producing good, flavourful, dense meat. Going to the sheep fair in Ashburton was great fun for me, a day out. For Sylvia, as a well-respected and experienced breeder, it was an important date in the calendar. That year's wether lambs would be sold and rams bought and sold to renew the bloodstock.

Left: A hideously plain schoolchild.

Main picture: The second farm – my heart's home.

Below: Even back then, I was drawn to an exotic costume and a bag of props.

Above: The Warren – my school from 1953 to 1960.

Left: Us gals marching on Sports Day.

Below: Me (third from left, front row) in The Warren's annual school photo 1959.

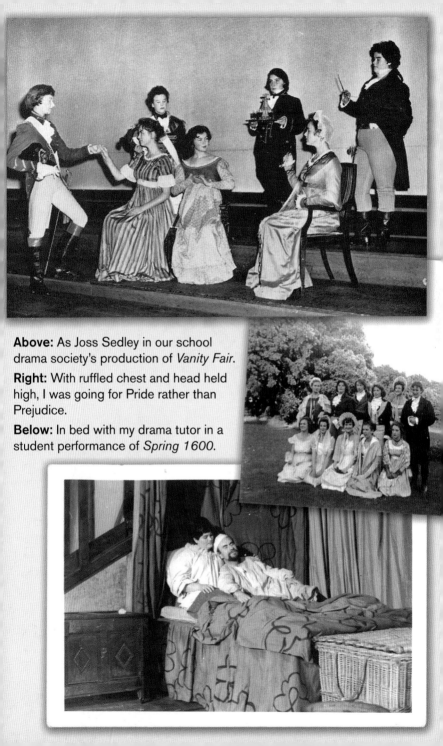

Above: As Joss Sedley in our school drama society's production of *Vanity Fair*.

Right: With ruffled chest and head held high, I was going for Pride rather than Prejudice.

Below: In bed with my drama tutor in a student performance of *Spring 1600*.

Left: Poster for production of *Hedda Gabler* in Los Angeles, one of the stops on our world tour.

Below: Some of the *Hedda* gang at Niagara Falls, looking none too happy with their costumes!

Right: Celebrating at the end of the *Hedda* run, with Jennie Linden and Fidelis Morgan.

HUNTINGTON HARTFORD THEATRE
1615 VINE STREET, HOLLYWOOD, CALIFORNIA 90028
Telephone 462-6666.   For Groups and Parties, phone Group Sales Department at 462-6666.
WEDNESDAY, APRIL 9th thru SATURDAY, APRIL 19th, 1975
Opening Night, Wednesday, April 9th at 8.00.   Mondays thru Saturdays at 8.30.   Sunday, April 13th at 7.30.
Matinees April 10th, 12th, 16th and 19th at 2.30.
OPENING NIGHT, WEDNESDAY, APRIL 9th and FRIDAY and SATURDAY EVENINGS
Orchestra and Mezzanine Loge $12.50; Balcony $10.00, $8.00.
MONDAY thru THURSDAY EVENINGS and SUNDAY EVENING
Orchestra and Mezzanine Loge $10.00; Balcony $9.00, $8.00, $7.00.
MATINEES: Orchestra and Mezzanine Loge $8.50; Balcony $7.50, $6.50, $5.50.
PRESENTED BY THE GREEK THEATRE ASSOCIATION, JAMES A. DOOLITTLE, GENERAL DIRECTOR.
Make check payable and mail to Huntington Hartford Theatre, enclosing stamped, self-addressed envelope.

By arrangement with the Governors
of the Royal Shakespeare Theatre, Stratford-upon-Avon England

PAUL ELLIOTT and DUNCAN C WELDON
for Triumph Theatre Productions present

THE
ROYAL SHAKESPEARE COMPANY
PRODUCTION
GLENDA JACKSON
in IBSEN's
HEDDA GABLER
English version by Trevor Nunn

with
TIMOTHY WEST
PETER   PATRICK
EYRE   STEWART
CONSTANCE CHAPMAN
PAM ST CLEMENT
JENNIE LINDEN
Directed by TREVOR NUNN
Design by JOHN NAPIER
Lighting design by ANDY PHILLIPS
ASSOCIATE PRODUCER: BERNARD JAY

Top: 'I'll scweam and I'll scweam' – as Marlene Ward in *Within These Walls*.

Above: No, I'm not stripping for Simon Williams in *I Am A Camera*.

Right: Fat Molly having a fag after entertaining the Nazi troops in *Enemy at the Door*.

Above: Feeling very superior as Mother Basil in *Once A Catholic* at the West Yorkshire Playhouse.

Left: An over-the-top wig and an Irish accent – a great part, as Carmel, in *Shall I See You Now?*.

Right: Mr and Mrs Eckersley (me with Roger Hammond in *Emmerdale Farm*).

Connie, the imaginative usherette in *Not for the Likes of Us,* was one of my favourite television roles. Her fantasies included being worshipped as a queen of a tropical island – with feathers, sarong and six-inch heels

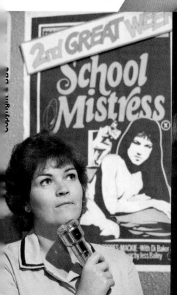

(centre right) – and as the subject of Suzanne Valadon's painting *La Chambre Bleue* (right). When she poses nude for an art class (top) – the most scary thing I have ever done on screen – she imagined she was Marc Gertler's *Queen of Sheba.*

Main picture: The habit of a lifetime? Playing a nun, again, in the film *Biggles*.

Right: I didn't know you could do that with a milk bottle! Uniformed in *Bottle Boys* – a comedy series with Robin Asquith.

Right: Demure looking, but hiding murderous intent. As Mrs Crockett in *The Clergyman's Daughter*.

After herding the sheep, from lorries to pens, and securing them, I'd skive off. It was a rare opportunity to see some shops. On my way home, I'd often bump into a local farmer I knew, who'd say, 'Where y'oum tew, Maid? Dew ee come to thicky old beer-tent vor a drap o' zider?' Despite my rebellious nature, even I was hesitant to get legless on scrumpy when there was work to do. We had a neighbour, an elderly retired general, who farmed across the valley. One market day, he stopped to give me a lift in his Land Rover. As we made our way up the hill over granite boulders and down to the track he said rather mischievously, 'How are the Popsies doing down there?' Not being versed in military speak I could only assume he was referring to the Aunts, which made me giggle. Nothing could have been less popsy-like!

Christmases for us Popsies came and went. The Nativity scene was always assembled with great ceremony on Christmas Eve, in a corner of the sitting room where it took up a considerable amount of space. To start with, baby Jesus was some three inches long (without crib) so, by the time the adults were added, Joseph, Mary, the three kings – Balthasar, Caspar, Melchior – and assorted shepherds, plus sheep and oxen, it had almost become the very centrepiece of the room. After that, we set about decorating what was left of the room with sprigs of yew and holly, a concession to the pagan origins of Yuletide. No Scandinavian conifer for us. After a bite to eat we would wrap up and go out to Midnight Mass. Coming into the warmth of the candlelit church smelling of candlewax and greenery, one's breath steaming from the cold outside, we were greeted by rosy-cheeked friends and neighbours, many of whom had helped to decorate the church. On our return, home-made mince pies were served with a small glass of sherry (I've been making up for this meagre ration ever since!). There was very little sleep for Courty, who got up a few hours later to put the bird in the Aga. We did have one Christmas episode where a goose was being reared for Christmas lunch but, when it came to the critical moment, no one had the heart to carry out the deed. Goosey had become one of the family and so we had to forgo the planned menu. The pork set aside for Boxing Day stood us in good stead and was a welcome alternative.

Although there were chores like milking twice a day over Christmas, we tried to organise things so that they were the most relaxed days of the year. Sometimes, on Christmas Day, neighbouring farmers with their families popped in for tea and the ceremonial cutting of the Christmas cake, but could never stay long because they, like us, had late-afternoon chores. While Sylvia's parents were alive, Boxing Day was spent at the vicarage near Ashburton where Sylvia had grown up. It was a large, early Victorian stone-built mansion in beautifully kept grounds. The vast herbaceous borders gave life to the somewhat austere building in summer but, in winter, provided us with garlands of holly that always seemed to be bursting with bright red berries. Inside, the house was as cold as charity. There was always a fire in the sitting room, more reminiscent of Scrooge's fireplace for all the good it did. We always arrived well wrapped up because the dining room was even colder. It was there that we had our second Christmas lunch at a vast rosewood table with an enormous matching tiered 'lazy Susan' which revolved, allowing one to take water, condiments and so on. At Christmas, though, it was topped with a large shallow bowl of holly sprigs in which stood candles and, on the lower levels, there would be sweetmeats – marzipan, dates, walnuts and tangerines. As well as these, silver boats contained cranberry sauce, bread sauce and gravy. On the table were silver salt and pepper shakers. There was mustard in an indigo-blue glass container sitting in a silver basket into which a tiny silver spoon had been placed, looking for all the world like an elfin soup spoon. As far as I was concerned Boxing Day was a duty rather than a pleasure, similar to visiting the headmaster and his wife. It was alleviated somewhat when Sylvia's sister joined us. Her name was Christine, but she was always known as Bobby, as a result of an interesting haircut she once had. She was always great fun; she never toed the party line, and could say things that neither Sylvia nor Courty would ever say.

Nothing could have been in greater contrast to those lunches at the vicarage than our Christmas lunches at home, where it was usually just the three of us sitting at the farmhouse kitchen table. The kitchen was always the heart of the home. There was something about the constant warmth from the Aga and the hiss of the oil lamps that took one to a place of comfort; a place where, in later years, Aunt Syl, Courty and I shared, without inhibition, our innermost selves.

As Viola in a student production of *Twelfth Night*.

Chapter Five

Practice Skirts and Leotards

Tell me and I forget, teach me and I may remember.
Involve me, and I learn.

Benjamin Franklin

Now eighteen, disappointed at not having the correct A levels to study veterinary medicine, I found myself leaving school with no idea which alternative career path to take. I loved acting but it didn't occur to me for one minute to pursue it as a career. Like Dick Whittington I headed almost penniless for London, signing on at an agency for temporary work in order to earn some money. Then it was off to the YWCA in Baker Street (now the Sherlock Holmes Hotel) to book in for the princely sum of £6 a week, full board. The Savoy it was not, but it was comfortable and central and full of professional women: musicians, actresses, even young daughters of titled families. After some months of varied and, in the main, boring jobs – filing, making tea and being a general dogsbody – I was no further in finding inspiration as to what I should do in the future. Out of the blue, my father, with whom I had continued intermittent contact, suggested that I assist him with his business in north London. He wanted me to become his personal assistant and learn the trade with a view to taking over the company in due course. I would work in an office above his factory, which manufactured such diverse things as soft and plastic toys, glove puppets and beach balls, the valve for which I believe he patented. The idea of staying in London appealed to me. I was beginning to make new friends and went to everything that my age and money would allow. There was so much on offer in the Big City. So, in a fit of foolish optimism, and thinking that an adult relationship with my father would be different, I accepted the job; it had to be better than working as a temp. In the event, I couldn't have been more wrong.

It was a disaster. I found myself holding the fort from about eleven in the morning, that being my father's interpretation of the sun going over the yardarm, and therefore time to start drinking. He left me trying to fend off calls from customers with queries and cope with problems on the factory floor, all of which I was ill-equipped to deal with. The problem with drinking the profits was that it didn't generate more profit, yet at his most successful he had attended trade fairs here and abroad and had major contracts with large companies such as Woolworths. He seemed determined on a course of self-destruction and we couldn't communicate any better than we ever had. I had to leave.

Once again feeling rootless and unmotivated, I turned to something that was familiar, a community structure, and applied to the Royal Air Force. However, after a gruelling three-day selection course at Biggin Hill, the RAF decided I wasn't officer material. There had been about a dozen of us and the only person who was selected happened to be the daughter of an air commodore, or someone as elevated. In the opinion of most of us she was the least likely candidate to become an officer, seeming to lack any authority at all!

So, on returning to London and no further forward, I started temping again and was offered a full-time job in publishing. This turned out to be with Macmillan, the well-known publishing house founded by Harold Macmillan's father. It was an enjoyable stopgap, if not the final answer. Harold was, by then, Prime Minister and so could not have any direct business interests and, consequently, I never met him, but I worked with Maurice, his son. Maurice later became Viscount Macmillan of Ovingdon and owned Highgrove House, later to become the home of Prince Charles. He was a lean, saturnine man, sartorially elegant and authoritative but with a slightly with-drawn quality. It made him mysterious and therefore attractive; we got on well.

One day the offices in Whitcombe Street were a scene of chaos, besieged by the press trying to speak to Alan Maclean. He was a senior editor but also the brother of the spy Donald Maclean, who had defected to Russia some ten years earlier, in 1951. This renewed interest arose when an investigation was closing in on Anthony Blunt, the fourth man in the Cambridge spy ring. We bolted the large wooden doors of our grand building and managed to get Mr Maclean out via the book-loading bay. He was merely a member of the Maclean family and probably had nothing to tell, but when did that ever get in the way of a good headline?

I used to visit the Aunts whenever I could, and during one of my visits I told them that I was still at sixes and sevens workwise. I had, in desperation, filled in an application form and got somebody to sponsor me to emigrate to New Zealand. This was almost certainly an attempt to escape my lack of direction. Of course, as Sylvia pointed out, it wouldn't have solved anything at all because I would have faced the same problems I had been having in England. The solution was not where I was going, but within me.

It wasn't long before the ever-wise Sylvia had a suggestion. While looking at a copy of the *Western Morning News*, she had seen an advertisement seeking an unqualified assistant teacher in a secondary school for girls near Tavistock, in Devon. She suggested that I apply for the post in the hope that it would lead me in a more permanent direction. At worst it was likely to be more rewarding than the work I had been doing. It was probably the right moment to leave London and, again, to have the comfort of home during the holidays. I applied for the job, and had an interview at a London hotel with the headmistress. A week or so later I received a letter offering me the position of assistant teacher for £50 a term, with board and lodging, and in September 1962 I started work at Sydenham House School.

It was ideally placed for me – Tavistock is a mere thirty-minute drive due west across the moor. My duties would encompass being in charge of a junior class of eleven- to twelve-year-olds, filling in when necessary for subject teachers, running non-specific classes such as general knowledge, plus debates and discussions. Being a boarding school, there were also many weekend duties such as supervising walks and church-going, as well as daily meals and bedtime routines. It was hardly onerous or deeply stimulating, but it was varied enough to retain my interest. After all, it was another new experience. Unfortunately, I could never persuade the powers-that-be to allow a Drama Society – nothing so subversive!

After my first term at Sydenham I returned home to Dartmoor for Christmas. That winter of 1962–63 completely broke the usual Yuletide routine. It was unbelievably harsh, and hit us just after Christmas. It was fortunate that the larder was still full and we even had half a bottle of rum and some cooking sherry in the cupboard, which were to come in handy as a restorative. There was a strange atmosphere the evening before the blizzard arrived; the barometric pressure had dropped alarmingly. The air was quite still, filled with an eerie gloom the colour of an early daguerreotype. Slowly the wind, as its direction swung round, began to howl low down on the ground, as though the earth were foretelling of what was to come. The dogs were restless and kept going to the door. We too were uneasy but there was nothing more that we could do to prepare for – we knew not what. As it was winter, the cattle were indoors and the sheep had been moved to more sheltered fields. They were used to being outside in the winter, even in bad weather; their thick fleeces kept them well protected.

The blizzard hit suddenly and battered us all night. We woke to find snow up to the downstairs windowsills and that's when the real work began. The priority was to dig our way out and check the animals. The depth of the snow meant that the sheep were in the greatest danger. We were able to account for all but five. We eventually found four huddled together, covered by snow against a hedge in the lee of the storm. The snow seemed to have trapped them in a sort of igloo, offering them warmth and protection. It saved their lives. Everything we did that day was slow. We were exhausted, hampered as we were by the depth of the snow and the sheer weight of it clinging to our boots. The fifth sheep was found a few days later by George, who was on his way to us. He had been trapped in his bungalow, blocked by the volume of snow packed against his doors and windows, and it had taken him time to dig himself out. Having no telephone, and concerned for our welfare, he was determined to reach us, a mere half mile away. The ewe was in a bad way, alive only because she had found some shelter. She was far too heavy for us to carry any distance and so we set about making a sledge, to which Violet was eventually harnessed, and the hypothermic sheep transported back to the farmhouse. She was ensconced by the warm range in the scullery and overseen by Courty who was always a dab hand at warming up frozen sheep and premature lambs.

We worked like dogs; the days were long, cold and exhausting. At lunchtime we took buckets down to the river to fill, our pipes having frozen solid with the plummeting temperatures. When it was too dark to work we returned home, hardly able to pull our frozen boots off. We lit the oil lamps – our farmhouse, like the previous one, had never had electricity – and hung kettles over the fire to fill our stone hot-water bottles. We pulled the rum from the cupboard to kickstart us into life and all had a nip, even Sylvia the confirmed teetotaller. Fortified and defrosted, we began the domestic chores which couldn't be shelved. Courty prepared supper while Aunt Sylvia fed the dogs and cats and I took the lamps and hot-water bottles up to the bedrooms.

My bedroom faced due east and even in the mildest of winters it was cold but, during this harsh spell, I had to prise my frozen sheets apart. I would wait until everybody else had retired to bed then creep downstairs to collect the dogs. They would supplement the heat of my hot-water bottle in order to defrost the sheets before I climbed into bed. They knew that upstairs was out-of-bounds and so it took a bit of persuading to remove them from their warm baskets by the Aga. Once upstairs, they soon settled down and it was not long before we all snuggled up together. I rose early and took them back to the kitchen before their nocturnal wanderings were discovered. Working dogs were definitely not allowed beyond that domain.

The only rooms we were able to heat were the kitchen with the Aga and the sitting room, which had an enormous open fireplace over which we boiled charred-black iron kettles, which dangled from hooks over the flames. This was in order to have sufficient hot water for washing clothes and dishes and bathing. Carrying heavy boiling kettles up a steep staircase to the bathroom was a hazardous business. Even the loo had to be flushed with a bucket of water. Our drinking water, coming from the river, also had to be boiled. Not an existence for the faint-hearted!

By the New Year, it was clear from the battery-run radio that the weather was not going to ease. This was a great worry because we were, by this time, running low on provisions, most particularly the stone-ground flour and yeast needed for bread-making. Some areas were getting food drops and aid from the Air–Sea Rescue helicopter, orchestrated by the local vicar, but our situation was not too dire at that point.

Apart from running down on food, we also needed help to move a lot of hay for feed. The farm was a few miles from the Outward Bound School in Ashburton and it was a day of great jubilation when about a dozen young men skied over with provisions and muscle to help out. They sat in the kitchen by the Aga, full of vitality and goodwill, happily munching scones with lashings of jam and cream and thawing out with mugs of hot chocolate. The weather had made it impossible for Dawes Creamery, our usual dairy, to collect our daily milk churns, so butter and cream were the order of the day.

We had been snowed in for some weeks and it was becoming increasingly urgent for me to get out for the start of the Sydenham spring term, which had also been delayed by the weather. A friend of the Aunts offered to give me a lift to the station as he too needed to get to Newton Abbot for business, the only proviso being that I was prepared to brave the snow to get to his house. He was an experienced and adventurous driver, having once taken part in the Monte Carlo Rally. Despite the icy conditions, he was game to put chains on his wheels and have a go at driving off the moor through narrow roads, the ten or so miles to Newton Abbot. Getting to him meant walking some one and a half miles through knee-high snow, up the track, over the moor and down to their house. It was a long and scary trek; nothing has identity in the snow. Landmarks that would normally have guided my path were obscured by a blanket of white. Even people who had lived on the moor all their lives later said that they had been totally disorientated by the snow-fall. Trudging through the deep snow in boots that became heavier with the weight of the impacted snow, I was further hampered by my suitcase. Not only was it heavy, forcing me to change hands frequently, but if I held it at arm's length I found that it dragged in the snow, which meant that I ended up carrying it on my shoulders. Exhausted, and by now very hot in my winter attire, I was relieved to reach their house unscathed. We took off in his red sports car almost as soon as I arrived, slipping and sliding down narrow Devon lanes, made even narrower by the piles of cleared snow, making them claustro-phobic and tunnel-like. We eventually dropped down from the high moor to the foothills and closer to sea level where the going got easier. Not surprisingly, all transport was disrupted by the longevity of the cold spell. I even had time to fortify myself in the station cafeteria. I had a mug of hot chocolate while I waited for the train to take me to London, where I was due to collect a group of schoolchildren and escort them back to Sydenham House School.

Sydenham, a beautiful old house set in a wooded valley on the fast-flowing River Lyd, had been rented out as a private educational establishment for girls of secondary age. For a house of such historic value and content, it was a bizarre setting for a school. The earlier part of the house, built in the fourteenth century, was improved in Elizabethan times to form the shape of an 'E', a classic example of Tudor architecture. My memory is of a house that looked modest from the front but from the back became an extremely grand manor house, with the grandeur of a stately home.

A long gallery, with an ornamental plaster ceiling, wainscoting and fluted pilasters, was used as a staffroom, where we played mah jong on Friday nights. At one end of the long gallery there was a glass-fronted recess containing a fine, well-preserved doublet and breeches of silk brocade. With these vestments hung the trappings worn by the horse taking its titled rider, the then owner Sir Thomas Wise, to the Coronation of James I, where he was created a Knight of the Bath. A rather appropriate title really as he doubtless looked a little grubby after his long ride! Beams of light shone through gabled and mullioned windows, lighting up the beautifully preserved and decorated oak staircases and panelling. To top it all there was a genuine Van Dyck hanging on the fifth-form classroom wall. For a history lover like me, it was paradise. No wonder I developed a long-lasting interest in Elizabethan and Jacobean times. It was akin to living in the period.

Much as it was a wonderful environment for a school, it was a singularly inappropriate use for a house of such historic value.

It was crying out to be in private hands, loved and restored, and in due time it was. The house came to mind once again when I read in the newspaper that a fire had destroyed a considerable part of it in November 2012. It was a shock to think of this wonderful monument going up in flames, taking so much history with it. What a terrible loss for the owners who had apparently renovated it to its original glory. How I wish I'd been able to see what they had done.

The school was run by a coterie of women aged between sixty-six and eighty-two. Looking back, it could only have happened in an age when many parents sent their 'gals' to private schools on the assumption that they would be well looked after by a trustworthy staff. As for the age and educational qualifications of the staff, or the academic standard of the curriculum, this simply did not enter the equation. The headmistress, Miss Strickland, whose name reflected her general approach to discipline, was, for all that, frail and bent. Most of the time she seemed to be imitating a chicken pecking at grain, nothing escaping her beady eye.

Miss Heath was an admirable eighty-two-year-old with an amazingly ample bosom – both age and bosom were somewhat of a handicap for a teacher in charge of games. Some days when I was passing the tennis court, set on the lawns that sloped away from the back of the house, I watched her tutoring members of the fourth form. I would be alarmed, not only at her puffing and panting, but by the independent activity of each mammary as it endeavoured to escape its moorings. What a cracker! She even died on the job. Well, not literally.

She lived in the school, had a brief illness and gave up the ghost during the night, much to the distress of the girls. She was a great favourite.

The science and biology teacher was known as Budleigh Dearie; so called because whenever she was asked where she lived, which was Budleigh Salterton, she would reply, 'Budleigh, Dearie'. She, like so many women who went into the teaching profession then, was a spinster, possibly due to the monstrous loss of men in the First World War. It was also a profession where those without specific academic qualifications were not barred. The biggest handicap for those self-same women, when teaching reproduction in biology lessons, was often a singular lack of experience, if any at all. The moral strictures of their youth went way beyond physical restrictions; for many the subject of sex may never have even been discussed. So, lessons would be centred on the anatomy of a rabbit and the production of a chicken's egg, rather than the nitty-gritty of human reproduction. Given that it was the early sixties, nothing seemed to have changed since my own schooldays. Thus we were sending girls into the world as ill-equipped as we had been. How could we have known that society was on the cusp of a momentous change? We were about to enter the Swinging Sixties.

During my time at Sydenham I made friends with a qualified teacher, Jo, who was not many years older than me. She lived on a farm some ten miles away and drove in every day. Her family was gorgeous, of Irish extraction, with a great sense of hospitality and humour. Many weekends I visited and was cosseted in their guest room on a feather mattress. On one particular occasion I stayed over because we were going on a Catholic pilgrimage the next day in a nearby town. Now, don't get me wrong, I am not that pious. The appeal of that particular jaunt for both Jo and me was the procession around Launceston Hill with the fingernail, or some bodily part, of St Cuthbert. As with many events that have serious and devotional overtones, behaving appropriately can be made all the more difficult if the person you are with is looking extraordinarily devout then, out of the blue, whispers a cheeky suggestion regarding the erstwhile fingernail. Jo took me so completely by surprise that I exploded with mirth and tried desperately to disguise it with a particularly emotional rendering of the Hail Mary.

I wasn't the only student teacher in the school; there was another girl who was filling in a gap year having applied for a drama course at a college near Exeter. She suggested I did the same. Why hadn't I thought of that? It fulfilled so much of what I was interested in. I applied to the same course immediately and was accepted for the following year. I wonder if she knows how much her suggestion changed the direction of my life.

❧

The end of the school year came and the aspirant teacher became the taught. I went to Rolle College, then an adjunct of Exeter University, to train as a drama teacher. Rolle College was later subsumed into Plymouth University, from which I later received an Honorary Doctorate. I was not only honoured, but delighted.

To add to my joy of being a student, I bought my first car with money I had been saving for some time. It was a convertible turquoise Sunbeam Talbot with column gear change and cream leather bench seats. It was so old it broke down with regular monotony. It was gorgeous and no car has ever come as close to my heart since. While living in a hall of residence I could afford to run it on my student grant, because petrol cost about 5p a litre in today's reckoning, although it seemed a lot at the time. To my sorrow I had to give it up in my final year for lack of funds.

For the first two years, halls of residence were convenient; at least one didn't have the responsibilities of domesticity while adapting to academic life. An added bonus was that we had three meals a day. By my third year I had digs with a family living in a large red-brick Victorian house in town. My landlords, Mr and Mrs Williams, had three sons, ranging in age from about sixteen to twenty, and a golden retriever. They were a lovely family and made me very welcome. I was a night owl and wrote my final dissertation throughout the hours of darkness. Ironically, my subject was the French playwright Jean Genet, whose work was also very dark. Finishing my dissertation was the reason that I stayed with them during the last vacation rather than returning home. As a consequence I had to support myself which, once again, meant finding a job because my grant wasn't sufficient to live on. I found some work deadheading carnations in a nursery greenhouse, but that was only for two days. On reflection, it is clear to me that I was not a dab hand at finding long-term employment. Rendered a pauper, I went back to my large, comfortable bay-windowed room clutching a loaf of bread, a pack of butter, a jar of Marmite, a packet of tea, a bottle of milk and a few cans of tomato soup. This was to last me for the next three weeks if I couldn't get another job. When I returned one day from a fruitless search for work, Mrs Williams had a word with me. 'Pam,' she said, 'I cleaned your room this morning and noticed that you haven't got much in the way of provisions, apart from bread and Marmite. Are you having difficulty finding a job? Have you got enough money to live on?' I fidgeted and dissembled, at which point she said, 'I'm feeding three strapping lads and a husband and one extra won't make any difference. You're welcome to join us.' I did so, despite feeling rather embarrassed at receiving charity and imposing upon them. None of them ever made me feel in the least bit in debt to them; they couldn't have been kinder.

I needed nourishment as the course was demanding. Rolle College had a vibrant and innovative approach to drama, embracing such things as the Theatre of the Absurd and mask work. The productions ranged from Samuel Beckett's *Endgame*, when I played Clov, to Sophocles' *Elektra*, Shakespeare, Victorian melodrama and, for a little light relief, Emlyn Williams's *Spring 1600* and a Cocteau farce. It was all very varied. I was in my element and fast becoming a performance addict. Even then I was never the juvenile lead, always a character part. If I ever managed to get cast in a role that was patently feminine, it was blousy or tarty and I loved it. Give me a nun or a tart any time!

Most of my friends were drama students, including a

somewhat maverick tutor with a wonderful voice and a way with women. He was great fun, though not very robust, having had tuberculosis when a young man but still smoking like a chimney. We all looked very sixties, pale faces and draped from top to toe in black, being frightfully existential. Hazel was my only non-drama student friend. She was a history student and living in the same hall. We continued to meet until her death some twenty years ago.

Distaff love, from the engaging-of-the-heart point of view, did not occur until those college years. It slowly dawned on me that I was falling in love with the girl I had met at Sydenham, the fellow student teacher who had encouraged me to join her on the course at Exeter. She was talented and sensitive; we matched each other intellectually and made a good team in our studies and friendship, but my devotion could never be admitted. There is no way one should risk losing a valuable friendship by declaring undying love to the object of your desire, a declaration that might endanger something so valuable. We remained friends for some years and even knew each other's husbands. One quickly learns that one of the greatest lessons in life is knowing when to keep one's own counsel. This modern need to expose everything about oneself at the expense of other people is not particularly palatable. It's not right to say something which can hurt and cause chaos in other people's lives. On reflection, I seem to have been drawn to successful intellectually dynamic women with drive but, for me, love has always been about the personality, not the sex of the person. In the main I have found men sexually fulfilling and socially stimulating, but there is a comfort in the company of one's own sex that is uncomplicated. What might drive a man to distraction would be completely understandable to a woman. Thus, in a domestic situation, there is a lot to be said for sticking to your own sex with, or without, a physical relationship.

The seeds of doubt were beginning to manifest themselves, not only with regard to my sexuality, but with regard to my future profession. To teach, or not to teach, that was the question. I acknowledged that teaching was a valuable and often rewarding profession; guiding the youngsters of today to the adulthood of tomorrow. Instinctively, however, I felt I was not the stuff of which good teachers were made. I was a doer, rather than a facilitator and guide, and I knew in my heart that I wanted to perform. My quandary was that I had already received three years of further education and needed funding to pursue a postgraduate course at drama school. My father was, once again, living the high life with Sally and we were rarely in touch at that time. Perhaps, because the farm had become my home, he no longer felt any responsibility for me; after all, I was an adult and old enough to see my way in the world. I had gone so far as to get a place at the Rose Bruford College of Speech and Drama. I applied for funding to many educational trusts with interests in the arts, but with no success. It was impossible for Aunt Sylvia not to be aware of my difficulties; after all, she had virtually become my parent. It was she, always living on a shoestring herself, who gifted me the college fees. There was a family trust from which she received a small income and she carefully saved this as a nest egg. Looking back, I realise how much she believed in me and it was a great joy to be able to repay this kindness in later years, when I was earning.

I absolutely adored Bruford's, run by another coterie of eccentric females. Rose Bruford, a small dynamic woman whose spirit permeated the college, always insisted on writing in green ink. Miss Bruford's right-hand woman and bursar, Mary Hennicker Heaton, was a tall woman with a strange gait that convinced us, silly students, that she had a wooden leg in which she kept the college funds. Bru's two main principles were to 'train actors who could teach, and teachers who could act'. She based the training work on the doctrines of Konstantin Stanislavsky who founded the Moscow Arts Theatre at the end of the nineteenth century. His principles were truth, discipline, character analysis and symbiotic connection between actors. His approach was adapted by Lee Strasberg at the Actors' Studio in New York, and was known as Method Acting. Some eminent film performers of today trained with him.

We swept through the corridors in leotards and long circular practice skirts to period dancing classes that transported us to another age. Each historical period was covered. For example, the relationship between God and man in the medieval period was emphasised with vertical movements (up to God and down to man), mirroring the beliefs of the time. The Tudor court reflected breadth in fashion and movement: wide and confident; England was a force to be reckoned with.

Choral speaking lessons, by Miss Mona Swann, were about

using the rhythm of words to create an orchestration with the human voice, similar to that of William Walton's *Façade*. Mona Swann's 'Waves . . . lap . . . lap, fish fins . . . flap . . . flap' et cetera had us in uncontrollable fits of mirth during a choral speaking session. So helpless were three of us that we were barred from the room for that lesson. She always eyed me rather suspiciously after that.

Mime was the ultimate physical discipline: silent characters in comedic and tragic situations like Leoncavallo's clown in *Il Pagliacci*, Charlie Chaplin, and later Rowan Atkinson's *Mr Bean*, the modern exponent of expression without words. It is an art form that requires physical control rather than speed, so appealed to me.

Stage make-up had me in a state of mucky confusion. The principle is that, on the stage, you are a long way from the audience and are illuminated with bright stage lighting that blanks out the features. Therefore, one has to create the features on one's face. The process of doing this is to paint the face an overall base colour, creating a sort of canvas. On to this canvas one paints the features with the appropriate Leichner grease-paint sticks: the eyebrows, the lips, lines of definition depending on the age of the character being played, the highlighting, the shading and accentuating of the eyes. To me, this is an extension of art that I have never been any good at. So it is no surprise that I have always found someone else, wherever possible, to apply my make-up.

I have James Dodding, one of my tutors, to thank for encouraging me to be brave and go into theatre. I was hesitant that a young actress who was not the traditional juvenile lead, not conventionally pretty, nor had the figure of a model, would even make it to first base. He told me character actors were always in demand, granted not always young, but that I should go away and research the number of actors who were unusual-looking, even quirky, those who weren't conventionally glamorous but had cornered the market. It gave me strength, I felt braver. I applied to various repertory theatres and, while waiting for a response, earned some money as a supplementary drama teacher in east London for a term, an experience that certainly confirmed that teaching was not for me.

During that brief spell of teaching, it fell to me to organise and direct a Nativity play devised with the senior children. I was considered a bit of a maverick, as it was based on a series of improvisations culminating in a television-style news report, direct from the Crucifixion; a sort of 'Jesus, This Is Your Life'. It went down like a lead balloon in the staffroom; the other teachers were expecting lambkins, lowing cattle, straw and a baby being worshipped by three men wearing crowns and frocks. I was summoned to the head. 'What was that travesty of our Lord's birth?' she demanded.

I then had to explain that I had talked to the teenagers in my class about Christianity and the life of Christ and they thought that, through improvisation, they could portray the cycle of Jesus' life. The important thing was that they wanted a punchy, modern interpretation, something gritty. I had found myself with a group of hitherto reluctant students suddenly imbued with an enthusiasm I'd not seen before. It was surprisingly exciting for a disinclined teacher. Those were the days when the school morning began with worship and prayer in a fairly rigid format, Christian instruction forming the only part of religious education. I had a minor problem with that Christmas production. There was a Jewish girl in the group who could have been excused from the activity had she so wished. However, she was a difficult and unmotivated child and I felt that it would not be helpful to leave her out. I gave her the choice of being in the play or being involved in some other way. I didn't want to put her, or her family, in an embarrassing position. The upshot was that she was very keen to do the make-up. She did it beautifully, in a way I could never have done. Suddenly I had a recalcitrant child onside, talking about doing make-up as a career after she left school. My words of justification to the head fell on stony ground but, as far as I was concerned, the entire exercise had been a great success. Score: Us one; Head: nil!

Anyway, I didn't have to fight the authoritative, rigid educational system of the time. I was off to be an actor.

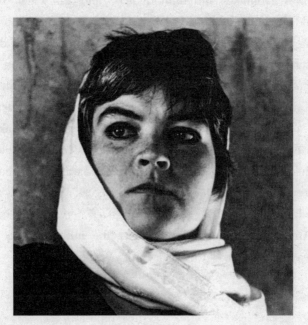

After my canonisation!

Chapter Six

Curtain Up

Speak the speech I pray you as I pronounced it to you,
trippingly upon the tongue; but if you mouth it, as many of
your players do, I had as lief the town crier spoke my lines.

William Shakespeare, *Hamlet*

Before I was able to take up my first acting job, I had to join
British Actors' Equity. However, there was already a member of
the union called Pamela Clements. So what do you call yourself
when someone has the same name as you? Duplicates aren't
allowed, presumably so there can be no confusion over contracts.
With the whole world of names at your feet, which one do you
choose? It seemed sensible to choose one that was neither too
complicated nor too difficult to pronounce. I tried several short
names: Pamela York, Pamela Moore, Pamela Shaw – they all
sounded a bit like the cast of a genteel repertory company in the
Home Counties. In desperation I canonised myself, and nobody
could have been more surprised than I when St Clement was
accepted by Equity.

With this membership under my belt, and an offer of work,
I started with Brian Way's Theatre Centre, an innovative
touring company based in north London. Brian believed in

involving children and young people in the theatre experience. He had about six small companies of actors who visited schools and youth clubs throughout the United Kingdom. We had three different plays for three different age groups: five to seven, eight to ten, and eleven upwards. They would all have the same theme, but a different content, the play changing every season.

It was the late sixties, a renaissance. A time of immense change in Britain, socially, politically and educationally. All the old structures were being challenged. The arts were encouraged and people were allowed to express themselves; drama was embraced as part of the school curriculum. Maybe cynics thought that children were just wafting about being trees and generally making mayhem but, on the contrary, it was exercising the body, expanding the imagination and exploring social interaction.

Each company had four young actors, two men and two women. I was about twenty-six and earning £7 a week, which covered digs and food and a few shillings over for luxuries. No money was needed for travel, each group being assigned a large van. Four of us sat in the front – no seatbelts needed in those days, you could even sit on somebody's lap if you felt like it. The back was piled high with costumes, props, rostra and the all-important ironing board, as well as our personal bits and pieces. We performed at two schools a day; sometimes the lunchtime journey between the schools could be as much as twenty miles. The lucky days were the ones where we spent the morning and the afternoon in the same school, then we could even have a leisurely school lunch, cooked by local dinner ladies which were, for the most part, delicious and welcome. The cooks in the north of England excelled themselves.

Between tours, we returned to the company's London base to rehearse new plays for the next school year and make more costumes and props. There was one occasion when we had to remake some costumes after a somewhat wobbly dress rehearsal the night before our first performance. We eventually left our base in London at about midnight, taking off up the A1 to our digs, close to the school, where we were due to perform at 9 a.m. the next day. I usually did the driving, not just because I was often the only driver, but because it took my wages up to the dizzy heights of £12 a week. This drive was one of the most terrifying I have ever done. I was in charge of three other people's lives and dog-tired. I kept nodding off over the wheel; even opening the windows wide didn't help much. I had to ask a fellow actor to stay awake with me, and to keep his eyes on me as well as the road.

Oh, the joys of driving that van. No power-steering, no synchro-mesh gear box and double-declutching to get down to first gear. Those wonderful arrow-shaped indicators that flipped up out of the side of the vehicle, like Dumbo's baby wings, would often get stuck long after one had turned the corner. If because of a mishap one of them was missing, down went the window whatever the weather, out went the arm and the hand performed a circular forwards movement for going left. For going right the arm went straight out at its peril, hoping that it would not receive the same fate as the missing indicator. Another of my duties during the tour was to top up the radiator and the oil and check the tyre pressures regularly. The saving grace was that we never had a flat or a breakdown, because the thing we feared most was having to unpack the back of the van in the pouring rain, to find the spare wheel. However, a most unexpected incident led to my having to unpack it in the middle of the night.

We were all woken up late one night by the irate landlady. The police were at the door and wanted to question the owner of the van. There were several officers outside and I, as the one in charge of the vehicle, was questioned and told to open the back of the van, which I did. It never occurred to me that someone would have looked through the window and seen a plastic bowl filled with rags stained with mock blood. For a moment I was a murder suspect. It took a lot of explaining, and unpacking the remainder of the props, to convince them that we were mere strolling players and everything was pretence. The face of the policeman, to whom I explained that the bloody rags were part of an Aztec ceremony, expressed bewilderment and incomprehension. However, having convinced the police that I was not a homicidal maniac, I was allowed back to bed.

My time with the Theatre Centre was one of immense learning. When you are playing to young people, who have differing powers of concentration and physical stillness, you need to capture and keep their interest. It taught us to hone the techniques learnt at drama school; to vary our vocal pitch, pace of delivery and movement. This was particularly pertinent with the teenage groups because their attention often wandered and, when it did, they were apt to be disruptive. The infant group was probably the most delightful to work with and the plays were structured around their attention span. They brought that element of wonder with them and very often the storyline would contain a magic element in which they participated. For one set of plays we hand-fashioned rudimentary musical instruments for the children to play at certain points in the drama. To elicit a hundred children's participation in this way encouraged them not to make mayhem of their own. The downside to this was getting the children to relinquish their instrument after the performance. To save the tears that might have ensued, we decided it was easier to make the handing back of the instruments part of the storyline . . . if they were not given back, the Magician's magic powers failed. So engaged were they in the story that this strategy was usually successful. Needless to say, there was occasionally some small person who held his crudely made instrument in particular affection and it broke one's heart having to take it away from him. Working with children was certainly an ongoing, organic process.

I was with Brian Way for a couple of years or so. It had been good experience to work with a company that had taught me so much. It was a bit like being in repertory, but with the added dimension of a freshness with each performance due, not only to each school being different, but also to learning to stage-manage on the hoof as one adapted to the differing working spaces.

When I was not on tour I had digs in Queensway, and led the capital-city life of the Swinging Sixties. A group of friends, usually girls on the 'look out', would go to clubs such as the Café des Artistes and Café de Paris. On more enlightened outings, we would enjoy music at Ronnie Scott's, the Festival Hall and the Wigmore Hall, as well as opera and ballet at Covent Garden. What a night it was when Rudolf Nureyev took curtain call after curtain call. We were on our feet, clapping till our palms stung but, after he'd taken twelve curtain calls, we had to leave for fear of missing the last tube home. During that period of avid theatre-going I travelled wherever necessary to see such eminent actors as Lawrence Olivier, Alec Guinness, Ingrid Bergman, Simone Signoret, Nicol Williamson and Peter O'Toole perform on stage.

Carnaby Street was leading popular fashion and was a mecca for both mod and hippy styles. Mary Quant was a no-no for me. I could never look like Twiggy. Mod styles were too fitted for me and, for obvious reasons, hot pants were out! It was a great relief when the hippy era heralded comfortable, colourful and flowing clothing. I was not exactly fat then (I was no Mama Cass) but I was well-built, as I once described myself in *Spotlight*, the actors' directory, much to the general hilarity of my actor friends.

There were plenty of boys also on the 'look out' and getting a boyfriend was never a problem. Heavy petting was acceptable and went about as far as it was possible. One must emphasise that when I was growing up, intercourse was considered unacceptable behaviour. We were all aware of the horrors of getting pregnant out of wedlock, and what that meant was that you did not give away the ultimate jewel in the crown. It must have been particularly difficult for young men but then, those same boys who wanted their oats also expected to marry virgins. Despite the rigid moral code, mistakes happened. Pregnancy outside marriage was a disgrace to be feared. Some parents were wealthy enough to send their daughters away when this happened, ostensibly to a finishing school. This was very often a place well away from home where girls could have their babies discreetly. The babies, taken afterwards, often without the mothers' consent, were offered for adoption. In many cases little consideration was given to the emotional trauma these girls were going through. During the term of their pregnancy, many had been treated like a sort of social pariah and then, after the birth, were expected to re-emerge happy and carefree, back into society and the marriage market, as though nothing had happened. Many of these young mothers were so traumatised by what had happened to them that they never spoke about their experiences, or the loss of their child, to anyone. Children who were adopted at that time should not feel anger towards their mothers, but pity. They need to understand the immense pressure these women were put under by the mores of the time.

The Pill was a recent invention and not widely available. There simply weren't the choices we have today. Of course, for some very close families, or where money was short, the adoption happened within the family. For others, it was the back-street abortionist as a last resort, if their own attempts at home failed. Home remedies were such things as downing a large dose of castor oil, or sitting in a very hot bath using a vaginal douche, filled with Sunlight soap and water, in the hope that this would break the cervical seal and bring on an abortion.

Widow Welch's pills (obtained under the counter from a Soho chemist) were another so-called remedy, to be washed down with a considerable amount of neat gin. The pills were originally made in London from 1887 until the late 1960s when they were discontinued. The Widow's advertisement claimed among other things to: 'Effectively Remove Obstructions' (a somewhat Victorian way of describing a foetus); 'Correct Giddiness and Nervous Headaches' (not tonight, dear); 'Useful in Windy Disorders' (certainly not tonight, dear); 'Alleviate Shortness of Breath and Palpitations of the Heart' (that was a good night, dear!).

Ma Welch's pills also claimed to be 'Safe all Year Round and in all Climates: 2s.9d. a box'. This miracle pill for all seasons included such things as apiol, borax, gin, gunpowder and lead. It was a miracle that anyone survived.

❦

So, Dear Reader, during this time of restraint, when did I finally relinquish my virginity? Not until I was nineteen, when I felt mature enough to take responsibility for that decision. He was an Italian naval officer. He looked divine in uniform and called me Paloma, not because he found it easier to pronounce than Pamela, but because he thought that Paloma, the Italian for dove, suited me. In hindsight he probably said that to all the girls, but at that time it was enough to make any maiden swoon. Whether it was the flowering of this girl's romantic soul, or sheer naivety, I shall never know, but it was heaven at the time.

Boys had already figured large in my life, especially during my early years. They were just there, at infant school, in my foster home, at Foxmead and other holiday homes. Another of my father's bright ideas had been to send me to stay with a German family not, as you might expect, in Germany, but in the Home Counties of England. Mama Lisa and Papa Alfred ran what seemed to me to be an enormous house overflowing with youngsters. I can't remember there being any other girls and, I suspect, it hadn't occurred to my father to ascertain the proportion of girls to boys. However, it was a great delight for me; I ran wild with the boys and was accepted as one of the gang. This wonderful camaraderie came to a painful end one day when we had biked down to the lake to sail a model boat, which then became entangled in the weeds. We waded out to free it, but to no avail. One of the older boys said he would swim out to fetch it and started to undress, when he suddenly became aware of my girly presence and, in a moment of boy-man authority, I was commanded by him to look after the bikes back on the path. From that moment on I instinctively knew that I was different. I was being ostracised, but I didn't really understand why and I wasn't going to question the leader I hero-worshipped. I think what I enjoyed so much about life with the boys was the sense of freedom, of equality, of the world being ours; a very different experience from the furtive explorations of the body during such games as 'doctors and nurses', all terribly innocent of course, part of growing up and completely untainted by sexual awareness.

I hadn't had a serious boyfriend until I was about sixteen. Then, the boy from Charterhouse School got the boot in favour of a mod with a scooter and very shiny suits. As time went on, I think the more earthy rock 'n' roll culture lured me. It was a wonderful counterpoint to the classical musical education I had received and fodder to a somewhat rebellious soul. This rebelliousness was a worry to the Devon Aunts who were in loco parentis. Particularly when my escorts started to include a local soldier who was later stationed in Germany, superseded by a very wild farmer with a Triumph motorcycle. Not many years after, he turned a tractor over and died slowly, pinned under the machine. It hadn't been a deep emotional relationship but, nonetheless, it did haunt me. The manner of his dying was horrific and unnecessary. It was my first encounter with death. Another longish-term boyfriend, who was a member of the Young Farmers' Association and a Young Conservative, had a car, the latter, I suspect, being the main attraction! It must have been a great relief for the Aunts to see me being picked up for a date by an upstanding member of the community for a change.

Nobody ever knew that while in the sixth form at the Warren I went out with a friend's father. He wasn't drop-dead gorgeous but had charm and a twinkle. We met when a small group of her friends were taken out by him on her birthday. He seemed to give me special attention and, more importantly for me, treated us as women and as equals. I remember that I was wearing a royal blue dress, made of a soft fabric with white-cuffed three-quarter sleeves and a broad white stand-up collar that framed my face. It sat over the shoulders, dipping to a 'V' at the bosom. He allowed us wine and cigarettes, an unexpected delight, especially because many of us were experimenting with Peter Stuyvesant cigarettes in the prefects' common room. Obviously this activity was prohibited at school, but as the room was in the attic with a large window in the roof, we could exhale without leaving the tell-tale smell of smoke. After lunch, this man took a very large Cuban cigar from a decorative cedar box presented to him by the sommelier and proceeded to show me, while the other girls were chattering among themselves, how to prepare it for smoking. Looking back, I realise that this could be interpreted as some strange form of sexual foreplay . . . he rolled it in his fingers, cut the end off and warmed the shaft! To my utter surprise he asked if I would like to try it first. Smoking a cigar was pretty unconventional for a grown woman, let alone a teenager. It was in my nature to take a challenge, so I took a puff. Oh, it was awful, but I wasn't prepared to lose face so soon. I was determined to persevere, but paroxysms of coughing forced me to give up after a few moments. He was amused, but I didn't feel demeaned by that amusement. As we were leaving, he took me aside and asked if he could take me out to dinner some time during the school holidays.

This flirtation was the beginning of several clandestine meetings and outings. He did not force the issue of a full-blown affair until one opportune evening when we were dining at a hotel. Much as I was prepared to play the game, which could have been a dangerous one with a less honourable man, I was not prepared to sleep with him. It was one thing to enjoy stimulating conversation, being wined and dined and treated like an adult but, as I mentioned earlier, sleeping with him just wasn't on the cards, even though his age and experience might have stood me in good stead. We were in touch until I was in my early twenties and then gradually drifted apart; relief and a fly-leaf in the book of experience for me, and a dead-end for the full-blooded male who was not going to achieve his ultimate goal. I now realise how provocative my behaviour must have seemed and how fortunate I was that his sense of morality had prevented him from taking advantage of my innocent, yet seemingly inviting, behaviour. I admit, with the wisdom of hindsight, that I was complicit, albeit in my innocent stupidity. It is easy to see how young people can fall for such flattery, particularly if they have been emotionally deprived during their formative years.

This was later followed by another relationship with a man much older than me, while I was at Sydenham House. He had been an agricultural officer in Kenya and we were introduced by a friend of the Aunts while he was recuperating in the area on his return from Africa. There was something very attractive about the lean, tanned look of somebody who had spent time in the African bush. It was one of those rare times when one has a bizarre and uncontrollable attraction to someone, which became manifest during our first evening out together. We dined at the Manor in Bovey Tracey. We talked, we laughed and somehow our difference in age and experience was of no consequence. Afterwards we went up on to the moor and looked at the stars. With no light pollution to obscure the firmament, the sky had an almost palpable velvet density, studded with diamonds, seemingly close enough to touch. He dropped me off at the farm gate. I was home later than I had ever been and afraid that the dogs might awaken the Aunts. Fortunately, the collies knew my footsteps and were silent. Quickened by my emotional response, sleep was long in coming. It is difficult to drift into the arms of Morpheus with a shaking body and a trembling heart. It was as much a sexual response as a deeply emotional one. We got on wonderfully well, which led to a physical relationship but one that was never fully consummated. He was convinced that his sexual performance had been damaged by the frequent and violent attacks of malaria that afflicted him and the powerful drugs he was taking to combat it. He was, understandably, deeply upset by this. It was malaria that had forced him into early retirement and his repatriation to the UK. For something that had such a dynamic start it somewhat understandably fizzled out. I wonder if my attraction to these two older men may have been the need to replace my emotionally and physically absent father but, perhaps, that is a little too Freudian.

Despite the unconventional relationships of my teenage years there were glimmers of conformity in my behaviour, due to my school and Dartmoor home life having settled into a stable pattern. The only, by now distant, thorn in my side was my father's erratic behaviour. When it pricked it could still be very painful. I had dreams of making a conventional marriage and fulfilling the functions of a dutiful housewife. After all, in the decade after the end of the Second World War, songs were about romance and women's magazines ran stories of perfect love. It was a post-war bubble of hoped-for perfection, a necessary counterpoint to the violence and destruction that such major conflicts bring, and it had a huge impact on me. Even maternal instincts surged occasionally and very forcefully, driven by raging hormonal changes no doubt. In adulthood these were tempered, as much as anything else, by the reasoning that unconventional parenting was no role model for parenthood. I was, frankly, scared of being a terrible parent, of inflicting on another person the same beginnings as I had endured. Possibly, also, a fear of being totally subsumed into the needs of a child, to compensate for this by being overprotective and controlling. If parents are too possessive, how can they eventually release their child into the world with an open hand and an open heart? I would think that separation is a thing that many parents dread but, when one gets the balance of love and boundaries right, you are less likely to lose them.

It was while I was still working with the Theatre Centre Company, living in a large terraced house in Bayswater, that I met a man who was taking a break from the Merchant Navy. A couple of actors I was working with lived in the same house and the four of us used to go out in the evenings together. Joy of joys, the merchant sailor had a motor car – always an attraction in those days. He was about my age and similar in looks to Prince Andrew, the likeness increasing when he wore his uniform. It was not long before we got to know each other better.

It was a passionate relationship. He always said that the greatest gift he had been given, in his early years of sexual experience, was to have a relationship with an older woman. She taught him how, what, when and where. We decided to look for alternative accommodation with more space and privacy and found a house a little further out in Finchley. Here we put down roots until we got married a short while later in 1969. Louis was estranged from his mother and stepfather and the Aunts were too far away to come to London, meaning there were no pressures to go for a white wedding in church, like so many of our friends were doing at the time. We married in our local Register Office, in Burnt Oak. My stepmother Sally was horrified when we told her we were not having an official reception. She insisted on giving us a wedding party in her flat so that she and my father could help us celebrate our marriage with drinks and a meal. It was kind and considerate of her and reflected our growing fondness for each other.

I never knew why Louis was estranged from his parents. Like some sort of fairy godmother, I was bent on reconciliation because he actually had a mother who might be concerned for his welfare. Maybe, as we were together and settled, he felt more able to make contact with her, or maybe he just gave in to my incessant nagging. However, despite that, it took quite a while and a lot of encouragement. One bleak winter's day, all the bleaker because the heater in the car had packed up, we drove up to north Norfolk, arriving tired and frozen at his parents' large detached house lying in some acres. A neat, well made-up woman wearing a twinset and pearls greeted us at the door. She was one of those people who did everything very efficiently, was always busy, a great cook and baker, but made everybody around her aware of the effort it took. I just wished she could have relaxed and related more to us, particularly to her son, but of course she must have been terribly apprehensive at this first meeting after so long. I had no idea what bridges they both had to cross, or if they would reconcile their differences, and I am quite sure they never did.

It was inevitable, for financial as well as for career reasons, for Louis to return to sea after we were married, but he was reluctant. However, working as an engineering officer on coastal shipping meant reasonably short periods of time at sea. No more than a month on duty and a number of days off in between; a perfect balance to retain the freshness of our relationship. The chance then came for him to join a cruise line fleet, which meant being away for three months at a time while he was doing an Australia and South Seas run, followed by a generous leave period. It was very difficult to adjust to this, particularly the returning, which made one tentative and rather nervous – like meeting someone all over again. I appreciate this must sound pathetic to those waiting for their spouses or partners to return from war zones, so often scarred by their battlefield experiences.

A few years after our marriage, we moved again, to a four-storey house owned by a friend of my stepmother's. She lived in the top half and we had the garden flat with a conservatory. Having a garden meant we could have animals; we opted for a cat because of our transient lifestyles, and so started a regime of cat owning.

By now it was the early seventies. I was doing theatre tours and starting to do small parts in film and television. One of the most bizarre pieces of theatre I did was during the Lamda Theatre of Cruelty Season called *The Last Dance of the Cormorants*. There were not a lot of cormorants involved but an awful lot of male dwarves who were sweet but very randy, to the point where one had to go to the Ladies escorted. It was a strange piece bordering on the sadomasochistic, maybe that's what set them off!

My very first television appearance was around the same time and was a Somerset Maugham play for the BBC. Charles Gray was starring, a very imposing and grand actor. He used this distinction, and a coldly aloof quality, to great effect as Blofeld in *Diamonds Are Forever* some years later. We were rehearsing in an Irish dance hall in Kilburn, because the BBC's rehearsal rooms in North Acton were fully booked with other drama productions. Oh, those glorious days when the BBC made their high-quality classic productions in-house! At lunchtime, everyone trooped off to the local pub that served real Guinness, except Charles. His assistant proceeded to lay up a trestle table upon which a freshly laundered and crisply starched linen tablecloth was placed, topped with silver cutlery and a small crystal glass of flowers. The manservant turned waiter placed before Mr Gray a light luncheon of cold meats and salad enhanced by a chilled bottle of Le Montrachet. Nobody was invited to share the repast, not even the director. Nor, come to think of it, do I remember him addressing anyone unless he had to. To be honest, I was amused by this eccentricity rather than being envious, and saw this from my lowly station in the cast as a goal to which I might aspire, although I never have, thank goodness. I have always tried to be an integral part of the cast and crew, both on and off stage. Where possible, it makes for a more cohesive and enjoyable creative process.

One of the highlights during this period was working with Joan Littlewood at the Theatre Royal, Stratford East. By the late sixties it was a famous and much-lauded venue, a mecca to which seasoned theatre-goers would travel to see her exciting and innovative work, tearing themselves away from the comfort and predictability of the West End theatre. I loved her; she was an utter and complete renegade, an explorer of experience like Freya Stark was an explorer of the Arab and African worlds. Her principles were left wing, but never in the dull grey Soviet-style of communism. She wanted to set up a People's Fun Palace, something akin to the eighteenth-century Vauxhall Gardens, but a place of learning as well as entertainment, music and fun. You could never imagine her idea of a people's palace in communist Russia. But for something so groundbreaking, the support it needed, the land and the funding, were not forthcoming at the time.

Nobody warned me not to ask Joan questions during the time she gave us notes (a critique of our perfomance). After the dress rehearsal of one particular production that included a series of sketches, I did that very thing; querying the relationship between me (playing a patient) and the other actor (playing a psychiatrist). In a flash Joan said, 'Change parts tonight.' It was the first night, I had to pull something out of the bag. Fortunately, I already knew the lines for both characters. I decided to play the psychiatrist as barking mad and physically uncontrolled.

The complete opposite of the over-controlling character the other actor had developed. It went down well with the audience, but I never opened my mouth in a note session again. It was said that if you even popped out to the loo during rehearsals, you were likely to lose your part.

One production Joan directed and co-wrote with John Wells, in Stratford East, was *The Projector*, with music by the now eminent composer Carl Davis. Joan and John, with their combined wit and intellect, cooked up a story that they leaked to one of the broadsheets. The story was that they were going to put on a recently discovered eighteenth-century play. This work depicted the destruction of houses in East London due to poor building methods by a speculator of the time. The villain of the piece, a Dutchman, was the eponymous projector, the equivalent of a modern rogue speculator, who buys land and puts up sub-standard housing. In reality it was a satire of the Ronan Point disaster in 1968 when an entire corner of a block of flats in East London came crashing down. This story had been swallowed hook, line and sinker by the journalist involved and Joan, with evident glee, announced that the origins of the play were a spoof, but not until after the first night.

Now, I have always been envious of actors who can make fellow actors corpse (laugh involuntarily) on stage but stay perfectly focused themselves. I was never any good at that, usually corpsing myself, but willing to have a go. However, one of my rare successes in the corpsing stakes was during *The Projector*. My character, a buxom, bawdy, brothel-owning madam, had a set-to with the Sergeant-at-Arms. He and his men were trying to evict me and my girls in order to demolish the brothel for development. The choreography was suggestive, with a long pole to do the demolition, and a lot of thrusting and withdrawing of said pole until it came to the point when the final thrust was about to be made, and my battle lost. At this stage in the action my character had to turn her back, lift her skirts, and moon defiantly at the soldiers, showing her bloomers. However, on that occasion, when I lifted my skirts there were no bloomers, only a proudly erect ostrich feather sticking out of my naked backside, reducing the soldiers and their commanding officer to very unmilitary giggles. From the front stalls came a familiar shriek of laughter. A shriek that was known, not personally, but from many film and stage perform-ances – Barbara Windsor! How prescient that encounter was – I couldn't have known that we would work so happily together twenty years later on *EastEnders*. She is a dear friend and has a heart that must occupy most of that little body. Babs was one of Joan's protégées, one of her 'nuts' or 'fruitcakes' as Joan called all of us, having worked with her on several productions.

During the run of this production, the Three-Day Week was brought in by Edward Heath's government. An agree-ment had not been possible between striking members of the National Union of Mine Workers, represented by the National Executive, and the National Coal Board. An increase in picketing included all power stations, ports, coal depots et cetera, and meant coal supplies became dangerously low. It was the middle of winter and electricity cuts were inevitable. We were not interrupted too badly by the cuts at first and were able to use candles onstage and floats downstage. These were the eighteenth-century equivalent of footlights, open containers of oil with floating wicks, hence 'floats'. It looked wonderfully romantic, but this was not enough to fill the house. Audience numbers dwindled as people stayed away, worried about returning at night to a cold and dark home. It tolled the death knell for the production, which regrettably closed earlier than it should have done despite talks of a possible transfer to the West End, which never happened.

Joan and I kept in touch and met socially at both her home in Blackheath and once at my flat in London where she turned up to my birthday party. She was escorted by her long-term partner Gerry Raffles, who looked just like Brendan Behan, and a sinister-looking short, muscular man who had just come back from Ulster. I was told he was SAS but, knowing Joan, it's much more likely he was an IRA man on the run. She was a true subversive who would have loathed the faceless, bland, self-interested power base of today.

I last saw Joan in 1994 when she was briefly over from France, where she was living at the time, and I was working on *EastEnders*. There was a shindig in her honour at the Theatre Royal, Stratford East and, when she saw me, she said, 'I wouldn't have thought you would sell out to fame, why don't you just piss off back to your television.' No amount of justifying myself and trying to persuade her that I was constantly endeavouring to retain my integrity as an actor would convince her. To her, commercial success was an anathema, unforgivable almost. Sadly, I never saw her again. Despite that last encounter, which upset me, I didn't hold it against her. Working with her taught me so much and I am pleased to have been involved with the Memorial Statue commemorating what would have been her hundredth birthday in October 2014.

Throughout the early seventies, following my rather lowly television debut with Mr Gray in 1970, I worked on about a dozen television dramas and had small parts in a couple of films, but it was hardly a full-time career. Actors spent a lot of time doing other jobs to pay the rent and, if those were not available, signing on. The two London dole offices most frequented by thespians at that time were Chadwick Street and Lisson Grove. It was great to meet up for coffee and a catch-up on what was being cast. There was a comfort in being with people who were also on the same journey. It made one feel less of a failure. At any one time, there were about 80 to 90 per cent of actors looking for acting work, much of it in regional theatre. Many towns had healthy repertory companies but drama itself was changing. Drawing-room comedies had been replaced by gritty working-class dramas. Actors who had a natural regional accent were now in demand. Film and television productions were changing as well. It was amazing how many actors, who had hitherto spoken received pronunciation, suddenly spoke with broad Liverpudlian or Newcastle accents. The reason one is cast, or not cast, is multifarious: physicality, physiognomy, timbre of the voice, balance within the cast itself – and one mustn't forget the ability to perform the role for which one is auditioning. However, there are some directors who have their own agenda: physical attraction being the obvious one or, conversely, not casting a dynamic woman they may perceive to be an intellectual threat. Nowadays, it is often easier to cast an actor who is flavour of the month and recognised by everyone, who may well be a good actor, but is not necessarily the one most suited to the role. It is lazy and unimaginative casting and often not very satisfactory from an audience point of view.

During this time, my husband and I were forging ahead with different careers; it wasn't as though he came back to a conventional married routine. I was aware that each adjustment after three months at sea was major for both of us, and would try to arrange it so that, free time permitting, I could meet him at the port to welcome him home. However, as time went by, I was beginning to realise that my teenage dream of being 'the perfect wife' was in increasing conflict with my career. I had the feeling that he saw me as ambitious. I have certainly never been ambitious in the sense of seeking fame through my acting. I simply wanted to act because it made me happy and fed my soul.

My perception of him at that time, which may have been wrong, was of a man who was quite content to stay in 'happy valley' and didn't want to climb the next hill to see what was on the other side, while I did. This is no criticism; simply that our paths, for whatever reason, were beginning to divide. It was probably fortuitous that we had decided not to have a family at this juncture. The first seeds of doubt about my marriage were forming but I chose to ignore them, hoping that I could still make it work. It wasn't until I went on a world tour, with the Royal Shakespeare Company, that the distance of thousands of miles allowed a very objective and clear view of what was happening with my relationship back home.

Playing Berthe in *Hedda Gabler* world tour.

Chapter Seven

Around the World in Ninety Days

Travel and change of place impart new vigour
to the mind.

Seneca

In the mid-seventies, I auditioned for the Royal Shakespeare Company to join a world tour of Ibsen's *Hedda Gabler* directed by Trevor Nunn. With a stellar cast, we all met up for a read-through on New Year's Day 1975, followed by a welcoming lunch at Chez Solonge. It was awesome! I was in the company of such eminent actors as Glenda Jackson, Timothy West, Patrick Stewart, Jenny Linden, Constance Chapman and Peter Eyre. It is amusing to reflect that the remaining 'minor' members of the company have all become successful in our own right: Celia Imrie (actress), Oz Clarke (authority on wine), Fidelis Morgan (author, director and actress) and myself (actress, presenter). It is also not surprising that such a springboard to our careers led to enduring friendships being made.

By mid-February, despite having a month's rehearsal and a week playing *Hedda Gabler* at the Richmond Theatre behind us, we were really still complete strangers. Granted, we knew each other in a performance sense but not personally, not what made each of us tick; quite a scary prospect when starting a three-month tour without our known social parameters. Would we all bond? Would it be like Sartre's *Huis Clos*, hell within a confined space? Whatever happened, it was going to be a learning curve in itself.

We flew Singapore Airlines. In those days, getting to Australia meant stopping at several places en route to refuel. We went via Athens, Bahrain, Sri Lanka and Singapore. The stewardesses, the Singapore Girls, dressed in beautifully patterned *sarong kebayas*, were attentive and charming. We were handed so many hot towels on that first flight that Peter Eyre, unsure about what to do with the increasing pile of cooling towels, was heard to say, 'I would flush them down the lavatory if it weren't highly likely that they would block the bowl and we'd be the first passengers to drown in mid-air.'

On all our stops we had to leave the aircraft. In Bahrain, there were a lot of uniformed armed guards with sub-machine guns, something we had never seen in Great Britain. I was somewhat alarmed because I was conscious that one of them was following me, down a long and deserted corridor, as I was going to the Ladies. I wasn't aware that there was anything particularly suspicious about me, but it was pretty unnerving. Fortunately, he didn't come in with me but waited outside.

We spent a night in Singapore, and all went out in the evening to the Car Park. That was its function during the day but, at that time, it became a food market at night with stalls selling all sorts of wonderful food. The bustling market was unlike anything I had ever experienced. The steamy night air was filled with the aroma of garlic, chilli, ginger and lemongrass. There was exotic food of every description for sale and ice-cold Tiger beer in bottles, misting up as the cold glass met the hot atmosphere. However, refreshment was not all that was for sale; everything was on offer. It was a well-known place to pick up whatever suited your desires. I was very jet-lagged and the only desire I wanted to fulfil was sleep in a comfortable bed.

After what seemed like endless days of travel, feeling pretty jaded, we eventually arrived in Melbourne, where we were playing the Princess Theatre. I remember the Australian backstage staff (the scenery movers and so on) with fondness, mainly because they were all so laid-back. Sitting under the stage, not the least bit interested in the intellectual happenings overhead, they would have a couple of tinnies and roll a few joints, waiting until their moment for action came. They turned out to be a great source of 'scoring the weed'. I had a lot of the Third Act off, so would have a relaxing puff in my dressing room until the final curtain. For quite a while the actors, still declaiming on stage, had been aware of wisps of smoke and an aroma reminiscent of the Flower Power culture. I hadn't realised that in the absence of air conditioning, the theatre's cooling fans were gently guiding my miscreant behaviour to the stage and auditorium. I was soundly reprimanded, and quite rightly so, by our leading lady. Not long after she was fondly nicknamed

Genghis, as in Khan, much to her amusement. I turned to the Antipodean grape for solace and have been a great aficionado ever since! Lots of people from the sixties smoked the gentle weed (and, of course, like many politicians, never inhaled). They were far from being drug addicts and never went on to anything stronger; for many it was only a short-term part of the burgeoning culture of peace and love. For the most part, today's equivalent is dangerous and cannot be compared to the natural plant used then. Still, it was illegal.

I digress from my journey. Melbourne was a very contained city in those days, with a suburban feel about it. The grid-system streets were quiet, compared to the vast cosmopolitan centre it has become. Most of my memories of those first weeks of the tour are pretty hazy – not so much from weed, I hasten to say, but from jet lag. There was an awareness, though, of a burgeoning literary and artistic presence. I do remember a serious European influence on the one hand and hippy tie-dye alternative on the other; oh, and iced coffee that was to die for. And standing at the stage door straining to hear Tina Turner singing 'River Deep, Mountain High' in concert at a neighbouring theatre.

In these early days, we had to concentrate on developing a play that was still in its infancy, as well as getting used to the members of the company with whom we were working. Oz Clarke, who was understudying all the male roles, was starting on a new path that would lead him into a different career, as a wine buff. While we were in Melbourne he could be seen poking about in the local bottle shops investigating Australian wine, which was virtually unknown to us in Europe at that time. Celia was my understudy as well as being a delightful assistant stage manager. Her main task as ASM was to make sure that all the props and everything practical were ready for the performance. During rehearsals Celia would go out and buy biscuits from her own meagre wage and serve them to us with tea. As far as we were concerned, this was the most important part of her role. She never asked for any payment so we assumed that the company funds were providing them. We probably still owe her a fair amount. Fidelis joined the company late, towards the end of rehearsals. She had the daunting task of understudying Glenda's part as Hedda and probably spent a lot of her time checking on Glenda's health! Although she was never called on, in her own right I believe she would have made a very strong and unique Hedda Gabler. She still makes me laugh when doing a frighteningly good impression of Glenda in full flood. Connie Chapman, who played Aunt Julie, was older than most of us and very experienced in theatre, television and film. She was so adventurous, game to do anything, mostly swimming in the nude!

When the time came to up sticks and go to Sydney, the cast were given the choice to travel by train rather than fly with the props, scenery and costumes. This request had been made by our leading lady so that we could see as much of the country as possible. With hours on the train we played the guessing game Botticelli, which proved to be a great bonding process for the cast. It was summer, and I suppose that I always think of Australia as it was then. Flat-bottomed, fair-weather clouds in broken ranks moving sedately across an azure sky, a sky we rarely see in the UK. The undulating landscape, made golden and arid by the hot summer sun, was dotted with groups of eucalyptus trees, the haunt of koalas – how I longed to see one.

It would be difficult not to fall in love with Sydney, an attractive vibrant city set on a jigsaw of bays and coves. It was wonderful to see water ferries used in the way we use buses, ferrying people across the water to the city and back. We were staying in Kings Cross, the equivalent of London's Soho, and playing the Elizabethan Theatre in the Greek area. Social life speeded up. We were taken on a trip to the Blue Mountains and rode the Katoomba funicular, the steepest railway in the world. It was a somewhat alarming experience, finding oneself suspended almost vertically down the side of a cliff, feeling too insecure to stop clinging on for long enough to take a photograph. The engineering company who built the railway sounded German, and somehow that gave me a feeling of confidence – *Vorsprung durch Technik*!

We went on a picnic, up the Hawkesbury River to a point where it is divided from the ocean by a mere spit of land. It was as I swam there that I realised the power of the Pacific. For the first time in my life I was tossed in the surf, like an old sock in a washing machine, having no idea which way was up and which way was down. Eventually, I was spewed out on to the shore, having thought my end had come. It nearly did when we went sailing on a large yacht hosted by the actor Warren Mitchell, who was working over there at the time. This is a very clear memory for me because I almost ended up being a shark's dinner! It was very rough out towards the Heads, not surprising really as one meets the open ocean at this point. A few of us were on deck enjoying the wind, the sun and the movement of the boat slicing through the sea when the call came to tack, in other words telling us to duck as the boom swung around. We all dropped flat upon the deck but the boom rope whipped across quickly and entangled my leg. Uppermost in my mind was the thought that to be dragged into those shark-infested waters meant certain death ... luckily, there were enough people on deck to tether the rope and loosen my leg and I escaped with only a rope burn and bruised dignity.

Sydney's most iconic piece of architecture, the Opera House, had opened a couple of years earlier. It is an amazing building, singularly fitting for a waterfront environment, with its curved roofs resembling white sails gleaming in the sunlight. Not surprisingly, it is now a Unesco World Heritage Site. We went there to see *Peer Gynt* with Jack Thompson, already a star in Australia, playing the lead and Pamela Stephenson, later to become Mrs Billy Connolly, playing Solveig. I later did an episode of *Within These Walls* with her which, I believe, was her first appearance on British television. As we were guests in Australia and also performing Ibsen, it was only seemly for Glenda and us to go backstage after the performance and for our leading lady to meet *Peer Gynt*'s leading man. This can be a difficult duty particularly when a production has been pretty dire. Ever the diplomat, Miss Jackson said, with hand outstretched, 'It is a very interesting piece,' to which Mr Thompson replied, 'Ah dunno, the nearer yer get, the thinner it gets.' So that puts you in your place, Mr Ibsen! His comment just about summed up the production.

Of course, Glenda Jackson was a massive star at the time, a luminary of the theatre and, after such films as *Women in Love*, *The Marat Sade* and *A Touch of Class*, a box-office star. Most audiences on this tour would only have known her through film and so it is hardly surprising that people would telephone the theatre with such enquiries as, 'Is Glenda Jackson appearing in the flesh?' and, in America, 'Are you showing Glenda Jackson in *Hedy Gabor*?' – a curious mixture of Hedy Lamarr and Zsa Zsa Gabor. Mind you, that is not quite as strange as the experience another Royal Shakespeare Company cast had when playing a theatre in Florida, around the same time. During a speech in *The Hollow Crown*, a strange humming sound was heard coming from the stalls. It took some time to locate and identify a woman crimping her hair with a battery-powered dryer. As an actor, do you battle through that or throw a tantrum on stage? The cast, including Sir Michael Redgrave and Sir Derek Jacobi, would have been dignified to the end, I'm sure.

As the tour went on, slowly and inevitably given the human condition, our emotional ties with home lessened their painful pull. Relationships formed within and without the company. Jenny Linden, who played Mrs Elvsted, was the only one who had brought home with her in the form of her husband and son. We had all been adrift, recovering from a sense of isolation from our loved ones, so painful at the beginning. Fidelis summed this up wonderfully well in a song she wrote:

We're hanging from the bottom of an upside-down world
Down under all the timeless, endless hours and miles
Remembering how it used to be when we were standing
on the top

I was you and you were me
And we were all and all were we
Today was now, tomorrow soon,
Now night is light and sun is moon.
Today your yesterday is her and I am on my own
And we are hanging from the bottom of an upside down world
Down under all the timeless, endless hours and miles
Remembering how it used to be when we were standing
on the top

Sydney was a pretty gay city even back then, and the seeds of the multi-day spectacle of the Mardi Gras were taking root. It was soon to become a mecca of fun, colour and outrageous alternativeness, known internationally. Into this very different milieu came a relative innocent who had the opportunity to have many Sapphic relationships, but didn't because casual affairs have never held any interest for me. I fell, not for some bush-whacking hunk, but for a woman. For the first time an unexpected emotion hit me like a bombshell, its shockwave engulfing me. Like an actor assumes another persona temporarily, so did I under the cloak of disguise that distance allowed. It was a time of discovery and abandon, of excitement and freedom. I wanted to woo and be wooed and felt no guilt. Like Icarus I was flying ever closer to the sun which, inevitably, would send me spiralling back to earth. That didn't have to be faced just yet because we were in Sydney for a whole month. That month went all too quickly and we were soon saying our farewells at the airport with promises of reunions back in the UK. I nearly missed the plane, so bereft was I at leaving.

We were en route to the States, to Los Angeles, the home of Hollywood and cradle of the film industry. As before, we had a few days off, while scenery, costumes and props were transported and the stage and lighting set up. It is rarely that actors benefit from circumstances; we are usually at the bottom of the food chain, contrary to many people's perceptions. As one of the *EastEnders* executive producers once pointed out, 'You are household names, like Jeyes Fluid and Andrex toilet paper.' In other words, fame doesn't equate with importance. This downtime allowed a few of us to stay over in O'ahu in Hawaii for a few days. We played the part of tourists to perfection. We toured the island in an open jeep, dined on a floating Chinese restaurant and sat on the beach until the early hours, where we got rather merry on cocktails that were like works of art: pottery bowls, their contents smoking like mini versions of the volcanic island we were on, full of multi-coloured decoration and fruits beckoning enticingly – their beauty disguising the lethal brew. The breakfast buffet groaning with tropical fruits was a far cry from seventies England, as were the blue-rinse elderly American widows disporting themselves, somewhat inappropriately, on poolside sunloungers. Occasionally, one of those wrinkled harridans would tuck dollars into the skimpy trunks of a very attentive handsome beach boy. One couldn't help but wonder for what service this remuneration was being made.

Our departure from Honolulu was delayed because another aeroplane had to be flown in from the mainland. We were not told why, but after a few cocktails in the airport bar, Tim West looked at me somewhat darkly and said he had just heard our original aircraft, a DC10, had a cargo door problem. The plane happened to be the same type as the one that came down in the 1974 Paris air disaster, at Ermenonville, killing everyone on board, because of a problem with the cargo door. It was a very recent accident and still fresh in one's memory; time for a few more cocktails. Not that I have ever been a nervous flyer, I have even piloted a light aircraft and loved it. One of the most exciting air experiences I ever had was crossing the Heathrow flight path in a helicopter, with a friend at the controls. We had to wait for the OK from the control tower and were given a minute to get across. I'm not too sure I could cope with such an adrenaline rush now. Late, and somewhat the worse for wear, we eventually took off for California.

My first impression of Los Angeles was akin to an out-of-body experience. She struck me as being a rather tired old whore with an illegitimate offspring called Oscar. What an experience, though, to walk down Hollywood Boulevard recognising and paying homage to the handprints of the stars. Seeing the famous Grauman's Chinese Theatre where, in May 1927, the premiere of Cecil B. DeMille's *The King of Kings* was screened. It has hosted other premieres including *Star Wars* as well as three Academy Award ceremonies and numerous other events. Our Englishness stood out as we walked from our hotel to the Huntington Hartford Theatre, where we were performing. No one seemed to walk in LA.

We were staying at the Magic Castle Hotel, one block north of Hollywood Boulevard. It was a series of apartments built around a pool, somewhat similar to the location in the film *The Day of the Locusts*. It was named in honour of the Magic Castle, the clubhouse of the Academy to the Magic Arts which was also a nightclub for magicians and magic enthusiasts. What excitement – we were invited to an evening of magic and fun at the Magic Castle. It was an opportunity to see professional magicians at close hand; we might even discover the tricks of the trade. Having great expectations of both Castle and Magic, it came as a complete surprise when we found ourselves traipsing through a series of small, ill-lit rooms. If there was any magic it passed me by and, if there were any magicians, I had clearly arrived in the middle of a disappearing act. It was the fastest jaunt of the entire trip and we, like them, did our own disappearing act.

Our first night at the Huntington Hartford Theatre on Hollywood and Vine was, by virtue of its location, a star-studded occasion. Peeking through the curtains, we were agog. How could we perform a play to so many people who had been our onscreen idols for decades? As ever, once you start a performance, the play becomes all-consuming but, after the curtain came down, there were more treats in store. We had a first-night party which was, unfortunately for the younger members of the company, a sit-down dinner. We were longing to roam around playing a sort of celebrity version of the game I Spy. After all we were in the company of such stars as Ryan O'Neil, Elliott Gould, Richard Dreyfuss, Julie Christie, Ellen Burstyn, Paul Newman, Joanne Woodward, Roddy McDowall, Bette Davis, Susan George, Sarah Miles . . . I remember George Segal coming to our table, and Greer Garson spending time being gracious and friendly to us, the junior members of the company. Now that is how to behave as a star. Glenda herself was a shining example in that she made sure that the lowliest members of our company were included in everything, to the point of supplementing outings for those on a meagre wage.

Probably because we were the Royal Shakespeare Company, and most definitely because Glenda was one of them, a plethora of other stars came to our performances and to meet her backstage: Barbara Stanwyck, Bea Arthur, Walter Matthau, Irene Worth, Ruth Gordon, Patrick McGoohan, Jon Voight, David Tomlinson, Cloris Leachman, Fred McMurray, Gregory Peck, Jack Lemmon and Douglas Fairbanks Jr, whom I was to meet later at an embassy party in Washington. I will never forget walking into the dimly lit room and being introduced to him, a man with such piercing blue eyes that they seemed to light up the room. I was transfixed and virtually speechless. How gauche that must have seemed, but he was utterly charming. The only other time I have been poleaxed by eyes (blue again) was at the wrap party for *Shoulder to Shoulder* in which Siân Phillips, who was married to Peter O'Toole at the time, had played Mrs Emmeline Pankhurst. I turned away from a conversation to see a louche Peter O'Toole leaning against a pillar, cigarette in one hand and a drink in the other. His eyes were fabulous, like blue topaz. He smiled at me and I was lost. He was gorgeous and he knew it. No wonder Noël Coward commented after seeing his performance as *Lawrence of Arabia*, 'If you'd been any prettier they'd have called the film *Florence of Arabia*.'

One evening, after a performance, a knock came at my dressing room door and Glenda's voice rang out with that inimitable delivery, as commanding off stage as on. 'May we come in, Pamela?' I was still in costume but de-wigging and dragging tissues, covered in Crowe's Cremine, across my face to remove my make-up, looking like something that had escaped from a Hammer Horror film. Presuming Glenda was employing the royal 'we', I said, 'Yes, do come in.' Through my mirror I saw a diminutive figure approaching at a staccato pace, hand outstretched. 'I did so enjoy the performance,' said Miss Bette Davis as I frantically wiped my greasy hands. I was not going to miss having the unseen print of that hand on mine. In fact I didn't wash it for days until bowing to the call of hygiene. More than anything else I couldn't drag my gaze away from the mad lip line of this small, but enormous, presence. I had thought her make-up was a clever character touch in *Whatever Happened to Baby Jane?* and *The Anniversary*. Where were her real lips under all that redness?

To see as much of LA as possible was a must. It would have been nice to attend a concert at the Hollywood Bowl, all lit and dazzling at night, but not only would that have coincided with our working hours, I am not sure the concert season was in full swing. The Bowl lost a lot of its glitz in the light of day, overlooked at that time by the dilapidated Hollywood sign, which had lost some of its letters. So unglamorous and so at odds with the status of the American film industry then. One thing Europe could not compete with was the American talent for theme parks. The Anaheim Disneyland in California was the first of many to follow. It was efficiently run, queues there one minute, gone the next and not a speck of rubbish in sight. The one ride that made me cringe was one called 'It's a Small World', a maudlin indulgence of singing multinational dolls perched on platforms, as we cruised down the river from one cave to another. However, one was aware of seeing amazing effects on most of the rides, like the 'Haunted House', which seemed way ahead of any technology we had experienced in Britain at that time. I loved the place and could have happily grown old in that fantasy land.

⁂

The day of our departure to Washington came. Glenda's Girls (Fidelis, Celia, our stage manager Ba Penney, Connie and me) along with Peter and Tim boarded the private Grumman Jet, known as the Faberjet, belonging to George Barrie who owned

Fabergé. He had produced *A Touch of Class*, Glenda's last Oscar-winning film, and made this beautiful aircraft available for her personal use in the States. With Glenda's usual company spirit, she wanted to share this.

The Fabergé colours are green and gold and this was reflected in the decor of the aircraft, including the bathroom where the green towels were embossed with gold Fs. Once in the air, Glenda cooked delicious strips of fillet steak for *sukiyaki* on a hot plate, which we devoured, sitting on leather sofas, while Fidelis entertained us on a keyboard that came out of the bulkhead. What a ridiculous life we actors lead. One minute catching a Number 30 bus to a draughty rehearsal room and the next flying low over Las Vegas in a private jet making phone calls. We'd heard of mobile phones, but had never seen one. In 1975 probably only multi-millionaires could afford them. What excitement – we were living the dream! The unpredictability of our business is one of the things that helps to keep us young, as well as open to a variety of life's experiences. Everything is grist to our acting mill.

Washington was a world away from Los Angeles in every sense, although one could argue that the political mask of Washington is comparable to the entertainment mask of LA. In the centre, broad boulevards run between columned buildings, edifices of power similar to that of ancient Rome and the Reichstag in Berlin. It was impeccable, not a spot of dirt or litter anywhere. To crown the glory of America's capital, the pink almond blossom was out, softening the unyielding sense of power, reminding one that nature is never that far away. How unreal it seemed, to be mixing in elevated and powerful society as we walked through the White House on a private tour. We were there to meet the then President of the United States, Gerald Ford, who unfortunately was delayed at a high-powered meeting, probably preventing World War Three. I would have been devastated if I had been deprived of Bill Clinton, who had tons more charisma and was a right-on President to boot. The White House pulsated power and it's no wonder I became such a fan of the series *The West Wing*. The Senate House, by contrast, seemed full of hustle and bustle and eccentricity. A continuing tradition in the Senate chamber is the maintenance of two small snuffboxes, decorated with Japanese figures, originally for the delectation of the southern senators. While the custom of taking snuff may have disappeared, the boxes still contain it. In keeping with this former Senate tradition, we were invited to partake. I had been introduced to it by an eccentric family friend and so felt confident enough to take a pinch, put it on the back of my hand and sniff – one nostril after the other. It is a most disgusting habit, and fortunately I didn't disgrace myself by dribbling or sneezing uncontrollably. We had lunch in the senators' dining room and it was here that John Glenn, astronaut and politician, who made history in 1962 as the first American to orbit Earth, came over to welcome us. It was extraordinary to shake the hand of a person who had pushed the boundaries of human courage. Action man in space he may have been, but he seemed singularly grey and undynamic on Earth. Instead of thrilling us with tales of space and life in a capsule whizzing around our planet, he bored us to death with the history of corn bread and bean soup – the latter no doubt aiding lift-off! He was so lacking in dynamism I began to wonder if he'd been taken over by aliens.

During the run of the play, we had time for sightseeing. Having no performances of our own on Sundays gave us a full day and a half off. We had to see the memorials to Lincoln and Jefferson. The latter had a strong impact on me. The quotation from the 1776 Declaration of Independence, carved on the wall behind the statue of Jefferson, is probably one of the most significant and poignant in the English language:

> We hold these truths to be self-evident: that all men are created equal, that they are endowed by their Creator with certain unalienable rights, among these are Life, Liberty and the pursuit of Happiness . . .

I felt a terrible sorrow reading those words, knowing that almost two hundred years later they had still not been acted upon.

One Sunday evening, Fidelis and I decided to go and see the film *Tommy*, which had just been released. I don't know what possessed us to take off into the outer regions of Washington, a far cry from the pristine and safe streets of the political centre. We didn't even know how we were going to get back to the hotel, hoping that we would be able to hail a cab. We came out of the cinema and, after walking some way in what we hoped was the right direction, we managed to stop a cruising taxi. Fortunately just in time because, driving a couple of blocks, we saw police cars and policemen with guns aimed at a couple of black men lying face down on the pavement in the full glare of the headlights, with their hands behind their backs. It was a disturbing sight and certainly not at all what we were used to. A very far cry from *Dixon of Dock Green*.

Another Sunday, a small group of us took off at dawn to travel to New York on the Amtrak Express train. Arriving at Grand Central Station, our first port of call was the Empire State Building. Gazing down at the city from its viewing platform, across the Hudson to the horizon, I felt how different the New World is from our Old World – its modernity, its landscape and architecture, busy, bustling, brash . . .

It was virtually unknown, at that time in English theatre, to have performances on a Sunday. Britain was still primarily a Christian country and the Sabbath still a day of rest. It would be almost twenty years before Sunday trading became legally permissible. So, joy of joys, we found that several theatres were open on Broadway. We got tickets for a vibrant revival of the operetta *Candide*, with music by Leonard Bernstein. It was a unique experience, sitting in a theatre where the audience seating had been pared down to half its capacity, in order to create extra staging, by bringing the whole performance into our space. Although it had been some years since I had read *Candide*, I loved the vibrant orchestration reflecting the satire in Voltaire's book. No wonder this musical has won so many awards over the years.

The evening was rounded off by dinner at the famous German restaurant Luchow's. Sardi's, the preferred eatery of the famous, had been our first choice but was closed on Sundays.

Now, I am an enthusiastic carnivore but, even so, found the unmitigated Teutonic meatiness of the menu a trifle daunting, made worse by having two vegetarians in the group. It was a little like being in a hunting lodge, all heavy wood, antlers and beer steins. It was aggressively masculine. Dishes included Königsberger Klops (sounds interesting . . . but just meatballs); Saddle of Hare with Preiselbeeren and Potato Dumplings; Baby Partridge (come to think of it, they are not too big when they are grown up) served on Pineapple Kraut; Planked Boneless Shad (Cole Porter's 'Let's Fall in Love' gave us a clue on this one but did the poor thing have to be planked as well as boned?). Exotic as it all sounded, it was a somewhat disappointing meal, made all the more disappointing by there not being a famous face in sight.

The next morning we decided to take the ferry to the Statue of Liberty. On the jetty, undeterred by our foray into European cuisine the night before, we purchased some strange fritters called *knishes* of Jewish Eastern European origin, in the hope that these would sustain us on our climb to the top of Liberty's crown – which they did.

Ever cautious, and with years of unpredictable English train times in mind, we said an earlyish farewell to New York and returned to Washington, well in time for curtain up at the National Theater. Our time in the city had been a brief but refreshing and stimulating jaunt – a welcome break.

Towards the end of our time in Washington, Tim West and I, both jazz enthusiasts, went to a downtown jazz club. As we sat at a wooden table in the atmospheric darkness, surrounded by the soulful strains of the saxophone, it began to dawn on both of us that, having been away for nearly four months, we were moving inexorably northwards towards our final staging post, Toronto; ever closer to the end of our journey, the inevitable return to the real world.

Once again, courtesy of George Barrie, we flew up the Atlantic coast in his Faberjet. Touching down in Toronto, having breakfasted on a meal of sand crab and Bloody Marys, so much more exotic than our destination, we were met by Canadian customs officials. Taxi-ing in grand style to a private section of the airport, in the aircraft equivalent of a stretch limousine, they must have thought we were a pop group and were mightily put out by the lack of electric guitars and drugs. I can't think of a collection of people looking less like purveyors of popular music. Having grudgingly accepted that RSC wasn't an acronym for a girl band and that we were merely strolling players, they let us go on our way. While we flew, our lovely props men were wending their way towards Canada in a lorry. Fortunately, the border customs officials were not as vigilant as those at the airport, because our chaps had smuggled two gallon-jars of vodka for me with the props. We were going to have a party.

Toronto struck me as being rather self-satisfied, convinced that they had got everything right that had been messed up in the States and, maybe now, time has proved them right. Most of us were staying in the Lord Simcoe, a comfortable budget hotel with appalling food. The one thing that delighted us were the slightly out-of-date waitresses' outfits, reminiscent of the Lyons

Corner House nippies: white lace-trimmed caps and pinnies with frilled bodices over very un-chic black uniform dresses. The image was enhanced by the great age of the wearers.

Niagara Falls was a must, so we all trotted off in high expectation, only to be escorted to an observation platform set in a cavern. To prevent us being drenched we had to wear wellies and macs, chosen from a row of pegs hung with assorted sizes. What a sight we looked clad in our somewhat nifty communal outfits. Being confined to a cave watching an albeit impressive wall of water passing in front of one, was more like being a visitor to a hydro-electric plant, all the natural beauty lost. It didn't compare with the experience of a breathtaking walk I took, some twenty years later, along the edge of the Victoria Falls in Zimbabwe. The one regimented and confined, the other wild and free. I was terribly disappointed and, judging by the souvenir photograph, so was nearly everyone else.

All life has lowlights and highlights but, as if to make up for the so far uninspiring stay in Toronto, the mega-highlight of the entire tour made its unlikely appearance shortly after our Niagara disappointment. Ella Fitzgerald was in town doing a show. Obviously, we couldn't attend; we had a show to do ourselves. The only alternative was to go to her band rehearsal in the afternoon but Ella, understandably, was known to dislike an audience at these. As luck would have it, we had the same publicist as she did and, with Miss Jackson's name, it was made possible for a small group of us to watch the rehearsal. We sat, entranced, in a darkened auditorium listening to this wonderful and legendary performer. The time sped by and, before we knew it, there was a whispered direction for us to leave to get to our own theatre for that evening's performance. We crept out of our seats, bent double, pretending not to be there. Suddenly, Ella held up her hand to stop the orchestra . . . oh hell, that was the very thing we had tried so hard not to do, disturb the rehearsal. She then, and I can hardly believe this as I write it, turned to us, smiled and, unaccompanied, broke into 'Every Time We Say Goodbye . . . I Cry A Little'. It was a moment I shall savour all my life. It is impossible to put into words but, even now, when I play her singing that track I still get goose bumps. It wasn't the last time we met this gentle and gracious lady. She attended a supper concert given by Jack Jones at the Royal York Hotel to which we had also been invited by Glenda. Ella arrived before us and apparently asked, 'Where are the girls?' Those same girls later played court to her like acolytes in Jack Jones's suite, where she sat enthroned like the queen she was.

May was upon us and so was Glenda's birthday and mine. We decided to give a joint birthday party in her suite at the Royal York, our birthdays being two days apart. Shopping for the party was a nightmare in the subterranean shopping malls, made essential by the ferocious Canadian winters, but we had help from Glenda's husband, Roy Hodges, who was over for the occasion. We all gathered for the party that night, assuming that Roy was unaware of the relationship that had blossomed, somewhat intermittently, between his wife and our lighting director, Andy Phillips. As Andy came into the party he was welcomed by Roy, who offered him a drink. 'I'll help myself,' said Andy, to which Roy replied, 'I believe you already have.' The room was full of company members and friends who, although they could not hear everything that was being said, were aware that a drama was unfolding. Eventually, Glenda made a speedy exit, stage right, into the bedroom followed by her husband. It became obvious that something momentous was going on behind that door which had nothing to do with the party. They were not the only players in this drama. I was sharing the birthday party with Glenda for a start. What do you do in those circumstances? Stay? Clear the room? Jump out of the window? What you really want to happen is for the ground to open and swallow you up. It is the sort of situation in which you are so embarrassed that you have an uncontrollable urge to giggle. Celia was smooching by a window with a director. Fid was frolicking under the table with an actor and I was longing to get under anything with anyone; preferably a table with a long cloth so I could hide. Even as co-host, I realised there was no way I was going to be able to save that party.

To cap it all, the Italian/American crooner Vic Damone entered with his entourage saying, 'Hi there! Is this where Frankie's party is?' I can only assume that he quickly realised his mistake because by this time our party had become more like a Feydeau farce and there wasn't a face in sight he recognised. It really was a case of 'Strangers in the Night'. He backed out as rapidly as he came in, presumably heading for the penthouse suite above, which had been taken over by Mr Sinatra.

Many lives were changed by that world tour. Some of us had tasted a freedom, a life in which the only strict parameters were professional. New experiences had come thick and fast. We had shed our responsibilities and the idea of knuckling down once more to a world of routine and dutiful domesticity seemed almost unbearable. Fortunately, returning to England did not mean the immediate disbanding of the company. We were returning to do a season at the Aldwych, then the London home of the RSC, followed by the possibility of a film of the *Hedda Gabler* production. This meant that I would be based at home and could sort out my domestic life; although, in my heart, I should have been honest enough to admit that to pursue the work I loved, my spirit might need to be free, to fly solo.

With the cast of the BBC's *A Horseman Riding By*.

Chapter Eight

Treading the Boards

I love acting. It is so much more real than life.

Oscar Wilde, *The Picture of Dorian Gray*

England in 1975 seemed so grey and drab, even though it was early summer. Facing up to reality back home took time. We had been married about six years and were still living in the garden flat. I was trying hard to make my marriage work. Despite my waywardness on tour, that heady experience had gradually faded as time had gone on, becoming more like a dream. A couple of months later, after a season with *Hedda Gabler* at the Aldwych, I went on holiday to Scotland with my husband. Putting his powerful motorcycle on the train, we took the overnight sleeper to Inverness. We rode slowly down the Great Glen, passing deep, still lochs shimmering in the early autumn sunshine. There is something mysterious about a loch; how easy it is to believe that the Loch Ness Monster is not merely a myth.

We had a happy holiday; there was a togetherness but, nevertheless, something had irrevocably changed. I think, because we both reacted so happily to Scotland, it led him to consider applying for a posting up there in the hope that if I got away from the influences of town life and my profession, we would settle happily into a domestic routine. At that time he was a Customs & Excise officer, and so it would have been relatively easy for him to transfer to a port or distillery in Scotland.

The beauty of the Highlands has taken me back many times, drawn by the rich greenness of a wild, wet, westerly coastline, with long golden strands and curving bays. Bays inhabited only by gulls, seals and birds that feed on the bounty of the sands and islands, each one with their individual charm and character. The people themselves seemed to have a zest for life and a welcoming spirit, but that wasn't the only spirit I got to know. I love the individual character of their malt whiskies. Each one, like wine, quite distinct, reflecting the region and its water; from the peatiness of a Laphroaig to the heathery finesse of a Dalwhinnie.

Back in London, after this break away, those of us from the world tour met again to film *Hedda*, but it really was the last time we would all be working together as a group. Not long after the film, I got a touring job with the Prospect Theatre Company, performing plays by Chekhov and Strindberg. By this time, my husband had applied for a transfer to Scotland. We had discussed this advancement in his career, which was great for him, but I said I had grave reservations because of my work. We both loved Scotland, but to be that far away from mainstream theatre and television at that stage of my career, was unrealistic. Although, in his heart, I am sure he was convinced I would join him. Before starting rehearsals, I had to go into hospital briefly for an operation, and he left to take up his new post. It was strange coming back to the house, it felt almost empty with just me and the cat. We spoke on the telephone and it was clear that he expected me either to follow him at the end of my tour, or . . . the alternative was never named. It was a strange blow. I felt abandoned, but that was totally unjustified. After all, it was my actions that had brought about this crisis, and the way out of it should have been a relief. Work helped to blunt those emotions and I drowned myself in the cup of performance and comradeship.

There were only three of us on the Prospect Company tour: Isla Blair, me and Paul Moriarty. One wet cold Monday found us in Oldham playing Strindberg's *Miss Julie*. Isla was putting on her costume for the performance that night and was half dressed in her corset, silk underskirt and wig when a woman walked in and said, 'What's this then? I thought it were Weight Watchers tonight!' She left and so did most of the audience, leaving us playing to about nine people. Fortunately, that was more than made up for by a later performance of the same play at the Corn Exchange Theatre in King's Lynn, Norfolk, when a few days after the performance we all received copies of an extremely academic book on Strindberg. Each book had individual tributes on the fly-leaf from a member of the audience extolling the performance, saying it was one of the most memorable evenings he had ever had in the theatre. We felt the same; it was one of those rare moments when one is performing and everything comes together and the performance transcends the stage. These occasions are so rare.

In Whitehaven I think it was, we were all in the same digs. I was lucky enough to be the only one of the three of us to have been given a 'superior' bedroom, though actually my bed was only about six inches wider than either of theirs. Paul, who was courting at the time, asked me if we could swap bedrooms as his girlfriend was coming to visit. Of course I acceded to his request. It tickles me now to think that my bed aided him on the course of courtship and eventually to marriage. Paul and I were destined to meet again when he joined the cast of *EastEnders* many years later, to play Peggy's amour, George Palmer. He, his wife and I had a reunion while he was working at Elstree.

One destination on the Prospect Company tour was Perth. It seemed sensible, indeed necessary, for my spouse and I to talk face to face. After all, we were both in Scotland and needed to discuss the future. I had already decided by this time that we needed to part, and it may well be that he felt the same. It was with trepidation and dread in my heart that I made the journey to meet him. It was terribly emotional and, like any decision made in an emotional state when both people are hurting, it would have been easy to have given in, to relinquish my hard-earned determination to forge ahead on my own. With difficulty we agreed to part. I should have felt elated at my newly found freedom, but I only remember driving back feeling drained, utterly and completely empty. We were divorced a few years later. However, having helped to reunite her with her son, I never lost touch with my mother-in-law, Hilda. She was more relaxed in later years when I visited her on my own.

One grey and rainy Wednesday matinee in 1976, I decided to lighten the day and, once again, try my hand at corpsing another actor. It was while I was playing Fräulein Schneider, in *I Am a Camera* by John Van Druten, and Simon Williams was playing Christopher Isherwood. At one point in the play, I had to deliver a letter to him. I pranced on to the stage, letter in one hand and in the other an enormous upright German sausage (NOT in the script), from which I took the occasional suggestive nibble. I handed him the letter and waited for his reaction, barely containing myself with glee and anticipation. By the time I noticed that Simon hadn't even seen the sausage, although heaven knows why, because it was about ten inches long and about three inches in diameter, I was in a state of barely controlled hysteria. I only just managed to squeak out the few words I had to say, before scuttling off stage still clutching the wretched sausage. I realised that I was still a novice in the art of corpsing other actors.

As a young actor, without the work pressures and time constraints of the leading actors, there was always time to watch, not just to learn one's craft, but to observe and enjoy the personalities these stars had become. Thus it was with Googie Withers. She swept into the lowly rehearsal room, a church hall at Waterloo roundabout, full-length honey-coloured mink coat swaying and every inch of hair and make-up in place. Pure

Hollywood! There we were, a gaggle of youngish actresses looking like nothing on earth, sitting around sipping endless cups of coffee and puffing away on fag after fag, waiting to get on with the first rehearsal. Googie spotted the actress Joan Benham, who was the same generation but more of a bridge-playing, decorously classic woman from Knightsbridge. Googie swept towards her with a couple of air kisses and a pat of her hair. 'Darling,' she said, 'how lovely to see you. I look such a mess after the journey up from Sussex on the train.' All I could think was that there must have been an obliging hairdresser on the 8.15 from Brighton. The whole scenario had become more like a matinee at Windsor Theatre and one expected that, at any moment, the usherette would come round with ice creams. Googie was 'old school', from a time of glamour, grace and 'nothing nasty in the woodshed'. Her personality and mode of dress seemed so wonderfully at odds with the part she was playing, that of prison governor in the gritty, tough environment of a women's prison in *Within These Walls*, of which more later.

Another iconic actress I worked with was Diana Dors. I had a couple of scenes with her in a Yorkshire Television series called *All Our Saturdays*. I must say Diana appeared more relaxed working with the men. I was the only other woman in the cast, though I can hardly imagine she saw me as a threat. I was somewhat taken aback and slightly embarrassed when the director took me aside after one rehearsal and said, 'No notes for you but well done for making Di work. She can be lazy.' I wouldn't have interpreted her work as lazy, but she did give me the impression that there was a very removed part of her which she guarded fiercely. I suppose this is hardly surprising when she had been a sex symbol in her youth and so had to endure the sort of publicity that attracts. The pity was that her vulnerability would have been so effective in her performances if she had allowed it to show more. Vulnerability and charisma are qualities that an actor cannot learn, either at drama school or during their professional life. It is either there or it is not. What a gift if you are lucky enough to have it and brave enough to use it. I know that Di had many plaudits for her role in *Yield to the Night*, but I have to confess that I didn't agree with those views at the time. Her performance lacked something . . . I think that something was 'herself'; such a shame because it was a showy gift of a part for any actress.

A William Trevor three-part 'Play of the Week', *Matilda's England*, gave me the chance to meet Celia Johnson, someone I greatly admired. Her performance in David Lean's *Brief Encounter*, with Trevor Howard, was an inspiration: a delicate choreography of repression, genteel emotion and pain. I watched her during our rehearsals and was entranced by this ladylike performer of another generation. She had the grace to socialise with those of us in the junior ranks, much to our delight. This gentility was reflected in her performances, but would possibly have limited her eventually, as screen drama was changing into a more socially realistic and gritty medium. One couldn't imagine her playing a raving psychopath or a hooker; but she was loved for the quality and type of performance at which she was so good.

The contract for *Matilda's England* was something that had unexpected consequences. Those were the days when strikes were frequent. Not among the acting profession, of course, because we could always be replaced. It was usually a union issue on behalf of electricians, set-builders or other workers in the front line of production. In this instance, the sparks went on strike. As a consequence the production ground to a halt before it was completed. Some weeks later, when peace reigned on the studio floor once more, the Beeb wanted to re-contract all the actors who were needed to complete William Trevor's play. The date, a month or two later, suited me fine and I signed a new contract. In the meantime I was in Manchester, doing a comedy with Hugh Paddick and Sheila Steafel. One evening, when I was in the bar of the Midland Hotel to meet some of the cast, a director from *Coronation Street* approached me.

'Pam,' he said, 'I've been intending to contact you, as there's a part coming up in *Corrie* that I'd like you to do.'

Great, think I. *Coronation Street* would suit me fine. 'May I see a script?' I asked, to which he agreed, with the rider that it was starting next month. Unfortunately, this coincided with the contract I had signed with the BBC to complete the William Trevor play. Well, that scotched his offer. Much as I would dearly have liked a part in *Coronation Street*, there was no way I could back out of a contractual agreement on a production, half of which I had completed already. No *Dallas*-style shower scene for my character. The fact that I didn't land up in *Coronation Street* was fortuitous, and not the only such event in my career. I spent a few weeks in Yorkshire on *Emmerdale* while Sheila

Mercier, the matriarch of the Sugden household, was unwell. I was wheeled in as a neighbour, although she was someone who had never been seen before, to look after the Sugden boys. Some time after the episodes were screened, the Yorkshire Television team, who had liked the characters, wanted to bring me and my onscreen husband back. However, since our appearance, the real ex-wife of my onscreen hubbie had been cast as a regular in the show. It just would not have made sense for them to be working in the same series. Game, set and match. It is interesting to contemplate that, had I ended up in *Corrie* or *Emmerdale* on a long-term basis, I probably would not have made the journey to Walford. Is there anyone out there who really thinks we have power over our own lives?

By now I was beginning to get interesting major parts on television. One late Friday afternoon, I was called to an audition at Bush House by the director Pedr James and the writer Mary O'Malley. They were casting the part of Carmel in a BBC play, *Shall I See You Now*, written by Mary. I was the last actor to be seen. Apparently Mary and Pedr, despairing of not finding their Irish Carmel, were preparing to fly to Ireland the next day to search for her over there. It had been one of the few occasions at an audition when I had bought into the casting game and dressed to look like the character. Unknown to them before I arrived, I also had the benefit of being half Irish. I got the part.

Shall I See You Now stands out in my memory because I was working on it when my stepmother, Sally, was dying of cancer.

She had in fact had breast cancer six years previously, usually a death knell in those days. When the 'all clear' came after five years, there were family celebrations. Unbeknown to her, it had spread and she was riddled with it, slowly becoming more skeletal. She died within the year, frail and wishing for death to put an end to her suffering. I remember her telling me, while she lay in her hospital bed, that she had asked the specialist to put a 'little lethal pill' under her tongue to allow her permanent release. After all, pain control and hospice care were not as they are today. Despite this, I still think people of sound mind should have the choice of deciding whether to live or be helped to die.

I may not have lived with my father and Sally but my relationship with her had, over the years, become much closer. Their marriage had somehow managed to stay the course, or rather held on by its fingertips. In the first years of her marriage to my father I behaved in a hideous fashion. If she took my hand to cross the road, I would pull away. Nor would I engage in conversation, I would just blank her. No wonder they sent me off to be looked after by other people. By the age of nineteen, while visiting them one day, I plucked up the courage to apologise to her for my previous behaviour. It was a good and bonding thing to have done. I began to realise just how much she must have suffered, not just from my treatment towards her as a child, but from the trauma of living with a man who was physically as well as emotionally violent when he was drinking. Sally always said, 'Your father is like Jekyll and Hyde. Before the marriage he is amorous, attentive and lavish but, the minute the band of gold is on your finger, he becomes Mr Hyde, a drunken, violent and demeaning bully.'

I realised that when you have wronged someone, admit it. The worst that can happen is to have it thrown back at you, but at least you have endeavoured to make your peace. Not only did she accept my apology, but she never held a grudge and during my working years in London I kept in touch with them. I received the news of her death during a rehearsal of *Shall I See You Now*. I felt sad, but glad that she was no longer in pain. Possibly, if Sally had lived, we would have had a continuing and closer adult relationship. She would have enjoyed being part of some of the later life I lived, which was something I could never do with my father. Deep down, I felt the wrong parent had gone. When my father died in his eighties, some sixteen years after Sally, the ghosts of the past died with him and I felt a sense of release.

In the late seventies the growing awareness of women's politics, of the striving for women's equality, started to impact upon me. I was not, nor ever have been, a rabid party-political person or card-carrying member of any political party. However, political involvement, in the sense of striving for justice and fairness for all, seems not only desirable but logical. As with so many movements in their infancy the Women's Movement was, in some instances, extreme. It is as though the pendulum has to swing all the way in one direction before settling to a reasonable middle position. There was a Soho commune where the women proudly sported the appearance of men. Adornment was spurned and dungarees and lace-up boots were the order of the day. Quite how dressing up as an ersatz man promotes the furthering of women's status in the workplace, and in society in general, is quite beyond me. I attended a lecture in London, given by a woman author and friend, who was verbally attacked for wearing make-up and jewellery, on the basis that she was adorning herself to attract men. Her response was that she wore make-up and jewellery because it made her feel good, it was for herself. She was celebrating being a woman. How can anyone take a group of women seriously when they want to call History, Herstory, when their research should have told them that the etymology of the word 'history' was originally from the Greek *historia*, meaning inquiry; the branch of knowledge that records and analyses past events. As for the use of the word chair, I think being addressed as a piece of furniture is far more derogatory than being called chairman.

Around this time I was also dipping a tentative toe into the gay scene and, not knowing any other way to explore this, I went to the most famous club of the time, the Gateways. It had become known through the film *The Killing of Sister George*. I didn't go alone but with friends, for moral support. Just as well, because I was completely overwhelmed by the strangeness and power of it. From the moment I walked down a steep flight of stairs into the club, I felt a stranger. I wasn't yet part of it. Gina, who ran the club, had been an actress and, even in her fifties, was glamorous and regal. She sat on a chair at the end of the bar, so obviously in control of everything that was happening.

She was married to a man called Ted who had originally owned the basement space, allegedly won in a poker game. He initially ran it as an arts club, a place where an eclectic group of people met on a regular basis. Later it became a welcoming haunt for disenfranchised minority groups. Then, in the late sixties, it was a women-only club run by Gina and her manager Smithy, an ex-member of the United States Air Force. Having discovered London through being posted to the UK, she stayed on to help manage the, by now flourishing, establishment. You didn't mess with Smithy, she was the muscle and Gina the beauty and brain.

One somehow started from the same premise as that of heterosexual socialising, because there was some fairly predatory behaviour. It could seem quite cliquey until one was accepted as not posing a threat, or being a curious onlooker. Not all the local residents were tolerant of the club's existence. A group of us were getting into my car at the end of an evening when we were attacked by a man wielding an axe. Fortunately, the damage was only to the car, but it scared all of us and the only way to escape was for me to drive the car straight at him, in the hope that he would move out of the way, which he did. Despite shaking like a leaf, I felt quite elated at having rescued us from a fate which could have meant injury or death.

Although these early years of the feminist movement saw the gradual breaking down of sexual roles, there was still a hangover of butch and femme roles in modes and manners. One evening, I was going out to dinner and, having a few moments to spare, popped into the club. There at the bar was one of the regulars, a very masculine-looking woman in a tie and waistcoat, drinking a pint of beer. Seeing me, she pointed and said in a wonderful gravelly London accent, 'Wivin' these walls? Good on yer. Luvit. The wife's 'ome now, watchin' it. She'll be down in a tick.' A sweet and memorable, but possibly the most bizarre, fan greeting I have ever had.

Within These Walls had become an iconic series, popular with lesbians because it was set in a women's prison. My appearances were two-fold. Having played one character in the first series, I was asked to play a different character in the second. Mona Bruce, who appeared in the entire series as Mrs Armitage, had written an episode with her husband Robert James in which there was a character they wanted me to play. When Jack Williams, the producer at London Weekend Television, asked me to play the part, I reminded him that I had played a different character in the first series. His reply was, 'You're an actress, aren't you, darling?' Oh, Mr Williams, if only more people who held our professional lives in their hands would give us such benefit of the doubt.

My life on the gay scene had been drifting along with the odd fling but nothing meaningful. It was running parallel with activities such as marching on National Women's Day and, often as not, trying to soften the argument being made by the militant feminists. It was during this time that I met and fell for an attractive woman who was intelligent, witty and fun to be with. Diana and I eventually settled into a happy and stable relationship. Looking back now, I wonder if it would have been wiser for me to have stayed on my own. After all, that was what I had fought so hard to achieve, having failed in the past to sustain a long-term domestic commitment. I confess to having a duality, wanting to love and be loved at the same time as wanting to be fiercely independent; but this was a relationship I couldn't resist. It was a new experience, exciting and different in every way, an entry into a demi-monde with someone I wanted to be with. The Aunts, with their usual non-judgemental attitude, took it in their stride. Not surprising in a way, since I was reflecting their own domestic situation. Even so, their concern was always for my happiness, however they felt deep down. My father said nothing, probably because he didn't know what to say, but Sally had once told me, with feeling, that she had met two women at a dinner party in Germany who were a couple. After talking to them she could understand the attraction of living in a domestic situation with one's own sex. A hardly unexpected reaction, considering what she was putting up with at home.

We had our own professions and got on with life at work, made a home together and had happy travels in our free time. We visited parts of the UK and had sun-seeking breaks in the Mediterranean. The exception was a jaunt to Russia in the year the Berlin Wall came down. We had the idealistic notion of being near history in action. We flew on Concorde, an unforgettable experience and one I wouldn't have missed for the world. It was a beautiful aircraft, the outside lean as a raptor but without the threatening attitude of a hunting bird. The narrow interior had leather upholstered seats. There was a machometer on the front bulkhead so that we could see when the plane broke the sound barrier. What a strange, almost uneventful, happening that was. Everyone watched the meter, waiting for the moment.

The End of an Earring

When it happened, it was rather like a bad gear change in a motor car, a little nudge backwards, then forwards and, as the aircraft went into Mach One, it just glided onwards almost silently. That seemed so strange to me because, on Dartmoor, Concorde's flight over us was accompanied by a loud bang as, a few seconds later, she went supersonic over the ocean. Diana and I spent New Year's Eve 1989 in Red Square amid Russians celebrating the brink of change. The onion-shaped domes of St Basil's Cathedral lit up against the dark sky made an impressive backdrop. Our feet crunched on the frozen ground but, despite the sub-zero temperatures, it was thrilling. The celebrating Russians shared their bottles of Georgian champagne with us like long-lost comrades. '*Prost*,' we said as we raised our glasses to toast their glowing future.

As a consequence of having met Mary O'Malley I was later cast as Mother Basil in her play *Once a Catholic*. Although I didn't attend a convent school myself, it wasn't strange to create the character of a nun. When I was in my teens I had flirted with the idea of joining the Roman Church, like my mother. In fact I became hideously pious after seeking the counsel of a Sister Monica, a teaching nun whose subject was history and whose intellect I loved. I think she was disappointed when I didn't convert. The reason I didn't may have been due in part to the influence of the Aunts, both pillars of the Anglican Church and vehemently anti-Catholic at that time. However, I based Mother Basil on Sister Monica.

The company was at the Leeds Playhouse for the run of *Once A Catholic* during the days when the Yorkshire Ripper stalked the streets and was killing women. I was the only company member with a car and was able to take people home after the show, as only shanks's pony and public transport were available. We had asked the Leeds Playhouse to provide transport for the actresses returning home in the dark after the show, but were told that the budget wouldn't stretch to that. It was essential for us to watch each other's backs at night. However, one free afternoon, one of the girls in the cast expressed an interest in going to see a film that I also wanted to see. Off we went in the daylight, coming out when it was turning dark. I offered, in fact insisted, that I take her back to her digs. She got in the car and, about half a mile up the road, told me to drop her off. I remonstrated, 'No, I think it's wiser to take you to your front door.' She explained that we were just across the road from the back entrance to her digs with a snicket or ginnel, in Yorkshire parlance, leading to the house. She got out and we parted company. The next day, the newspaper was full of an attack in the same snicket. I felt absolutely sick and raced to the theatre where I found her safe and unharmed, but shocked. The assault had taken place a mere ten minutes after she had walked up there. The victim had been injured but was alive. Those were dark days, years in fact, for the people of Leeds and it was a great relief to everyone when the perpetrator, Peter Sutcliffe, was caught, tried, convicted and incarcerated.

While I was on stage in Leeds I received the news that Hilda, my mother-in-law, had committed suicide. She was by then a

179

widow, very frail and in considerable pain due to an arthritic condition of her neck, made worse by an operation to alleviate the problem. She travelled in an attempt to take her mind off the discomfort and ease her loneliness. None of the men she met subsequently were enduring, but maybe this was because she just didn't find the right person. Her death, and the manner of it, knocked me for six. I was sorry I was unable to attend either the inquest, or the funeral, because of my acting commitments. However, I was in touch with her solicitor, who told me the inquest had revealed that Hilda had locked herself in the house, put on her nightdress, made herself up and taken an overdose. She had left a note saying, 'I only want someone to love me.' She left me two very nice rings, a modern one made to her own design and the other Victorian. That gesture touched me deeply.

Barely a year after Sally's death I was to lose someone even closer to me. How strange it is that some productions are heightened by emotionally dramatic events in life. I don't paint or, up to this point, write anything more than a letter, so all I can dedicate to those that I love is that which I do; the play that I am in at the time of their deaths. I was filming the series *A Horseman Riding By* in 1978, the first of a trilogy by R. F. Delderfield. Like Dickens and Walpole, Delderfield could have been writing for the screen; their books are so visual, so full of action and so rich with story. It was a great pity that the other two books in the trilogy were never filmed.

We had some weeks on location in Devon, where the piece was set. It enabled me to see the Aunts and to spend some time with them. They were much older and less able to cope with the rigours of hill farming, which was a harsh life and it had always been a struggle to make ends meet. A time came when it was no longer possible for Sylvia to find the £6. 19s. 0d. for a six-day week to keep George on and she had to ask him to find work elsewhere. They had worked together for years and had a mutual respect for each other, born of their knowledge of the land. It was heartbreaking for both of them. The only way to get the labour she so badly needed had been to take on youngsters who wanted farming experience, or students from Seale Hayne Agricultural College. They had the enthusiasm and energy, but not the experience. This meant an extra unforeseen burden on her, having to be tutor and supervisor alongside her own work.

How fortuitous my working in Devon turned out to be, because it was not long after that Courty had a massive stroke, following a ridiculously minor operation on her toe, and died. Fortunately I was able to get time off to read at her funeral. I felt upset and angry that such a minor reason to go into hospital should have ended up the way it did. Her death was the first one that impacted, in a major way, on me. Spending so much time outside with Sylvia, doing what I perceived to be the enjoyable things, probably meant that I hadn't always appreciated Courty's qualities when I was young, but I had made up for this as I grew older. She was kind, gentle and tolerant to a fault. Despite there being no electricity and no modern machinery, the house had always run like clockwork. Clothes and bed linen were washed by hand, dirty farm clothes scrubbed on a washboard and then rinsed in the river. The house was cleaned with an ancient carpet sweeper, brooms and a duster. She beat the cake mixture with a hand whisk, pushed meat through an ancient mincer for rissoles and cottage pies, with never a murmur of discontent. Outside, she tended the vegetable patch, fed and cleaned out the chickens and collected the eggs. The almost moribund lambs were warmed back to life in the plate oven of the Aga and orphaned lambs, kept near the house, had to be bottle-fed and inevitably became pets. This relentless routine, getting slightly easier over the years as the farming stock reduced in size, was, nonetheless, carried out by her until she died. The little leisure she had, when she was not at her weekly whist drive, was usually occupied with charit-able work in the community. She'd bake for the church and other fundraising events. She was popular and greatly missed when she died.

As for Sylvia, Courty's death left a great chasm. In a blow she had lost both her companion and her workmate. The one who was completely inconsolable was Alice, Courty's little Jack Russell and faithful friend, who guarded her through the night on the end of her bed. Had Alice died before her, Courty would have been equally inconsolable. It's strange how one can be heartbroken, yet pragmatic, about a human dying of natural causes but, when a beloved pet dies, the mourning can seem out of proportion. I think this must be because one can't converse with an animal, one can't explain why someone has left it, any more than one can reassure it when hurt, or likely to die.

Treading the Boards

Aunt Sylvia died more than thirty years after Courty, a few days before her ninety-second birthday. She had been adamant that she wished to die at home, which was quite understandable but, for her to do this, it became necessary to make some fundamental changes. Much against her protestations, oil lamps gave way to the installation of electricity and the famous Aga converted from coal to oil. Thus she would no longer need to stoke it and lift heavy coal scuttles three times a day. Not only was she frail by her late eighties but her eyesight was failing. Despite her initial resistance, it didn't take her long to realise that coming into the modern world was the only way she could stay at home and remain independent.

She had a pacemaker fitted when she was seventy, which gave her another ten years or so of good-quality life, enabling her to keep on a small flock of sheep – a joy for her. However, this was followed by two more pacemakers. These may have kept her heart going but they did not rejuvenate Sylvia's ageing body which, by this time, was failing fast. She had battled against the obstacles of being a female farmer in a man's world, eventually becoming chairman and then president of the Whiteface Dartmoor Sheep Breeders' Association, and so it was sad to see her have such an undignified last few years. They were hard for her and for those around her. Thank goodness she had support, when she needed it, from many members of the surrounding community. However, without the constant, kind and loving neighbours who lived up the hill, I doubt that she could have spent her last years at home on the moor.

Sylvia was wonderful but, like all of us, she had her faults. She could be remarkably thoughtless when it suited her. She was very obstinate and wilful at times. Courty would often say to her, 'You listen, but you don't heed.' She had no concept of 'a stitch in time', preferring to wait for a leak to bring the ceiling down rather than fix it the moment the leak became apparent. It was during one of those many leaks that I lost the only photo I had of my mother. She never got anything serviced, which meant that when something stopped functioning she had to call a specialist in to help, incurring greater expense, and one which her limited income could ill afford.

She preferred, as I have already mentioned, to accept the word of a man over that of a woman, much preferring male company to that of most women. This may have been based on the fact that she believed men to be better educated than most women of her generation, although there were many highly educated and intelligent women of her age living on the moor.

Having been a pillar of the Church when Courty was alive, Sylvia came to question its precepts in her latter years. It was a long and painful process for her. Ultimately she abandoned Christianity and its rituals completely, believing it to have become totally divorced from the simple goodness and truth of the teachings of Christ. She spent years trying to fathom out the nature of God – or rather 'G.O.D.' – using only the initials as she couldn't bring herself to speak the word. However, she believed that the wonders of the natural world, the sheer power and beauty of the moor on which she had lived, surrounded and protected, could not exist without a Creator.

In her youth she'd been an avid reader of crime novels but in later years had a library comprising mainly reference books. As well as continuing to read modern books on Christian interpretation she read the Koran, the Talmud, the teachings of Buddha and many other religions and beliefs. She studied Mayan astronomy, the life of the Hopi Indians, geology, crop circles, ley lines and the alignment of ancient monuments and megaliths. Her interests spread far and wide and it was these endless studies that brought her the peace she had once felt from Christianity. She believed firmly that the spirit never dies and that love was the only true dynamic through which mankind should and could live.

On her mantelpiece she kept a framed photograph I took of Courty with a short extract of Hindu scripture from the Bhagavad Gita attached to it. Next to the photo was a sealed jar containing a piece of bread from the loaf Courty baked on the day of her death, and which I now have.

Despite the frailties of her body, Sylvia's mind remained young and open to enquiry and folk of all ages were drawn to her wisdom and good counsel. She was as much a part of the moor as the very ground on which her ashes are scattered.

The story of her early life is testament to that.

Sylvia and Courty: bored stiff at a wedding reception.

Chapter Nine

The Well of Contentedness

Never the spirit was born; the spirit shall cease to be never;
Never was time it was not . . . End and Beginning
are dreams!
Birthless and deathless and changeless remaineth
the spirit for ever;
Death hath not touched it at all, dead though the
house of it seems . . .

Bhagavad Gita

I came to know Aunt Sylvia much better over the years, and much more so in later life. I discovered a fascinating history. Her father Montague, the middle son of three boys, read Holy Scripture at Lincoln College, Oxford. He did not get a first, as was expected, but a somewhat mediocre degree. This may have been due to bouts of depression he had from time to time. He became a parson in a mid-Devon parish shortly before Sylvia was born, in 1914. He was an incredibly tall man, very thin and stern-looking. I was terrified of him as a child, even though Sylvia, who adored him, always said how wonderful he was with children. That adoration between father and daughter, so different from my own, was mutual and maybe blinded Sylvia to his shortcomings. She always blamed her mother for holding his career back, but perhaps his temperament and lack of achievement at Oxford was also in part to blame.

In fairness to him, her mother Geraldine was a woman of gentle but frail bearing, but never 'quite right'. Sylvia always maintained that her mother's 'difficulties' stemmed from her wedding night because she remembered overhearing her Aunt May say, 'Geraldine returned from her honeymoon a very disappointed and frightened woman and she has never recovered from it.' One can only assume that, having no brothers, Geraldine had no idea about the male physique or what love-making and procreation were all about. Added to which, it is very likely Sylvia's father had no experience of premarital sex either and thus no idea how to set about making love to an innocent woman. Apparently, from then on, they had separate rooms.

I think Sylvia believed that her father, at some point, must have laid down the law insisting that they had a child, no doubt a longed-for son. However, that was not to be – Sylvia was the result. This was followed by a further attempt and another daughter, Christine, later known as Bobby.

I remember how tender Sylvia's father was with his wife, despite the difficulties in their marriage. Deep down he must have been a sensitive if troubled man because it was he, rather than Sylvia's mother, who ran the household as well as a busy parish, becoming father and mother to the girls and nursemaid to a fragile wife. Fortunately he was aided in this task by their housemaids, cook, gardener and handyman. Their two daughters could not have been more different. Bobby was wilful, capricious and attention-seeking. Hardly surprising, given that Sylvia was the exact opposite, being the apple of her father's eye, she could do no wrong. I was entranced by Bobby, she was great fun, a tremendous horsewoman. She married twice and had enjoyed various tumbles in the hay with one or two of the local farmers. I felt a kinship with this rebel soul when I was a difficult teenager, much to the concern of the Aunts.

Sylvia always said that Bobby took after her Aunt May, a wealthy woman who had also been similarly spirited; finally shocking her parents by marrying Bill, their chauffeur. Despite being called Bill the family always referred to him as 'Darlin'' because that was what he called Aunt May. It was certainly a somewhat curious marriage in that Darlin' would drive his wife May around in her Rolls-Royce, while she sat in the back with her pet Pekingese, Beady Eyes. Furthermore it didn't look as though poor old Darlin' got his oats either. Sylvia used to stay with them from time to time. On one occasion, while helping her aunt to make the matrimonial bed, she was surprised to notice that, rather than pulling the top sheet up over the whole bed, it was folded in a very ingenious way so that ne'er the twain should meet! Aunt May certainly never had children. Darlin', however, made up for his lack of conjugal rights by keeping a mistress down on the south coast. There he spawned a family to whom, when he died, he left a great deal of money. Money he'd inherited from his wife when she died.

The End of an Earring

Among other stories that Aunt Syl told me about her Aunt May, two stand out in particular. May had a favourite maid called Gladys, similar in age to herself. On one occasion Gladys had a nasty carbuncle on her leg and, when asked why she was limping, she replied, 'Oh Madam, us 'as got a terrible carbolic on me leg, 'tis proper painful.' The other story I remember hearing about was when Gladys, by then quite old, was serving the dessert at a dinner party. In truth, she should probably have retired well before then. She came in dressed as usual in her black dress, frilly white apron with bib and lace cap upon her head, carrying cook's masterpiece: a jelly which, once released from its mould, stood proudly erect on its silver salver. But, like Gladys's legs, it was very wobbly. Gladys, who was clearly having a great deal of difficulty keeping the jelly under control, was heard to say, 'Oh dear, Madam, this 'ere jelly is proper tremulous.' Now whether the dinner was taking longer than usual, or whether Beady Eyes was getting bored and hungry and lusting for a piece of sweet jelly, will never be known. He was sitting as usual beneath Aunt May's chair, waiting expectantly for little titbits to be proffered him by his adoring mistress from time to time. Just as Gladys was about to lower the fruit-studded jelly on to the sideboard to be served, Beady Eyes, shot out from under his chair and nipped poor Gladys on the leg (thank heavens it was some years after the carbolic incident). With a shriek, all Gladys's attempts to keep the trembling work of art on the dish abandoned, the jelly and dish crashed to the floor. All eyes, especially those of Beady Eyes who was on his way to sample the offering gently spreading over the carpet, were focused on the ruined jelly as the distraught maid departed in tears, all dignity forsaken.

When Sylvia was about five, her father was offered a living on Dartmoor. The day the whole family visited the area for the first time, they took a wicker basket piled high with luncheon goodies and picnicked by a brook in the parish. Sylvia knew, instinctively, that she had found 'home', and was overjoyed when her father took the position. From that moment on, any time spent away from the moor was a wrench. It wasn't long before Sylvia first felt that sense of separation, when she and her sister were sent away to a private preparatory boarding school in North Devon, an experience that lasted barely a term. Sylvia remembered this as a time of terrible homesickness and longing for the moor. The two of them, along with the other pupils, were poorly treated and malnourished. Eventually, Sylvia became ill and was sent home. I was never absolutely certain what the nature of that illness was, but I think it was rheumatic fever. I know that she needed full-time nursing for some months. As a result the school was investigated and shut down very soon afterwards. Bobby was sent to Cheltenham Ladies' College, but Sylvia never went to school again. She was taught by various governesses thereafter, feasting on their knowledge and gaining an eclectic education.

Despite what could be interpreted as an indulgent childhood, she was clearly an interesting and engaging child. While on holiday with her parents when she was about twelve, she met a

Sylvia, aged eight.

man old enough to be her father. She always referred to him as
W.H.S. and, although they never met again, they kept up a
correspondence concerning the changing seasons and the cycle
of nature for almost forty years until his death.

Sylvia was in her very early teens when Dorothy came into
her life; she was about the same age as Sylvia's mother, but
childless. Many of the important people in Sylvia's early life

'W.H.S.'

were simply referred to by their initials, and Dorothy became DF (Dearest Friend). Dorothy also found her delightful to be with and it was not long before she took on the role of the mother Sylvia never really had. She was a New Zealander who had come to England, fallen in love with Dartmoor and built a house there called Tumbley. DF had a husband, from whom she was separated. Sylvia used to say that he would turn up from time to time to see his wife. She always knew when he had visited because she would arrive at Tumbley to find DF in tears, although DF never talked about her husband or what had passed between them.

Dorothy loved Sylvia, now a budding and attractive teenager, as a daughter. It was she who recognised Sylvia's love of nature; broadening her knowledge, teaching her the names of flowers and shrubs which grew wild on the moor; about birds, their songs and how to recognise their nests and eggs. All of which would be noted meticulously by Sylvia at the end of each day in one of her many diaries.

They packed their rucksacks with binoculars, notebooks and picnic lunches and would ride up to Benjy Tor together where, overlooking the wooded Dart Gorge, they would look at ravens, those birds of myth and legend, and their nests. Sylvia loved this place, where two tributaries, the East Dart and the West Dart, combine to flow through the Gorge. It was where she wanted her ashes spread when she died. They would tether the horses and sit in the heather nibbling hard-boiled eggs and ham sandwiches. On warm summer evenings they camped by the Dart. In the mornings they built a fire on the rocks beside the river, cooking breakfasts of duck eggs and bacon in an ancient frying pan, seeing iridescent flashes of colour as the kingfishers swooped down in the hope of catching their own fishy breakfast. They swam in the clear icy water feeling the velvety brown trout brush against their legs.

At Easter they would pick baskets of pale yellow primroses for the church, the yellow heads and crisp spring-green leaves sprouting from the rich-red soil of the Devon hedgerows. Primroses, and the tiny Devon violets that grew on banks and in rock crevices, were Sylvia's favourite flowers. When the bluebells were out, so abundant they formed swathes of blue over large sections of the moor, she and DF would sit on a lump of granite, worn smooth and comfortable by harsh moorland weather over millennia, wondering at the sea of colour. Their love for each other was mutual and deep.

By the time Aunt Sylvia was about sixteen she was undertaking many of the parish duties a clergyman's wife would usually have carried out. She helped her father with his correspondence, arranged functions and typed his sermons. They were both night owls and discussed religion and philosophy until the early hours. It was DF who noticed how tired Sylvia was getting and it was she who suggested that the rector employ a secretary, or one of the parishioners, to help him.

It was probably about this time that it must have slowly dawned on her father that his elder daughter was no longer wearing dresses or skirts as befitted a young woman of the day. Sylvia had taken to wearing trousers, a jacket and a tie, about which Bobby made disparaging comments in front of the family; an ideal outfit for horse riding, but not acceptable as everyday wear. In so many ways it seemed that she was becoming, without realising it, the son her father had longed for, similar in some ways to the upper-class Englishwoman Stephen Gordon in *The Well of Loneliness* by Radclyffe Hall. It was only much later in life, when Sylvia had lost some of her innocence, that she realised how much she must have added to her father's sorrows and how distressed he must have been by what seemed completely normal to her. She had no knowledge of same-sex love or that she was different in any way from other girls. It was not long before her father asked DF to talk to her about friendships and the importance of marriage and having children. All of which went completely over Sylvia's head although, curiously, at this time she did have a male suitor called Cyril. They had known each other as teenagers and he had fallen headlong for her. Unbeknown to Sylvia, he had already approached her father to ask for her hand in marriage. The rector must have been delighted, because he apparently gave his blessing and encouraged Sylvia to accept him. At this stage I think her father thought there might be a reprieve from his worst fears. However, Cyril's proposal, and all his future ones for many years after, fell on stony ground. She was fond of Cyril, very fond, but not in that way. Strangely, it didn't seem to occur to him that she was not, as others suspected, the marrying type.

In her late teens Sylvia helped out at country holiday camps run for children from deprived city areas. It was at one of these that her father's worst fears finally came true. She shared a hut with a woman she had worked with at a previous camp. One sultry night they were awoken by a fierce thunderstorm that broke with tremendous force over the campsite. The rain lashed down on to the cabin's tin roof and flashes of lightning burst through the thin curtains. It was pretty scary and her hut mate, who was terrified of thunder, crept into Sylvia's bed for comfort. As the storm abated Sylvia found herself being gently caressed, culminating in an awakening that was as powerful as the storm had been, leaving her fulfilled and in a state of sheer wonderment.

It was not long before her father and DF knew she was in love with Audrey, or A as Sylvia called her. To Sylvia it was as meaningful as a betrothal, so natural that she had no inkling of the

196

distress that those around her were going through. Her father and DF were devastated. I think that Sylvia, as an old woman, felt that this, coupled with her father's disastrous marriage and enforced celibacy, caused the breakdown he had some years later when he was forced to take a nine-month sabbatical from the parish. For Dearest Friend, there was no solace. She saw the girl she had nurtured and treated as her own daughter drawing away from her, obsessed with someone whose personality was likely to bring Sylvia nothing but sorrow. Sylvia was too infatuated to notice that DF, the woman who had given her so much and to whom she would one day long to turn for comfort, was broken-hearted. Gone were their chats over the curry suppers they shared together around the fire at Tumbley, curries full of raisins and spices hitherto unknown at the rectory. All these became a thing of the past.

Audrey.

Dorothy was absolutely heartbroken. She sold Tumbley, her heart's home, and went back to New Zealand. Not only had she loved Sylvia, but her wisdom and experience had formed the bedrock of the girl's life, far greater than anything Sylvia's parental home could offer. It would be some years before Sylvia's world started to crumble and the only person she could have turned to, the one who would have given her solace, would no longer be living nearby.

Youth can be cruel. Sylvia never forgave herself for the hurt she had done Dearest Friend. Despite this, they still corresponded lovingly, until the day DF died.

So completely in love was Sylvia that she was blind to the tortured soul that lay within the bosom of the woman who had captivated her and who would, one day, break her heart. It had been blindingly obvious, both to her father and DF, that the relationship with the capricious and sometimes objection-able beloved could never last. Sylvia was a frequent visitor to A's family home. They were wealthy and lived in Surrey. She was always amused by the special treatment afforded the autocratic father who presided, resplendent with beard well-clipped and combed, at the end of the table. In front of him was his special chutney, or whatever had been preserved and reserved for Papa only.

Sylvia loved A's only brother, Humphrey, who was a pituitary dwarf, a condition in which a lack of growth hormone prevents maturation. Even as an adult, he looked and sounded like a young teenager. It was agony for him as a grown man to be regarded as a child in public, without the social standing that would normally be accorded an adult. Sylvia recognised in him an intellect and sweet nature that were always there despite the continual difficulties he faced. Although Sylvia was aware of A's merciless taunting of her brother and found it very distressing to witness, she never confronted her about it. How ridiculously blind and even forgiving love can be. Despite his difficulties, Humphrey gained a first at Cambridge, eventually becoming a monk. As was usual for Sylvia, she corresponded with him by letter until his death. It is amazing that even during her tough farming years she found the time and energy to write so many long and interesting letters to so many people. What a wonderful book her 'little scribbles', as she called them, would have made.

Sylvia and her amour eventually set up home together on a farm in Devon; Sylvia farming, with A fulfilling the wifely role, running the home as Courty would do some years later. Sylvia would get up early to bring the cows in for milking, taking the churns up to the gate to be collected by the dairy, before returning to a wonderful cooked breakfast. Out again for the morning chores and back for lunch, the main meal of the day; followed, after the evening milking and calf feeding, by a high tea. For Sylvia it was a time of bliss; she was doing work she loved and was utterly fulfilled in mind and body.

At some point during their life together they decided to adopt a child, a boy. His fate, or it may well have been a blessing, was similar in some ways to that of my father in that this child was the one to be selected to leave the family. At least my father

Humphrey with his mother, nephews and niece.

had been able to keep his surname and given name and thus, to some extent, his identity, but this child had both his names changed. Perhaps, in some situations, a fresh start and identity is the best course – only the child concerned can answer that. I am pretty sure it wasn't Sylvia who was the prime mover in the adoption, because she was still underage; nor did she have the money and influence to obtain whatsoever she desired, as A did. All I know is that Sylvia, who always regarded herself as lacking maternal instincts, adored that boy. Until the end of her days she referred to him as 'the child of my heart' and, despite her protestations, loved him as a son. In the same way as DF had guided her young life, so she too guided his. They rode over the moors revelling in nature and each other's company. For Sylvia their relationship was the icing on what appeared to be a perfect cake, but a black cloud was slowly appearing on the horizon. Audrey's behaviour was becoming increasingly volatile. Sylvia and her adopted son often found themselves as co-conspirators, having to cover up things to avoid A's wrath over some supposed misdemeanour. If truth be told, Sylvia was becoming slightly troubled by this but it seemed in no way to diminish her love for A.

The storm that had been gathering broke with the arrival of The Old 'Allett to the village. He was, I think, an ex-naval officer but I may be wrong about this. It was Sylvia who always referred to him as The Old 'Allett. He made a beeline for the two women. Maybe, like some men, he found the Sapphic lifestyle something of a challenge and wanted to see if he could break them up. Sylvia was never sure what the motive was, but break them up he did. To her dismay and utter disbelief, she discovered that A was having an affair with him. For Sylvia, who regarded her own relationship as permanent, this seemed hardly possible. Suddenly, Audrey had better things to do than look after Sylvia who, by now, was too emotionally stressed and too exhausted by her farming commitments to cook for herself, or to look after the house. She concentrated what little energy she had on keeping the farm up and running; the work she had so much enjoyed had become a Herculean task. More often than not she returned to an empty home, cold because the Aga had been unattended and left to go out or, just as bad, to a sullen and resentful lover. Life had become unbearable. To complicate matters A's terminally ill mother, of whom Sylvia was very fond, was now living with them.

Fate had at this point decided to step in. She put in position the woman who would eventually lead Sylvia out of the Slough of Despond, in the form of a private nurse engaged to look after the ailing woman . . . enter Mrs Molly Court! She was a down-to-earth, warm, no-nonsense Yorkshire woman; even-tempered, with an irresistible twinkle and a soft northern burr. It was not long before Molly, shrewd as always, summed up the situation between the two women. Sylvia's unhappiness was palpable. Molly was aware too that Sylvia wanted to visit A's mother who was, to all intents and purposes, her mother-in-law, but knew that A had banned Sylvia, not only from the sick room but from all contact with her mother. Molly's keen eye could see the cause of Sylvia's distress was far more than her inability to visit the dying woman, and she knew whose fault that was. Like so many others before her, Molly came to dislike A. Despite not being in much of a position to help Sylvia, she came to love and respect the young farmer.

Some weeks later, Audrey's mother died. Her duties finished, Molly left the remote Dartmoor farm but not without having made friends with one or two people in the village, who kept her up-to-date with Sylvia's situation. Not many months would pass before she once again walked up the path to the farmhouse door, to take charge of the household and Sylvia.

Molly was no fool. As she had predicted it was not long after she departed that A upped sticks and left to be with

The Old 'Allett. She took almost every stick of furniture – she probably felt justified in this because much of it would have been paid for by her. She showed not one bit of kindness towards the girl with whom she had lived for some years, not just stripping the house but, far worse, taking Sylvia's beloved boy from her. She, who had had no legal right at the time of the adoption, could not claim him jointly. Added to which, A made it clear that she wouldn't allow Sylvia to see him again. I am not sure how old he was at that time but probably in his early teens, not a good time for your life to be thrown into uncertainty once again. It was a blow that Sylvia never really got over. Her grieving was made worse by her anxiety for the boy's long-term welfare. She had no idea what stories Audrey might spin and she so much wanted him to know the truth. To tell him that she loved him above all else, that he had lit up her life, that Audrey's leaving was not her fault and that she had been powerless to stop his being torn from her. She wanted him to know the excitement she felt at the end of each school term, knowing that he would be with her for the holidays. Even in great old age, when she did have a chance to talk to him, to tell him everything face to face, she could not trust herself to speak. She was afraid that she might break down in front of him, fail to find the right words to explain what had remained in her heart since he had left. Her one joy, near the end of her life though, was to know that he had found happiness and remained a keen countryman, horseman and birdwatcher. Those were shared gifts that Audrey could never take away from either of them. Of course, in every relationship there are two sides to a story and this, for obvious reasons, is only one side. How much easier it would be if one could be a fly on the wall, to know the objective truth.

Some months after A had left the farm they leased, Sylvia was nibbling on a piece of toast, mouldy at the edges but covered in Marmite in an attempt to disguise its age, when there was a knock on her front door. There stood Molly, suitcase in one hand, a sturdy paper bag in the other and a yellow beret perched on her head. 'I'm here to look after you,' she said as she walked through the door. Plonking her suitcase down in the kitchen, she washed her hands and took a frying pan out of the cupboard. Opening the bag, she pulled out a loaf of fresh bread, butter, eggs and some bacon and proceeded to cook Sylvia the best breakfast of her life. She never left.

Molly had not always been a cook and housekeeper but had led a very different life. She had been married and divorced and, being a fully qualified private nurse, had led a sophisticated and cosmopolitan life, nursing wealthy private patients at home and abroad – a skill that was often to spill over into caring for sickly farm animals. This move away from a world of financial independence and comfort to one of hard living and austerity on a Devon farm was not a difficult one to make. She was following her heart. The only hot water and warmth came from the Aga and there was no electricity. A simple chore like ironing would involve heating smoothing irons on the Aga, using them alternately as one became cold. The irons were very, very heavy and her wrists bore testament to that in later years. None of these privations was a deterrent.

The Well of Contentedness

From that moment on they settled into a contented routine, Sylvia running the farm and Molly the household. They lived together in a partnership until Molly, who was fourteen years older, died. Molly had truly loved Sylvia and, in time, Sylvia came to love her very deeply but without the intensity, the passion and the desire that she and Audrey once had. For some years they shared a bed, whether to keep warm or because of their need to let out spare rooms to paying guests, I never knew. I am sure that, even without the heady love she had once known, there must have been moments of physical togetherness.

Thanks to these two remarkable women, my life had a stability that might have been the envy of a more conventional family unit. A stability that equipped me to face the 'slings and arrows', the rejections and the vagabond life that are all part of my precarious profession.

Enter Pat Wicks.

Chapter Ten

The Distant Call of Bow Bells

I wander thro' each chartered street,
Near where the charter'd Thames does flow.
And mark in every face I meet
Marks of weakness, marks of woe.

William Blake 'London'

Possibly the production that challenged me the most was a BBC television 'Play for Today', *Not for the Likes of Us*. I went to meet the director Tim King and producer Stephen Gilbert, a strange creative partnership. Tim liked his films European and intense, while Stephen loved the heyday of the musical, with the likes of Fred Astaire and Ginger Rogers. The part was mine. It was the lead role, not something that character actresses experience often. The script, written by Gilly Fraser (whose work I would perform again in future years in *EastEnders*), was a gift. I loved it. There was just one glaring problem and that was in the final scene. Connie, the character I was to play, had to take her clothes off as a nude model in an art class. I discussed this with Tim and Stephen, and with great sensitivity they did say that if I really couldn't countenance baring all, the camera could pan down focusing on my kimono as I took it off, rather than on my body. Much as this was a welcome way out, I knew pursuing that course would compromise the script. The play was about a woman who was drowning in her life, taken for granted by her family and working herself to the bone; feeling physically unattractive and invisible.

Connie is shown some nude drawings by a young girl she is working with. She is curious and at the same time horrified; they are of naked people who are far from her idea of physical perfection – wrinkly, old and saggy. Connie is encouraged to visit the National Gallery to see how artists portray women. She looks at works such as Mark Gertler's *Queen of Sheba* and Suzanne Valadon's *La Chambre Bleue*. Much to her surprise, each of these paintings is a celebration of big women. Connie takes the plunge, confronts her fears and becomes a nude model, braving the non-judgemental gaze of the student artists. To lose seeing this moment of Connie's bravery, of metamorphosis, would negate the essence of the play. I knew to be faithful to the play that I had to strip, dammit! When asked if there were any requests regarding the filming schedule while on location, I said, 'May I do the last scene first, to get it out of the way? I don't want it hanging over me during the shoot, like the Sword of Damocles.' As a consequence, the tone was set for the remainder of the filming. Nobody could lose face, whatever happened, not after I had bared all!

Following the screening of the play I had the most unexpected response from men, complete strangers, who had watched it. I found that when I was out shopping, at the petrol station, or just doing those everyday things, I had winks, nods of affirmation, in-the-know looks and smiles; approaches that a woman of my maturity wouldn't receive without instigating them but, of course, being naked onscreen was probably seen as that very thing. Imagine my surprise when a local policeman, whom I knew in passing, knocked on my door the morning after the screening. With a very big smile, dressed in mufti and smelling of aftershave, he said, 'I saw you on telly last night . . . I really enjoyed it. Can I come in for a coffee?' Whoops! Not an easy situation but, quickly recovering and with as much aplomb as I could muster, I made the excuse that I had a casting session in town and was on the point of leaving. If anything, I had anticipated possible responses of antagonism, even horror, from a viewing public used only to seeing lithe nubile bodies on screen. What did become clear to me was that there were plenty of men around who liked large women. Some press was a little hurtful but, in the main, most critics understood the essence of the play, which was, of course, far from gratuitous. Thank you to the critic Elizabeth Cowley, who unwittingly poured balm on my wounded soul by referring to the character as having 'the face of an angel and the body of an ageing Rubens nude'.

Some weeks after the screening of *Not for the Likes of Us*, Gilly Fraser introduced me to a friend of hers called Tony Holland. He later co-devised *EastEnders* with Julia Smith, noted for her work on *Dr Finlay's Casebook*, *Z-Cars*, *Doctor Who* and *The District Nurse*. I had worked briefly with Julia on *Angels*, a series about hospital nurses. Life is a strange journey of fate and serendipity.

In spring 1986, I got a job in *EastEnders* for three weeks. I had been aware even from 1984 that the BBC, with Jonathan Powell as head of series, was in the planning stages of a series called *E8*, the working title at that time, subsequently changed to *EastEnders*. Around the same time, the BBC had acquired the old ATV studios at Elstree, in Borehamwood, a suitable base for a bi-weekly ongoing drama. I thought being part of such a series would be ideal for me as an actor, added to which I knew and liked Julia and Tony, the creators, and their work. My agent put my name up for one of the original characters, Pauline, but was told that the producer had already cast that part. It turned out that Julia had chosen Wendy Richard, the only cast member at that time with a previous high profile. She played Miss Brahms, a regular character in the comedy *Are You Being Served?* That scotched my plans – but sometimes things come to those who wait.

In 1985 Hugh Miller wrote an *EastEnders* book for the BBC, to tie-in with the series, in which Pete Beale's ex-wife Pat was mentioned. It wasn't until the following year that they decided to bring her in on a temporary basis to stir up the Beale household. The character, later to be played by me, was loosely based on Tony Holland's mother, whom I did eventually meet after I joined the show. Tony happened to mention that his mother had a home in Norfolk, not far from where I was living then. She was a blonde, buxom, well-preserved woman in her sixties. Her name was Pat and she had some of the qualities of the Pat I was already playing in *EastEnders*. I know nothing about her past, only that they had lived, when Tony was a boy, a stone's throw from Europe's longest street market in Walthamstow; an extraordinary coincidence because, like his mother, I too had lived in Walthamstow before moving to Norfolk. I have a feeling that he and his mother had drifted apart and so I was never sure if Tony had told her that he had loosely based the character on her. I have often wondered since whether some of Pat Holland's story was reflected in the fictional Pat's history but, maybe, he had just used the name Pat in the same way as he had used other family names. He had an Aunt Lou and two cousins, Pete and Pauline.

The first I knew that I was to be Pat was a couple of months after I'd moved out of London, to East Anglia. Most of the recent productions I had been working in had been on location, or at studios outside London. So it had seemed like a good moment to make a break from the metropolis and go back to country life, with Diana coming home from her London job at weekends. My actor friends thought I was mad: 'You won't be available for auditions, you'll be losing work,' blah, blah. My response was, 'Most of the work I have had over the last eighteen months has been through direct offers, I haven't needed to audition.' I reminded them of the actors' superstition that if you move to Shepherd's Bush, you'll never work for the BBC; live in Shepperton, you'll never work at Shepperton Studios. It wasn't long before I ate my words – my friends had been right.

❧

I was sitting at home when the phone rang. It was Mike Gibbon, a director who had become a friend after we'd worked together in television and film. After the initial pleasantries he said with some hesitancy, 'I don't suppose you watch *EastEnders*?' 'I certainly do, when I'm at home,' I said. 'I like it. It's gritty and real; reminds me of the early days of *Coronation Street*.' At which point he blew a sigh of relief and said, 'May I courier a script to you straightaway? We start shooting those scenes in a few days' time. Let me know what you think as soon as you've read it.'

I knew him well, so was somewhat surprised when the script hadn't arrived by midnight. Some time later, there was a knock on the door which I opened to reveal a bedraggled man in leathers and a motorcycle helmet, wet to the skin and holding the precious package. I had forgotten that a London-based courier would have difficulty finding a house in the middle of the countryside in the pitch dark. The poor man had been trying to find the place for hours and, apart from anything else, appeared rather surprised at how few people there were in the countryside in the middle of the night to ask for directions.

I sat up and read the scripts and loved Pat's edgy character, her vivacity and bitchiness, and I knew the part was for me. The telephone wires were red-hot the next morning. I called the director and let my agent know that a casting director from the BBC would be contacting him to make a formal offer and to negotiate terms.

With only a few days to spare, I tore up to London to have talks with the costume and make-up departments at Elstree Studios. Reading the scripts, I had already painted a picture in my mind of how Pat should look: brassy, plunging neckline and slingback shoes. Her heyday would have been the fifties. She would have been made up to the nines, with wonderful azure blue eyeshadow, shocking pink lipstick and THE EARRINGS which would, in time, become iconic and almost more critiqued than my performance.

Pat was, in the main, everything I am not. To play against your own personality is a joy for an actor. Pat is vulnerable, so that is probably the only quality we share. I love developing and working on a character through the text, teasing out the signposts the author has given in order to understand the character's behaviour and motivation. I based Pat on two people: a blousy shop assistant who served in a Hackney bakery, and a bus conductress I once spied on a Number 38 bus, with spiky bangs and dangly earrings. That is what actors do, they are like parasites; they create a character, feeding from the people around them as well as from their own experience. There is something exhilarating about being able to inhabit any character: a doctor, a whore, a queen – it is endless.

I am not sure whether Hugh Miller ever wrote Pat as being a smoker but when the producer, Julia Smith, asked me if I thought Pat would smoke, I replied, 'I think she would put anything in her mouth she could.' Many times there were circumstances in the action when the costume department would suggest that Pat wore trousers. I was firmly against this.

Pat was of the generation where women didn't wear trousers, especially women of her type and build. Having agreed Pat's look with the powers-that-be, my metamorphosis began with a day at the hairdresser's, trying to get my hair the right sort of hard-blonde colour needed for the character. The next day, with lines learnt and preparation done on the character herself, I was as ready as I could be to go to work.

The series I was going into had been running for fifteen months and was extremely successful and popular, attracting high viewing figures at that time. It was conceived as an ongoing drama concerning the daily lives of families and people in the East End of London. They live around Albert Square, in a fictional borough called Walford. We see their troubles and conflicts played out over time, indeed all the things that can divide a community but, when the chips are down, can also bind them.

Co-creator with Julia Smith, Tony Holland was a breed of scriptwriter that has long gone. In the early days there was a tight core of scriptwriters who had regular meetings. They sat in a smoke-filled office, around a fag-laden table over bottles of red wine and discarded coffee cups and boy were they creative! That closeness meant a continuity of storyline, a complete understanding of each character's speech pattern and idioms born of their personality and background. The writing was, in a sense, much more personal to each actor than it is now. That is because there was a permanent core of actors in *EastEnders*; there wasn't the same turnover of cast members. Neither was there the turnover of material, which eventually demanded more and more new writing blood to feed two hours of screen time; the equivalent of a movie a week. With Tony's creative imagination, the storylines were plotted far into the future. He was a past master at long-term secrets and lies, which is a courageous thing in a time of instant gratification. To keep a story running with interest over a long period can be gripping and rewarding for the audience, especially when they are the only ones privy to the secret. It creates an additional tension and deliciousness when each viewer feels they are the only person in the know. Tony first used this technique in the *'Enders* storyline with Den Watts being the father of Michelle's baby. Christmas 1986 made television history when his episode, in which Den handed divorce papers to his wife Angie, attracted over thirty million viewers. When an event was predictable, such as the 1987 General Election, he left enough room in the prerecorded episodes to include election coverage. Including such events makes the episodes seem real and up-to-date. An unforeseen event has to be edited in at very short notice. That immediacy was no better illustrated than later that year, when an additional late episode went out at half past eleven. Everybody is in the Queen Vic and, just before midnight, Den, the landlord, tells everyone to be quiet as he turns on the television to see Big Ben, in real time, sounding in the New Year. Nowadays, with a greater turnover of actors, that sort of long-term planning is possible only with a few of the regulars.

I found Julia was a martinet as a producer; she wouldn't allow any of her cast to get grand ideas above their station as mere actors. She was impatient with directors who didn't get the job done at the allotted time and to her satisfaction, without needing additional blocks of filming time. In fact there was a situation in which a director got the sack before she finished the episode and Julia took over. Conversely, when directing she took as much time as necessary. Sometimes for big episodes such as Christmas, she would have as many as three remounts (additional blocks of filming time). She was supportive of her cast in her role as director – she became one of us and would defend us to her last breath – but the moment she put on her producer's hat she once again became a martinet.

⚬❧⚬

When Pat first arrived in Albert Square, there were numerous characters whose lives and stories were part of her history. She was probably the one person in *EastEnders* who was related to, or had a family connection to, most people. Pat and Angie had been school friends so, when Pat returned after being away for some years, she stayed with her at the Queen Vic. Pat had been to school with Pete Beale, his twin sister Pauline and Den Watts, when Angie was a junior in the same school. They were all local children. Pat eventually married Pete Beale (Pauline becoming her sister-in-law) and they had two boys, David and Simon. Pat married Pete on the rebound from Frank Butcher whom she met, much earlier, at a Butlin's holiday camp. She had fallen hook, line and sinker for him but Frank was with somebody else. Despite this, she carried on having an affair with him, in the hope that he would make their liaison more permanent. When this didn't happen she went off the rails, clubbing, drinking and sleeping around, and had many a set-to with her mother-in-law Lou. She and Pete eventually divorced, he married Kathy, and they had a son, Ian. School friends Den and Angie married and took on the tenancy of the Queen Victoria public house, where Pat's son Simon now worked.

Pat's first few scenes are with Ian Beale (played by Adam Woodyatt), Den Watts (Leslie Grantham), Ethel Skinner (Gretchen Franklin) and Dot Cotton (played by June Brown, whom I already knew because we had worked together before, and got on well). Pat comes up behind Den in the market, putting her hands over his eyes and saying his name in a familiar way, 'Denny Watts?' There are drunken scenes with her old schoolmate Angie Watts (played by Anita Dobson), vicious and violent scenes with her ex-husband, Pete Beale (played by Peter Dean), and less than fond encounters with her son Simon (played by Nick Berry). Both sons, Simon and David (played by Michael French), as we learn later, are bitter towards their mother for her lack of maternal affection and selfish behaviour.

Over the three weeks Pat is in Walford, she sets the cat among the pigeons, with her drinking and talent for making trouble. Angie and Simon both want to see the back of her and both give her some money to enable her to be gone for good. Pat returns to Essex, to Brian Wicks, a man to whom she had once been married; a violent man who had knocked her about, no doubt intolerant of her inconstancy.

So that was Pat's time in The Square. It had been an enjoyable job but that's an actor's life, in one door and out the other. What an irony, that just when we think our path in life is prescribed, there is a sharp turn in the road. In the summer of 1986, I was offered a part in the BBC series *Dancers*, by director Pedr James, with whom I had worked previously. It was nice of him to remember me. I had enjoyed working with him before and it was gratifying that he wanted to cast me again. I read his script and accepted the part. Not many days later a friend of mine, who was a writer and writing for *EastEnders* at the time, telephoned me with some news which rather took me aback. Apparently, they were storylining for Pat's return to The Square but the scripts were still at an early stage. It was a compliment that the character was wanted back, but what do you do when you are privy to information you are not supposed to have, as well as being committed to another job? I needed to know the facts before deciding what I should do and asked my agent to make some discreet enquiries. If it was true that I was needed to play Pat again, and I certainly had a yen to develop the character further, then I was in a real quandary. I thought long and hard about the pros and cons of joining an ongoing production, because commitments like that can change your life. Many actors would feel that hesitation to be foolish. In an uncertain profession like ours, they would bite a hand off for such an offer, but I was the sort of actor who baulked at a commitment of more than six months. I also had some awareness of the high media profile such a programme, viewed by millions across the country, brought the actors and I wasn't sure I wanted that attention either. My ambition, small as it may seem, was to enjoy the challenge of acting roles, rather than aim for fame.

The Distant Call of Bow Bells

Strange the things you recall when reflecting on events in your life. I have just remembered meeting an elderly actor way back in the 1970s. He claimed to be a psychic and told me, to my utter amazement at the time, that a part would come along that was made for me. I would play a brazen and brash London character, who would be successful, similar to that of Elsie Tanner in *Coronation Street*. What he said stayed with me for a couple of hours, but I hadn't thought of it again . . . until now. The only claim to similarity between us is that we were both in soaps and both played larger-than-life women, but Pat Phoenix was a true sex symbol.

I hadn't signed a contract for *Dancers*, but I wasn't prepared to let Pedr James down. Besides, in those gentlemanly days, a verbal agreement was almost as binding as a written contract. I told myself, after the first sleepless night, that there was no point worrying about something that might never come to fruition and slept like a top. My agent called me up the next day to say, 'Pat's back, the BBC want you. They would like you to think it over but, as your agent, I think you should take it.' Another sleepless night!

As I thought it over, it became very clear to me that it was an opportunity I could not throw away at this stage in my career. I spoke to Pedr about his production versus *EastEnders* and he released me with his full blessing, 'Go East, young woman!' However, now that it was on the cards I really had to think long, hard and dispassionately about the implications of joining a cast whose minor, as well as major, off-screen exploits and lifestyle were daily fodder for the tabloids, seemingly more gossiped over than Hollywood in its heyday. After all, there was in the cast a convicted murderer who had served time, the odd actor who got carried away by the fame, as well as the usual array of high-octane nightlifers.

Many of the actors were taking advantage of businesses that were prepared to pay good money to people with high television profiles, to make personal appearances. These could be in shops, nightclubs, markets, restaurants or social clubs, for example, but not to be confused with the non-paid charity appearances to which one had a personal commitment. I never did much of the former, unlike some of my colleagues, who made a killing in the early days. Those were golden years before the BBC clamped down on many appearances or work outside the show. This was, perhaps, understandable, because some were abusing the system by arriving at a Monday morning's rehearsal, having flown or driven back from a gig in a far-flung part of the British Isles, tired and unprepared.

That sort of media profile had never been given to a programme before, even a long-running one such as *Coronation Street*, probably because *Corrie* was a few hundred miles away from the journalistic activity of Fleet Street. The culture of paparazzi was still in its infancy but growing fast. Most of the actors just wanted to get on with their job and their lives. Let's be honest, we are like everybody else; it's only the high profile that creates the interest. Contract artists in the old days of Hollywood had the benefit of protection from the studio bosses to maintain their godlike image to the public. Scandalous gossip was suppressed as far as possible. We were a poor relation and very unprotected then.

So it was that I, who only liked short-term contracts, said 'Yes' to *EastEnders* and landed up staying with the production for over a quarter of a century. How ironic is that?

With Mike Reid.

Chapter Eleven

Chimes of Walford

Sir, if you wish to have a just notion of the magnitude
of this city, you must not be satisfied with seeing its
great streets and squares, but must survey the
innumerable little lanes and courts. It is not in the
showy evolutions of buildings, but in the multiplicity of
human habitations which are crowded together, that
the wonderful immensity of London consists.

Samuel Johnson,
quoted in James Boswell's *Journal of a Tour to the Hebrides*

I returned as a regular cast member of *EastEnders* only a few months after my first appearance in 1986, and working at Elstree Studios created its own problems. I was living 120 miles away, so daily long-distance journeys to the studios were out of the question. Our schedule in 1986 was almost more of a nightmare then than it was when I left *EastEnders* in 2012, even though we were only doing two episodes a week at that time, rather than the current four, not including additional special-event episodes. Reluctant to move house for the sake of a job that was unlikely to last for ever, I rented a room from a friend in leafy Hampstead, only twenty minutes' drive from Elstree.

After all, Pat may have been a useful vehicle to take the story forward, but she could also have been a flash in the pan in terms of longevity.

The difficulties of living in London, in rented accommodation, and going home for thirty-six hours at the weekend soon became apparent. It was not long before Diana and I bought a house closer to Elstree, which benefited both of us workwise. Despite this, our life together was not destined to be for ever. This may well have been due, in part, to an unenviable quality I possess that can smother a close relationship. A tendency to over-care, to over-mother, to think and do for the other person, possibly making them feel inadequate at times. This, coupled with my getting very well known during the years that followed, brought pressures of its own; on health and on our relationship. This was made more difficult by my being in the spotlight with Michael Cashman, who was in *EastEnders* at the time, and many other actors and well-known people who were involved in a campaign against the Amendment to Section 28 of the Local Government Act (1988).

I will support any struggle that allows people to be equal and true to themselves, and many people who would not hitherto have been politically active were galvanised into fighting Clause 28, which they considered unjust. The Amendment barred local authorities from 'promoting' homosexuality. One of the focuses of Conservative concern was a copy of a book, *Jenny Lives with Eric and Martin*, which had been written by a Danish author, Susanna Bosche. This had been written as a teachers' guide rather than a textbook and, according to some newspapers at the time, had been found in the library of a school in a Labour-controlled Inner London Educational Authority. The Arts Council, who distributed government funds to the Arts, was very worried. Sir William Rees-Mogg, the Government's appointed Director-General, instructed legal counsel to advise him. The barrister concluded that, 'Clause 28 was a Pandora's box for mischief makers.' One of the concerns was that this Act could end up being a self-censoring piece of legislation. For example, a local authority, for fear of breaking the law and being fined, might not allow the staging of such plays as *The Killing of Sister George*, *Privates on Parade*, *Plague over England* and *Separate Tables*, or allow libraries to stock such books as *The Well of Loneliness* and *Maurice*. As it happens, Glyndebourne Touring Opera was forced to abandon a production of Benjamin Britten's *Death in Venice* for that very reason. Despite rational argument and debate, hysteria won out and what was referred to as Clause 28 became law on 24 May 1988; it was repealed in 2003.

To keep opposition to the legislation alive and to make a high-profile gesture, Ian McKellen put on a show to celebrate the works of well-known gays and lesbians. This show was directed by Richard Eyre at the Piccadilly Theatre on 5 June 1988. I was there performing a sketch with other members of the *EastEnders* cast. The theatre was full of the most eminent performers (many of whom were not gay), freely giving their support and time, firing arrows of righteousness and wielding swords of justice. It was a most amazing night.

As a consequence of our failure to prevent Section 28 passing into law, a handful of focused gay movements evolved, one of which was Stonewall, named after the Stonewall Riots in New York's Greenwich Village in 1969. It has become the largest, and many would say the most successful, lesbian, gay and bisexual rights charity in Europe. In fact, I was one of the original committee members of the movement but, later feeling increasingly out of touch with the world I was endeavouring to represent, I resigned my position.

At home things became increasingly unhappy and, ultimately, we both withdrew into our own pain. It was time to let go, for each of us to make a new life. It is a sorrow when you meet someone who has meant so much, only to realise it cannot be for ever, that you both need to reclaim your own lives. Those who have the courage to love, also need to find the courage to grieve when that love is waning. Being alone again was another great adjustment but work occupied time and the mind.

As I have already mentioned, Julia Smith had worked on *Dr Finlay's Case Book*, known in the trade as Dr Finlay's Book Case. So she based our schedule on theirs, saying, 'What is good enough for Dr Finlay is good enough for us.' This horrendous routine involved us starting our shooting-week on a Friday. We filmed all the exterior scenes beforehand, so that we knew what the weather was like. This was important for continuity with indoor scenes, filmed later. For example, if it had rained during the outside filming, when doing the interior scenes one needed to come indoors either wearing a mac, or sprayed with water to indicate the inclement weather outside. At the same time as filming, we were also rehearsing the episodes. It was quite complicated because if an actor was wanted for filming, they were grabbed from the rehearsal room and driven to the lot behind the studios to do an entirely unrelated scene and then back to rehearsals. This to-ing and fro-ing went on all day. The lot contained the entire exterior set, comprising Albert Square, the Queen Victoria pub, the homes of the characters, the market, the launderette, the cafe, Dr Legg's surgery, the car lot, Bridge Street, the allotments, the war memorial and the Dagmar – all designed so wonderfully by Keith Harris. The lot was later extended to house George Street and Walford Tube Station. The studio had open days at one time, and I always remember how surprised visitors were to find that the exterior of The Square was just a mass of frontages. 'Where do the characters go when they walk through the front door?' was their response. To which we had to explain that the interior scenes were picked up at another time, most likely on another day, inside the studio.

Due to the fact that filming had to be a priority, the rehearsal schedule sometimes went a bit awry. Those were the occasions when naughty little actors, with time on their hands, would get up to mischief. Very often the air in the green room would be blue with unrepeatable humour. After finishing in the late afternoon on Saturdays, Sundays were free, which actually meant working on the script and learning lines. One had to be 'off the book' by Monday afternoon for the producer's run-through in story-order, as well as a technical run-through in filming order. Monday morning was used to rehearse anything that had not been covered by Saturday. Notes (covering scenes, staging, performances, running time et cetera) were given to the director on Monday evenings, and rehearsals planned for Tuesdays based on these. This gave us a chance to hone performances. Wednesdays and Thursdays were studio days. In those days we started quite late, at ten in the morning on the studio floor; after costume and make-up, that is. Most of the women's make-up and costume could take an hour or so to complete but, because there were quite a lot of us to be dressed and made-up, we usually got in well before ten. The boys tried to get away with as little of this as possible, some often arriving rather close to the wire. We rehearsed on camera until lunchtime but nothing was actually filmed until the afternoon. After two hours of filming, we went back into rehearsal mode until suppertime. Following this, the remainder of the day's work was recorded until ten in the evening.

If a director was lagging behind, or a producer wanted last-minute changes, it could be a nightmare. What wasn't shot, couldn't be screened. I remember several times when five minutes were left to shoot a whole scene on the last day. On one occasion an additional scene was written for Pat and Den after the supper break. Of course we didn't have a chance to learn it, having been on set all evening. How I wished they had just told us what the scene was about, the objective of the characters and the length of it, and got us to improvise. After all, we knew our characters well enough. I suppose, however, being a very technical medium, the cameramen and the boom operators in the sound department need to follow a camera script, to know exactly what is happening at any one time. It was a very tiring routine with almost no opportunity for a social life. My great regret was that I could rarely agree to go to a theatre performance in London, or out to dinner, because we were never sure exactly when we would finish work. How I value all those friends who have not struck me from their address books but have waited over a quarter of a century for me to emerge into the real world!

During that first year, Pat is creating havoc between Pete and his wife Kathy (played by Gillian Taylforth) and the Beale matriarch Lou (played by Anna Wing), claiming Simon is not Pete's son; starting an 'is he or isn't he?' game in which Pete's brother Kenny (played by Michael Attwell) is implicated and, ultimately, even Den! It was great fun being villainous and I wondered how much hate mail I would receive or, indeed, how much antagonism I would encounter on the streets. It surprised me that this didn't occur, but it may have been due to the fact that the audience could understand this volatile and damaged creature's behaviour. I remember asking Julia, the executive producer, when I first returned to The Square, how such a destructive character could be integrated into the social structure of the Walford community. To which she replied, 'We'll peel away the layers of the onion skin and show the audience why she behaves as she does, putting up her fists before engaging her brain.'

The following year Julia and Tony decided to bring in Pat's lost love Frank; the one and only true passion of her life, the loss of whom is the basis of her rootless and disruptive behaviour. She receives a letter from Frank out of the blue asking her to meet him. The chance arises when she goes off to a darts match

in south-east London with the rest of the Queen Vic ladies'
darts team called 'Flights of Fancy'. Pat certainly has a flight of
fancy when she goes AWOL, flying as fast as her slingbacks will
take her, up the Greenwich Tunnel to meet him.

It was time to cast Frank. Tony Virgo, one of our producers,
asked me to feed in any ideas I might have for casting. That
could have been dangerous . . . I'd have chosen George
Clooney (he would have been in his mid-twenties then, but I
always wanted Pat to have a toyboy!). I was keen for Tony to
consider and meet Chris Ellison, whom many people would
have known from *The Bill*. His physique and demeanour
seemed just right for the character. After checking his schedule,
it was a no-no; he wasn't available. In the meantime Tony had
seen Mike Reid in a dramatic role on television in *Big Deal*. He
was impressed with his performance and depth of character-
isation as well as his suitability for the part and convinced me.
How right he was.

With sheer hard work and adrenaline, Mike had carved out
a successful career on stage and TV, making people laugh. The
sidestep to drama was not as gigantic as it may seem. After
all, the one thing that every good comic has is timing, an
important aspect of all performance arts. Mike was in for only
one episode and so a screen test was not deemed necessary. We
met for the first time in a hotel near the Tower of London for
a read-through. After the initial introductions, we sat around a
conference table with our scripts. Across the table I looked
at this big man, clearly quite nervous and so unlike the person
I came to know. He seemed even more stressed when we

started the read-through and, as the day wore on, I began to realise that this man was a doer rather than a reader. In time I learnt that he used to record his entire script on to a cassette and learn it audially, often in the car, something I have never been able to do.

The next day, our first scene was on the quay by the *Cutty Sark*, where Pat and Frank kiss for the first time in more than twenty years. Unchained from the table and the script, Mike came into his own. It was only when he was acting that one knew he was ideal for the part. It was quite chilly for a summer's day and we were not wearing warm clothes. Our lips met in that nervous, cold manner of strangers. Well, that's what we were, having been introduced to each other only the day before. But that is what actors do, the most personal things on the slimmest of acquaintance. Ever after, Mike, when he wasn't being even cheekier, would call me Lizard Lips. Pat and Frank go on to reminisce and sing 'their' song, the 1952 Jo Stafford number, 'You Belong to Me'.

While having lunch, he shows her a photo of his youngest child, Janine, and tells her that his wife June has died, proposing that he and Pat get together. She gets up and walks out, believing him to be like all the other men she has known, just using her. She has no intention of being a nursemaid, a washer of socks, a keeper of home.

As Mike came in to play Frank for only one episode, that might have been all we saw of the character. It was evident though, to Julia and Tony, that this partnership had legs and would work long term. In 1988, Mike accepted a longer contract. Pat and Frank finally get together, eventually taking over the tenancy of the Queen Vic. Mike and I decided that he would play the landlord as 'mine host', all bonhomie and not a lot of work, while Pat runs the pub and does the hard graft behind the bar. She even takes her responsibilities as far as going on a book-keeping course! With the knowledge that she's now at the centre of the community comes a sense of social status. This sense of belonging increases when, a year later, they travel to their wedding at the register office on a horse and cart, and she takes her first steps to respectability on all fronts.

Now, it may have been the happiest day of Pat's life, but it was one of those storylines many of the cast dread; one in which everyone is on parade virtually the whole time but, in fact, doing precious little. We shot the reception scenes in The Square over three very shrill windy days in May. Those scenes were due to be aired six weeks later, in other words in midsummer. Consequently the cast was forced to wear light summer clothing, had to sit at trestle tables that threatened to take off in the wind, and were frozen. I was lucky enough to be wearing a two-piece costume for the ceremony and so had been able to sneak a Damart vest underneath it. One is always a victim of the elements whenever filming outside. The considerate costume department held a stock of thermal undies for those occasions when our light clothing enabled them to be concealed beneath. Wendy Richard and I were frequently to be seen walking around the lot with our long johns down to our ankles, which were hastily tucked up above the skirt line whenever we were actually filming.

Gretchen Franklin, who played Ethel, was probably the warmest one at the wedding, having done an impromptu knees-up which, at the age of eighty, was nigh on miraculous. She was a game old girl but with a tongue as sharp as a razor. She didn't suffer fools gladly and wasn't over-complimentary about fans. So sick was she of receiving letters asking for a 'singed' photo that she burnt the corner of a signed photo of herself and sent it to the no doubt uncomprehending autograph hunter. She adored the little pug who played Ethel's 'little Willy' and who frequently cocked his leg against Pat's bush, just outside her house, quite rePUGnant! Gretchen always had him on her lap and in shot but, like all his breed, he snuffled and snorted, adding unexpected dialogue to scenes. As if this wasn't bad enough he smelt like a polecat, due to his somewhat overactive anal glands. As he was at a more elevated level than most dogs, one was acutely aware of the effluvium; not easy to act a scene trying to raise one's voice above the grunting and, at the same time, trying not to breathe. His condition was probably not improved by the bribes of sausage titbits handed to him regularly by Gretchen, to ensure his full attention and devotion.

Sausages, and their kind, were off the menu for me after a scene, one freezing cold February morning in 1987, in which Pat is mugged in The Square and left unconscious. I had to lie on the icy ground and wait for Willy and Roly, the standard poodle belonging to Den and Angie, to find me. In order for the dogs to be attracted to my prostrate form I had been lathered with sausage fat. Now, we all knew how much Willy loved sausages; if I thought my relationship with him was rocky before, things were truly shocking now. He was only inches away from my nose, added to which I had to remain motionless while he and Roly licked me all over. I may love animals but this was one step too far!

There are a number of suspects in this mugging, Den, Pete and son Simon, but it turns out to be the Walford Attacker – some hitherto unseen serial criminal invented to keep up the suspense of the storyline. Pat ends up in intensive care, not as you might think asphyxiated by Willy, but due to a head injury. The plan was that Pat would have some scenes in hospital with a shaved head, fully bandaged. However, the hospital set had to be constructed, lit, et cetera and what did we have? A strike! It was great for me because I sat at home by the telephone waiting for a call to summon me back to the set. The dispute, and the consequent backlog of work, meant that I was on standby for a couple of weeks.

In the meantime, Julia had asked me to go and see her. 'How do you feel about being semi-bald on camera?' she asked me. Pat would have to wear a wig when she comes out of hospital, and Julia wanted a scene in which Angie whips the wig off Pat's head in a moment of playfulness, much to Pat's embarrassment. It meant that I would be seen with half an inch of regrowth, which frightened the life out of me, but I remembered having seen a production of *Playing for Time*. In that, all the female inmates of a concentration camp have shaven heads. I found it gave the characters a profoundly touching vulnerability. I suppose, because the hair is an adornment on a woman's head, being without it makes her feel naked. It gives her a sort of defencelessness. On that strength alone, I was prepared to go for it. At that time the Beeb ran regular make-up courses in-house, which included hairdressing training. I was alarmed at the thought that my hair was to be shorn by someone who had only wielded scissors for about two weeks. Fortunately, the tutor was an eminent West End stylist and it was into his hands I was committed. Thank goodness, because I have rarely been so apprehensive, but he was quite wonderful talking me through the process as I trembled in the chair. The next hurdle was a wig for Pat, similar to one she might receive from the NHS. It was a short curly thing that didn't look too horrendous but caused great hilarity among the boys in the cast. Thereafter, Nick Berry and Tom Watt, who played Lofty, would jump out at me at inappropriate moments and shout, 'Wiggy!' After that I was known as Wiggy by many members of the cast. What naughty boys!

Wendy Richard and I were friends during our working day but never very close away from work. To some of the young actors she appeared a little grand, with a long cigarette holder and an attitude that said, 'Don't mess with me.' If you cut through that, she had a big heart but could easily take offence. For example, she would make a pot of tea in her dressing room on studio days between rehearsals and filming. She wouldn't have her favourite daily tipple, Moët, until her day's work had concluded. It was quite an honour to be asked to 'take tea' but once I wasn't able to pay court because I had an additional scene to learn, and was frozen out for the rest of the week. But while she could be antagonistic towards actors that she didn't like, or perhaps didn't rate, she and Bill Treacher (playing Arthur Fowler), despite their differences, made a truly memorable onscreen couple for eleven years.

Wendy and I certainly bonded over our love of dogs, and when her dear Cairn terrier, Shirley (named after Shirley Brahms in *Are You Being Served?*), died, I cried for her. I was so sorry that, after the death of her little dog, the BBC couldn't let her take on the ownership of Betty, the little terrier that was Pauline's onscreen pet. This was additionally poignant at a time when she was having a recurrence of the breast cancer that led to her death, in 2009. Her funeral in central London, near her home, was a sad occasion and very well attended. The thing that surprised me most was, that – instead of a grand rare-wood coffin with gold handles, she chose to be buried in an eco-friendly willow one. I realised at that point that I hadn't known her very well.

❧

It was a joy having Mike Reid as my onscreen husband. We, as characters, complemented each other physically as well as emotionally. Off-screen, there was an enormous bond of humour and respect between us. Mike and I always said it wouldn't matter if we went completely off-script, we'd just know what was needed to be said and when to say it. He was a driven man, as many comics are, with a big appetite for life. He could demonstrate stress in everyday things, equal to his largesse – a man of extremes. Sometimes I would say, 'Mike, you're going to have a heart attack if you carry on like this.' We were once stuck in a traffic jam on our way to Television Centre, in London. It wasn't the easiest journey from Elstree Studios and we had a deadline to meet. Mike was getting progressively more purple in the face, banging his head against the steering wheel. Short of pushing him out of the driver's seat and taking over myself, there was nothing I could do but endeavour to console him with calming words. It was not surprising that a year later he was the first member of the cast to have a mobile phone. At least if he was ever held up in traffic again he could telephone ahead to say he was going to be late. Telephones were hardly mobile in those days, being bigger than a house brick with an old-fashioned handset sitting on a cradle. It was very heavy, but we all gazed at it in envy. Did it make him any calmer? I doubt it.

Mike continued to do some of his stand-up shows while working on *'Enders*, and what surprised me about his act was that it did not contain swearwords or blue jokes at that time. His attitude was that it may have been offensive to women in the audience. I always found this rather amusing because his wife Shirley, like many of us in situations of stress, swore like a trooper! He was an old-fashioned gent, who stood up when women entered the room and walked on the outside of the pavement when he was in the company of a woman. However, he had to bring his act into the modern world, which was a decision made reluctantly, I suspect, although probably necessary in commercial terms.

The audience loved his ad-hoc phrases that became part of the *EastEnders* scriptwriting canon: 'What are you – some sort of pilchard? Some sort of ice cream? Some sort of doughnut?'

There were other phrases he used like 'Parking a leopard' (throwing up), 'Flat bugle' (flattening someone's nose), 'He's a wave short of an ocean' (probably when he was talking about Ricky!).

It was Christmas 1991 when I asked permission from the BBC to do a pantomime. The panto season was short, and so they gave me time off either side of my normal Christmas break. In that way I wouldn't be absent for too long. I swapped my earrings and slingbacks for a fairy dress, wand and tiara to play Good Fairy in *Robinson Crusoe* with Eric Sykes at the Congress Theatre, Eastbourne. I had been a great fan of Eric's and there was no way I was going to miss working with a comedy legend. I loved his scatty, off-the-wall humour and always watched *Sykes*, the series he did with Hattie Jacques playing his twin sister. Our friendship during that run was not, I think, based on the fact that I was physically similar to his previous co-star, more that we shared a love of malt whisky! Even years later he would see an interesting malt in a shop and send it to me. His deafness and deteriorating eyesight must have made stage-work increasingly difficult. Going into the wings, dark after the bright lights on stage, meant that he had to be guided backstage to his dressing room. Despite that, I never saw him fuss or grumble about it.

The other comedian I loved was Les Dawson, and I have always regretted not working with him. He asked me to appear in his production of *Dick Whittington* in Plymouth, but I couldn't get time off from *EastEnders* in that instance. It was his last pantomime and it was graced by Michael Aspel's appearance on stage to catch him for *This Is Your Life*. To me, watching Les Dawson or Tommy Cooper and not laughing out loud would be as impossible as eating a doughnut without licking your lips!

It's very rare for *EastEnders* to have episodes in which there is a time-jump. They are one-offs, a different style of drama, titled differently and screened independently. The first one in 1988, *Civvy Street*, was such a stand-alone. It fills in the background to some of the inhabitants of Albert Square during the Second World War, with Lou (my mother-in-law-to-be) and her close friend Ethel as young women. Dot, the other close friend, was too young during that period to be included. In 2004, I was involved in a one-off special called *Pat and Mo*. It was an hour-long story, filling in the relationship between the two characters through flashbacks to their youth, something quite novel for *'Enders*. Again, it was screened quite separately from the normal episodes and, consequently, missed by many viewers. Such a pity, because it explained a lot of reasons for Pat and Mo's behaviour towards each other. Needless to say, Laila Morse (playing Mo) and I fought to keep that history alive. The two girls who played us as young women were very well cast, Emma Cooke playing the young Pat and Lorraine Stanley playing a young Mo. It would have been impossible for us to play characters that young, especially given that Pat was Miss Butlin's when she was sixteen – she had been a looker! It transpires during the hour-long piece that Mo is married to Pat's beloved brother Jimmy. Frank is married to June and Pat is beginning to feel jealous and more and more isolated. She slowly slips into wayward and drunken behaviour which alienates her further from her brother. She feels completely ostracised, and, when Jimmy is dying of cancer she is not informed. On finding out, she thinks that Jimmy must have died hating her. However, Mo has a letter from Jimmy which she should have given to Pat, but has kept over the years. At the end of the piece Mo is on her way to deliver it to Pat, but changes her mind; a so much better ending for a continuing drama. Never close doors, then you have somewhere to go.

Laila Morse is a true Londoner, whereas I can only claim to be a distant half. As the sister of Gary Oldman, she knows all about the business. She was not trained as an actress, having got into it by playing the part of Janet in Gary's film *Nil by Mouth*, which won a BAFTA. She didn't find *EastEnders* easy at first because she was extremely nervous; the pace at which the work was covered made the pressure even greater. Her performances rely on her own natural talent and delivery, which meant she sometimes found it difficult to repeat lines and the performance endlessly, as one has to do when filming. That's where training helps because so much of an actor's work is technical. I gave her all the support and encouragement I could and she was appreciative of it. Moodle (my nickname for her) and I worked together happily and with fondness, unlike our onscreen characters.

Distant location shoots were not that common in *'Enders* either, and are possibly less common than they used to be, due to financial cutbacks. A certain percentage of the audience felt that it didn't work, seeing the characters they knew so well in the context of Albert Square on unfamiliar territory. However, we liked filming away from The Square because it gave us a chance to concentrate on a particular script and shoot in a more filmic way, using a single camera. In the studio we usually worked on a multi-camera system, which meant that there were three or four cameras filming a scene, with the shots being controlled from a separate gallery by the production team. *EastEnders* was one of the few drama series still using multi-camera. Filming in this way saved time, although it was slowly giving way to more use of the single-camera technique. When I first started in television, at the end of the sixties, the studio productions looked very flat and lacking in depth. It was a little like being in a theatre with the cameras in a static position in front; rather like an audience watching the actors performing on stage behind a proscenium arch.

One location shoot was in Paris – there were some very happy actors on the day that was announced. It was a three-strand story involving, among others, Mike and me. Pat and Frank were going to look for his daughter Diane (played by Sophie Lawrence), who had run away from home. The whole shoot started somewhat inauspiciously before we even crossed the Channel, when the actors and crew were put up in what can only be described as a dilapidated old people's home. It was redolent with the smell of cabbage and furnished with plastic chairs that had alarming slashes all over them and some worrying stains. There was, of course, a reason for us staying in this accommodation. The Beeb in its innocence had not realised that an entire crew needed somewhere to stay during the Sandwich Open golf tournament. Every hotel in the area was fully booked and so were all the restaurants. The so-called guest house offered us a supper of white fish and over-boiled cauliflower served on a white plate, somewhat reminiscent of school or hospital meals.

My make-up call was the earliest I had ever had on location, just after 4 a.m. Around 6 a.m. we all boarded a boat sailing to Calais. Not just one crossing as you might expect, but with two return trips backwards and forwards across the Channel, in order to film onboard and arrival scenes in Calais. On the outward trip, we went across to drop a cameraman off in France while the rest of the *EastEnders* team remained onboard to do more scenes on the return journey to England. Once again we didn't get off but stayed onboard to complete more scenes on our way back to Calais, where our arrival was filmed by the cameraman we had abandoned earlier that day. Going backwards and forwards had, by this time, taken most of the day and we were tired and hungry. Happy to be on terra firma at last, we discovered there was more filming to do. Then, joy of joys, we were allowed to go to our hotel, which was on the seafront, very plain but very welcome and only a short walk from a restaurant where we feasted on seafood.

The next morning, after a scintillating film shoot in a supermarket, we boarded two ancient coaches and set off for Gay Paree. Surprise, surprise, the first coach blew up on the way, smoke billowing from its rear. Everyone clambered out and waited while the driver of the stricken coach, with a lot of

Oo la las and *zut alors*, summoned a breakdown van and a replacement vehicle for us. Off we went once more to what was becoming less like Gay Paree by the minute.

As if to make up for what had been an unpromising start, the hotel La Terrasse in Montmartre, overlooking the Montmartre Cemetery, was comfortable and very nice. I had just enough time during our stay in Paris to wander around a small section of this cemetery, paying homage to the great and the good, resting in their grand and gothic tombs. During the shoot, one of the cast had a birthday and all of us, cast and crew, went to a fabulous Art Deco restaurant in Pigalle. There we had a wonderful banquet of lobster, crab, langoustine and all manner of lovely fishy things, way surpassing our Calais feast, all downed with first-class French wines. At the end of the meal each of us got ready to pay our share, only to be told that Mike had paid for all of us. It was the most generous gesture I have ever seen in a working situation.

By the time the day of our return dawned, we had been away for almost a week. However, some of us had finished work a day early and wanted to get home, only to be told that we were returning the way we had come out: by bus and boat. Apparently the Beeb had a deal with the ferry company. Mike threw a wobbly, backed up by the rest of the cast who had no more filming to do, and insisted that we flew back from Paris. Mike and I were rewarded with a sojourn on the flight deck. Those were the days when there was little need for tight security and passengers were sometimes invited to meet the captain. We stayed there for a somewhat bumpy landing at Heathrow, only to be accused of having landed the plane ourselves as we emerged from the flight deck.

It is often said that behind every comic is the spectre of tragedy, and this was never more apparent than with Mike. His life may have had its fair share of laughs but it also had more than its fair share of tragedy. While he was working on *EastEnders*, his twenty-four-year-old son, Mark, committed suicide by setting fire to himself. A few months later, his six-month-old granddaughter (one of Mark's twins) was found dead – a cot death. I can remember quite clearly sitting in the make-up chair while Mike was already on set. Jillie Sutton, our artists' liaison officer, came into the room. Her face was grey and in a shaky voice she asked where Mike was. We told her and she went into the studio to find him. Some minutes later the studio door was flung open and Mike appeared in a terrible state, almost ranting, raising his fists to heaven. 'What have I done? Why me?' he beseeched. Everybody in the room was not just speechless, but incapable of reacting, because we were not privy to what had caused his terrible grief. Perhaps it was just as well we didn't know at that stage what had happened, because what could one have said to somebody who has just lost a son and a grandchild? The only way to help was for us to be there for him, and take on with a good heart the extra work that his absence made to the schedule. There was always a sadness in Mike, the mask of tragedy alongside that of comedy.

In 1994 Mike took a break from *EastEnders*. Not only had he borne tragedy in his own life but he was portraying a deeply depressing storyline. Frank, by now a second-hand car dealer, is having a nervous breakdown on screen due to the accidental death of a young homeless man on his car lot who dies in a fire; a fire that Frank pays Phil (played by Steve McFadden) to start, in order to get some insurance money. This storyline, of a man being burnt to death, was horribly close to the events in Mike's own life. The tragedy in life and the tragedy in performance became too much, heaping ashes on ashes. How such a story was given to Mike to perform I'll never know. It was downright inhuman. I was sorry to see him go. It was sad for the show, but right for him.

At a party with Tony Caunter.

Chapter Twelve

Albert Square Dance

Life would be so much easier if one had a
copy of the script.

Anonymous

Pat is left destitute with a home and children to support and almost has a breakdown herself. Frank has gone. She realises that she has to get on with her own life. She meets another car dealer, a successful one this time, called Roy Evans, played by Tony Caunter. Roy's introduction to Pat is her storming into his office to give him a dressing-down about a faulty car he has sold David, her son. She doesn't draw breath and he is rather attracted to this ballsy woman. Flowers and the returned car, wrapped in ribbons, are the result of this altercation, but she doesn't want to know. After all, Pat is very used to men only wanting one thing. After some weeks of his persistence, she relents and has dinner with him. Their friendship develops to the point where they go on a cruise together, on the firm understanding that there is no hanky-panky. However, she's rather taken by his reluctance to have his wicked way. After all, it is a strange relief for Pat to have a friendship with a man whose sole motive isn't sex. She grows steadily fonder of him. Little does she realise that his reluctance to put their friendship on a more physical level is because he is impotent. He confesses this to Pat and, as their relationship deepens and he relaxes, her experience helps him to overcome his problem and they end up living together. But it can never be a love match; he is not Frank.

On Christmas Day, 1995, Roy and Pat are expecting Father Christmas to pop in and entertain the children. The front door bell rings and her son David answers it. Who should be there but Frank, returning to resume married life as if nothing has happened. It was good for 'Enders to have him back for a few months but not for Pat, whose life is turned upside down, once again. She is, justifiably, resentful of his abandoning her to cope. When he returns once again the following year, Pat is married to Roy; opting for a marriage of comfort, security and predictability rather than one of excitement, passion and uncertainty. Frank woos and marries the current landlady of the Queen Vic, Peggy Mitchell, played by Barbara Windsor. It created a potentially fiery quartet, giving us some dramatic story lines and, ultimately, meaning that I had a lot more work with Barbara.

Barbara joined *EastEnders* in 1994 to play Peggy, a character who had been seen in a 1991 episode played, at that point, by Jo Warne. We were all in awe of such a famous person joining our cast but she seemed, to my surprise, rather nervous. It was very endearing. Most of her initial scenes were with Steve McFadden and Ross Kemp playing her sons, Phil and Grant, leading to Peggy taking over and running the Queen Vic. As I had run the pub as Pat, Barbara was keen to get some advice about working behind the bar. For a start, the beer pumps were almost too stiff for her to move. To add insult to injury she had to jump up in order to reach the glasses, which were hanging high above the bar. I hope I gave her what help I could but only her heels could give her the height she needed!

I didn't really get to know Babs in her early years in *EastEnders*, mainly because on a series like this one tends to be working within one's own family group. Consequently, one gets to know those actors better. We did have some cracking jealousy scenes while Peggy is married to Frank and Pat to Roy. I suppose the initial ice-breaker between us was in 1999. Babs and I, along with Mike and Tony, had episodes focusing on our characters. Always a great compliment, but nerve-wracking in its challenge. Babs and I were aware of this, and spent time working on the dialogue together outside rehearsals. It is always good to work with actors who are supportive of their fellow performers and willing to spend time honing their scenes. Pat and Peggy are thrown together and, as a consequence, share some home truths. Meanwhile, Frank is saving Roy from killing himself due to his insecurity over Frank and Pat's continuing bond, which he had believed to be a thing of the past. Their jealousy and acrimony culminate in a humungous fight between Peggy and Pat: '. . . you bitch . . . you cow, you bitch . . . you cow', *ad infinitum*, with slaps interspersed with the odd flying object. It so captured the imagination of some youthful viewers that, soon after, an edited version was posted on YouTube as a rap. How about that? Two mature birds, entering into street culture – not bad, bro!

Some months later the four of us had a memorable location shoot, this time in Spain. The story was that Terry (played by Gavin Richards) and Irene (played by Roberta Taylor) had rented a villa and wanted to share it with a couple. Due to crossed wires, two married couples turn up at the airport: Frank and Peggy, Pat and Roy. It was a cracking script, lots of undercurrent, lots of comedy, a good director and six actors who knew their characters like the back of their hands and got on with the job – but it wasn't without incident. On a glorious afternoon, when we had finished filming beach sequences and had broken for lunch, the director Paul Annett choked on a fishbone and had to be rushed to hospital. It was quite scary but, despite that, we had to get on with the job. This was an episode that would have been difficult to pick up at a later date on a cold beach in Clacton. Our lovely Number One cameraman, Dave Bowden, came to the rescue. With camera script in hand, a little additional inventiveness and jokey encouragement from all concerned, he carried on filming. We were delighted with all that we had achieved under our 'new director'. Paul returned late in the afternoon, having had the fishbone removed, and promptly said, somewhat hoarsely, 'Is that all you've done?'

One evening, nearly everyone had gone to bed after dinner because of an early start. Mike, Tony and I were not working until later the next day, so thought we would make a night of it. Barbara bowed out because she had a lot of outstanding script-learning and an earlier start. The three of us trooped up to my apartment, ensconced ourselves on the balcony under a warm starry sky, the air filled with the scent of *dama de la noche*, and didn't stop laughing for five and a half hours. It was one of the funniest evenings I have ever had, just drinking, smoking and telling stories. Tony and I still talk about it now. How I wish Mike was still with us.

A couple of days later Pat and Frank revive their previous passion and end up in bed together. We were already in a state of helpless giggles at the situation. The bedroom in the location villa was tiny. Mike and I were not exactly small and the very narrow double bed hardly contained one of us, let alone two. To make matters worse, the cameraman and the boom operator ended up in the bathroom in order to get as much perspective into the bedroom as possible, the cameraman having to stand on the lavatory seat to make room for the camera and the boom operator. We were all helpless with laughter and any camera shakes on that scene were not due to the earth moving.

Still, something obviously moved for Pat and Frank – before long they're planning to run away together but Peggy finds out. She reveals their intention to everyone in the Queen Vic, culminating in her slapping both of them across the face. Babs was very nervous about doing this; like me, she hated doing onscreen slaps. These can easily be simulated, as in the previous set-to Peggy and Pat had, but in this instance, for technical reasons, we did it for real. I assured a nervous Babs to just go for it, and did she . . . mine was a very genuine reaction, I felt it. I wasn't hurt, but one of my earrings was; it flew off in the mêlée! All I could think about was that losing an earring might muck up the continuity: earring on – earring off – earring on – et cetera. Fortunately it didn't. The upshot of this public humiliation is that Pat leaves and Peggy throws Frank out.

Pat is now sitting in the pouring rain on a bench in The Square. She is torn between her love of Frank and her awareness that he will never change. He will always be a man who has the best of intentions; never a realist, but a dreamer. She's been publicly shamed, her life and the future of her marriage are in jeopardy. As Frank is leaving, he calls out to her, 'Pat, I love you,' words that she wants to hear so much but, at the same time, doesn't want to hear. She's in anguish. As he gets into the car and drives around The Square she runs out of the gate and calls his name. It is never quite clear whether Pat wants to tell him to stay or wants to say goodbye. I played it ambiguously. That was deliberate because one must remember that, for all his failings, he has always been the only man for her.

We were shooting those scenes at night and couldn't depend upon there being torrential rain, as required in the script. Consequently, we had a thirty-foot water bowser that stretched across The Square to provide us with a downpour. It was far more ferocious than natural rainfall as such effects need exaggeration on television. Very often, when it is actually raining, it doesn't always pick up on screen. It was one of those uncomfortable shoots, thankfully rare, but nevertheless memorable. Quite hideous working for several hours soaked to the skin, hair plastered to my head, chilled to the marrow in a wet woollen coat with a fur collar that looked like a dead cat –

ever after known as Pat's wet pussy by the costume department.

When the cameras weren't turning, the first assistant director forbade me to leave the set to warm up during a break in filming. To add insult to injury, even the concerned and lovely costume and make-up departments were denied access to me in order to stem the flow of cold water pouring down my neck, soaking me to my underwear. I won't mention his name, just that he was diminutive with a bombastic Nazi-like approach and an obvious dislike of actors. That was the first of two occasions, during my entire time at *EastEnders*, that I have been up to the production team and said, 'That man should not be working in a creative medium and, if he appears on the set again, you'll have to choose between him and me.' The other person was a director who, for some reason best known to himself, had to manhandle all the actors into position on set, rather like overgrown chess pieces. Now, if actors are not comprehending directions, he is failing as a director. Being manhandled all day, not knowing if one can move freely from the allotted position as part of the action or wait to be moved, is somewhat of a hindrance to the acting process. The latter did work there again but, by strange coincidence, I was never in any of the episodes he directed. Truly, I'm not a diva.

After Frank's departure, Pat's life plummets in every sense of the word. Roy will not take her back; in fact he throws her out of their house into the, still, torrential rain. Once more, she is on the streets and destitute. Always a survivor, she finds herself a

B&B in a less than salubrious area of Walford; changes her earrings, puts on her lippy and gets on surviving. As time passes she contemplates the possibility of going to live with her son, Simon, in New Zealand. He sends her the fare and she is on her way to the airport when Roy, doing the full car chase, catches up with her taxi and asks her to come back to him. She relents, despite the fact that he tells her the ground rules must change. Later, at home, he divulges that he has never liked her earrings. Upon which she takes them off and puts them in the wastepaper basket. That scene got a lot of audience attention; sack the earrings? That was comparable to axing a character. Life continues much as before but with a slightly less brash Pat. However, she knows a secret. Roy's son Barry is married to a girl called Natalie, who is having a fling with Pat's stepson, Ricky. Complicated? I should say so! As ever, Pat's loyalty is with Ricky, after all, he is Frank's son. Eventually Roy finds out and, discovering that Pat knew, he assumes that not only is her allegiance with Ricky but that she must still love Frank. He has a fatal heart attack.

The scenes showing Roy being taken into the ambulance on a stretcher were shot in a blizzard or, should I say, we attempted to shoot them in a blizzard. The problem was that the actors could hardly see each other, the cameramen could hardly see to shoot, let alone see Tony playing Roy, who was by now, in reality, almost dying of hypothermia on the stretcher. All exterior filming was halted at this point. That was a problem because, later that night, I was due to film an out-of-sequence shot for a different episode. It was a crane shot showing Pat in The Square, yet again solitary and homeless. The lead-up to her being homeless this time is due to her stepson Barry's mental breakdown following the discovery of the affair and his father's death, for which he blames Pat, calling her a whore and suchlike. Finally he throws her out of the house, as Roy has died intestate. We resumed filming by the time it was dark. It had stopped snowing, leaving a virgin carpet of white in The Square. We turned this to our advantage. I had suggested to Tim Mercier, the director, that the image of Pat's solitary footprints, marking the snow as she walks away, would be a fitting end to the episode.

Pat picks herself up once more, landing a job at the bookmaker's. She's good at that – after all, she did a book-keeping course when she and Frank got the licence for the Queen Vic and has a head for figures. Added to which she has the ability and front to handle the customers in that mainly masculine environment. She's loyal and supportive to her young boss, a minor gangster who is later murdered. To her surprise, he has left his house to her in his will. In one fell swoop she has regained stability and a roof over her head.

⁂

It is five years later when Frank comes back into Pat's life. Not to see her, but to try and get her to change a witness statement she has made for a trial that would incriminate his daughter, Janine, for murder. To Pat's surprise, she hears Frank calling her at the courthouse. As usual he has made the first move and, breaking down her defences, persuades her to have a drink and a chat. Inevitably their past and her feelings for him win out;

they spend the night together. The next day she discovers the truth: he is there for Janine rather than for her, and the silly man has even brought along a teddy bear for his grown-up daughter. Pat's worst fears are confirmed; he has used her and is, as ever, still living in cloud cuckoo land. However, the case is dropped when Pat decides to tell the truth. She withdraws her witness statement and so can no longer appear for the prosecution. The freed Janine leaves and doesn't even see her father sitting outside the court; eventually he's abandoned by both his women. He tries to make it up with Pat as she leaves, parting with, 'Take care of yourself, babe.' Pat replies, 'I'm sixty-two, I'm nobody's babe,' to which he counters, 'You'll always be mine. Right up to my last breath, and beyond.' She never sees him again.

Without the influence of Frank's presence, Pat and Peggy's relationship continues to be up and down, but is beginning to develop a warmth born of common experience and under-standing. In fact they are off on a girlie weekend when they receive news of Frank's death. Despite the recriminations that often follow such a situation, they give each other mutual support during the funeral. This storyline was written specifically because Mike Reid had died suddenly in Spain some months earlier, in July 2007. The audience would have known that a person who had played such a high-profile and loved character was dead. Of course, the last thing that anyone wanted was to offend the family. So his wife Shirley and their children were asked if they felt that a storyline encompassing the death of his character, Frank, was appropriate. For the sake of everyone, but mostly the audience, some resolution was essential, as well as the recognition of such a great character.

Mike's funeral at Great Dunmow Church some months before had been an emotional occasion, not only for his family, but for his *EastEnders* family as well. Consequently, Frank's funeral scene was a very difficult one to shoot because we were truly reflecting the reality of the actor's death. It was hard not to show our real feelings but, as actors, we had to keep it together, only recapturing the emotional reality that each character in The Square would have felt at Frank's death. Oscar Wilde had a point when he said, 'Life imitates art far more than art imitates life.'

Pat nearly misses going to Frank's funeral, not because it was intended, but because I was ill and off work for some weeks. I have for the most part lived a life free of illness, disrupted only by childhood falls, knocks, strains and misdemeanours. Throughout the autumn of 2007 I was suffering from what I thought was a frozen shoulder and, believing in alternative medicine, went to a chiropractor who strapped it up. This stiffness started to descend down my back but I optimistically believed that my impending vacation would put things right. After all, sun, sea, swimming, relaxation, a healthy regime . . . what could be better? By day five of my holiday, I knew something was very wrong. I could barely move, had no muscle tone and, as a consequence, became increasingly depressed. As the days moved on I realised that I was incapable of returning to work. In despair I called Elstree Studios and spoke to Carolyn Weinstein who handles all artists' liaison. She was wonderful as always. She instigated meetings with the production team to enable them to start rewriting upcoming scripts, allowing me to get back home for medical tests and assessments.

Upon my return from holiday, I was met by a family friend who was a doctor in Oxford. He immediately took bloods, asked questions and said, 'I'm pretty sure I know what is wrong, but the blood test will confirm it.' Thanks to him, within two hours I had that confirmation. I had polymyalgia rheumatica and temporal arteritis, an inflammatory connective tissue disorder. What a relief at last to be able to put a name to what was wrong with me. So here I was, somebody who barely took even as much as an aspirin, having to take the only drug known to alleviate the condition, steroids. Unfortunately over the years I have not been able to come off either the steroids, or the array of additional drugs necessary to prevent the bone thinning and osteoporosis that the steroids accelerate.

The management at *EastEnders* was kind enough to suggest that the episodes written for Frank's funeral could be rewritten without Pat if I wasn't up to it. Tony Jordan, the writer and producer, and John Yorke always said that Frank and Pat had the only true love story in *EastEnders*. I agree. Consequently, how could the character leave this world without his grieving love? The production team was wonderful, scheduling short filming days for me which, fortunately, didn't seem to inconvenience anyone madly. It meant we worked sensible hours on location, which was a rare occurrence. I suspect it was a bonus for everyone, except the production managers, whose budget for those episodes was probably a tad bigger than usual.

❧

After Frank's death, Pat and Peggy's relationship goes from strength to strength. One of the most bizarre scenes that Babs and I have had to play was Pat and Peggy commandeering an ice-cream van to get Heather (played by Cheryl Fergison) to hospital when she goes into labour. After parking the van in the hospital car park, Pat and Peggy discover a bottle of vodka in the freezer. By the time they have polished this off with ice cream and children's sweeties, stuffed full of hyper-inducing additives, they are pretty high. I believe that the story was originally written with drugs, rather than alcohol, in mind. I had assumed that the Beeb had cold feet over this. After all, it could have been seen to be making light of a serious subject before the watershed and I later discovered it would have impinged upon another serious storyline concerning drugs. Given the brief Babs and I had, we had to make it crazy enough to be loyal to the script, realistic yet humorous. We talked about how to play the scene. As two fairly hardened onscreen drinkers, half a bottle of vodka wasn't going to touch the sides. However, armed with the rather feeble alternative, that the sugar and additives in the sweets would exacerbate the effect of the alcohol, we decided to go for it, playing it as though we had drunk far more. Contrary to our initial fears, we had great fun with this scene. We must have got something right because the reaction from viewers was, and still is, that of sheer enjoyment at seeing two older characters retain their onscreen integrity while behaving in a foolish, funny and affectionate way. It is so rewarding when members of the audience come up and show their obvious delight in something one has done.

True to form, Pat doesn't consider retreating to a nunnery in her later life. She carries on in much the same way, having a fling with Patrick (played by Rudolph Walker). He's a man with a taste for rum, a laid-back style and a twinkle in his eye for the girls. He and Pat have had a flirty relationship for years, but now she takes it a tad further. By this time, Pat is working as an administrator in a Portakabin on the second-hand car lot, and she invites Patrick for a drink in her office. Here he finds her wearing a fur coat, ostensibly to keep out the cold. The naughty woman welcomes him by opening her fur coat to reveal that she has nothing on underneath. Patrick's eyes nearly pop out of his head, and it's not long before she has her wicked way, even in her own house on one occasion. It all ends rather nastily when his wife, Yolande (played by Angela Wynter), finds out. The affair stops, as so often in *EastEnders*, with a few face slaps. Rudy is a charmer, sweet and calm to work with, and looks quite divine in his cricket whites as himself, not in character I hasten to add. It was a delight to do the *Antiques Road Trip* with him after I left the show and to meet up again on a BBC art programme in 2014.

Back in The Square, Pat still hasn't learnt her lesson, and later has a fling with Norman Simmonds. They knew each other previously because he is Janine's uncle, always known as Half-

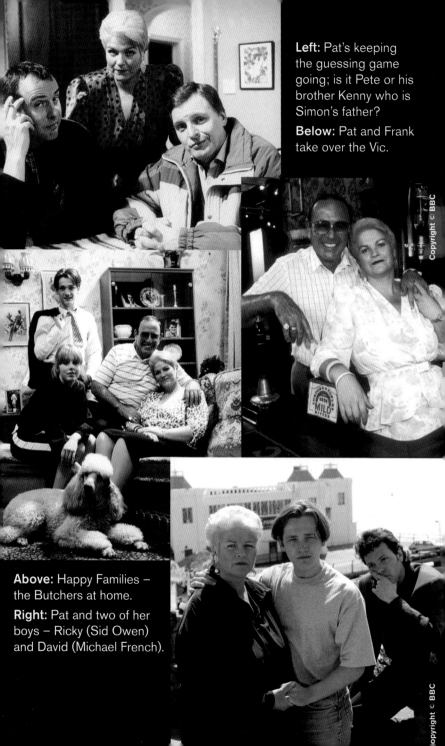

Left: Pat's keeping the guessing game going; is it Pete or his brother Kenny who is Simon's father?

Below: Pat and Frank take over the Vic.

Copyright © BBC

Above: Happy Families – the Butchers at home.

Right: Pat and two of her boys – Ricky (Sid Owen) and David (Michael French).

Copyright © BBC

Left: Pat and Peggy behaving badly in an ice-cream van!

Above: On location in Spain: Roberta Taylor, Gavin Richards, Barbara Windsor, Mike Reid, me and Tony Caunter.

Above: The Butcher family attend Frank's funeral

Left: The Jackson-Butcher clan – a very extended family.

Left: Her Majesty is introduced to an East End boozer during her visit to Elstree Studios

Below: A Stonewall meeting with Stephen Fry, Ian McKellan and Suede

© REX / Jeremy Selwyn / Evening Standard

© REX / Edward Hirst

Stone
workin lesbian

Left: A new me.
Right: Honoured to have received my honorary doctorate from Plymouth University at Exeter Cathedral.

© Ian Derry/Mirrorpix

© Chris Court/PA Archive/
Press Association Images

Above: Good Fairy – in pantomime with Eric Sykes.

Left: Tattoo of Pat on a fan's arm. Ouch, that must have hurt;

Below: Giving it my sultry all on the Christmas Party Special made by the EastEnders cast.

Clockwise from left:
Caught, and just about to be landed, by Mr Aspel; The guv'nor giving me moral support at *This Is Your Life*; With my drama tutor from Rose Bruford, Jimmy Dodding; I couldn't keep a straight face when my friend Paul O'Grady turned up as his wonderful alter ego, Lily Savage.

Opposite page, clockwise from top: Presenting a series at Whipsnade – this pygmy hippo seemed to take a shine to my familiar shape; A break for a snack after opening the new penguin pool at Whipsnade; Ideal day; *TV Times* fixed it for me to be a vet for the day, assisting the real vets at the Royal Veterinary College; A photo shoot for a dog magazine at a friend's house, where I was upstaged by her many Scotties – wonderful!

© Kindle Entertainment

© REX / Neil Genower

© REX / Ken McKay

Clockwise from top left:
Hooked on glamorous parts –
me as the villainous Mazola in
CBBC's *Leonardo*; Receiving
a lifetime achievement award
at the *Soap Awards 2012* –
and remembering not to cry
or gush on for hours; Having
a giggle with Ross Noble
and Ardal O'Hanlon on *That
Sunday Night Show*; With vet
Sean Wensley from the PDSA,
giving advice to dog and owner
during 'Pam's Problem Pets' on
This Morning.

Pint because of his stature. It is very invigorating for the regular cast to have actors coming in to play guest or recurring roles, like George Layton who played Norman. It makes such a difference if they are 'old school', as one has a bit of luvvie culture in common. In the meantime, Pat has continuing problems with Frank's daughter, Janine, and the stress of their increasing antagonism brings on a heart attack. Having been persuaded to have a pacemaker fitted she makes a full recovery.

Life at Elstree can be somewhat enclosed and it is easy to lose touch with the acting profession at large. However, tales of the business abounded when Martin Jarvis joined us for a couple of months in 2010 to play the smarmy journalist Harvey Freeman. Martin, Barbara and I had great fun playing scenes that were bordering on farce but believable, I hope. It was chaos when we filmed in Carnaby Street, the public taking pictures during shooting and coming up to speak to us. Harvey Freeman chats up both Pat and Peggy, unbeknown to each other and, when it comes to light, they join forces to humiliate him. This situation cements Peggy and Pat's friendship and so it comes as a great surprise to Pat when her best mate leaves Walford without saying anything, let alone a goodbye.

With age, Pat's personality is softened. She is not so defensive in her relationships, though she can still have a good old set-to with any of the adults who cross her. This gentler side is shown particularly in her relationships with the youngsters on screen. I always felt, in developing this side of her personality, that she is much more accepting and tolerant of youths than adults, compensating perhaps for her lack of maternal

The End of an Earring

behaviour with her sons. She is not judgemental; she's been there, done it, got the T-shirt. To be working with young children is very enjoyable but can be exhausting. For a start, one's own performance can take a back seat because it is necessary to constantly encourage them and find ways of retaining their attention at a personal level, both off the screen as well as on. More recently, of course, working with Pat's great-grandchildren on set more than made up for my not having young ones at home. In terms of keeping oneself young, and in touch with the culture of today's youth, working with them is a reward in itself. I was surprised, but always chuffed, by young fans writing in and sharing their problems with me. I even had letters from some saying they wished that Pat was their own nan.

Worries about money, her home and her sons causes a further deterioration in her health. This is exacerbated by the arrival in The Square of Derek Branning (played by Jamie Foreman), a threatening and dangerous man who has a violent history and a grudge against Pat's son David. It was interesting to play Pat being fearful of a man for a change, helped by Jamie's menacing portrayal of the character.

❧

It will be evident from everything I have said so far that being in an ongoing series is akin to being part of an extended family. Some you love, some you are not so keen on, some you find difficult to work with but, at the end of the day, it is a job of work and you have to get on with it. My onscreen family included Michael French playing David Wicks, with whom I loved working; not only is he a good actor who makes demands on himself, but he has great onscreen presence. He can also be very naughty! He is one of the few people who not only corpsed me on set, but had me in a state of something approaching hysteria. The sort of laughter that bursts out of your body at the most inappropriate moments and that you can't contain. In fact, to regain any control at all you have to leave the set. This was impossible during a party at the Fowlers' house when Michael put a bunch of watercress in the hair of one of his least favourite characters. It went unnoticed for the entire scene, apart from the two knowing miscreants who were choking with laughter. Fortunately we were just extras in that situation. With time on their hands, that is when actors can get up to mischief, which we did occasionally in the Queen Vic, particularly when Bill Treacher was on set. He was a past master at making other actors corpse, looking so innocent in the process. Fortunately his endeavours had less potentially dramatic consequences than Leonard Fenton's anecdotes. Unlike Dr Legg, the character he was playing, he was a marvellous mimic, particularly of animals, regaling us with stories and sound effects. Indeed, sometimes one would be running a scene and hear an hysterical poodle in the distance, thanks to Leonard. The greatest misfortune was that it was fatal for him to tell a funny story standing up, because as soon as he had delivered the punchline, he would fall over, presumably because of the exertion of telling the joke. So we either caught him or did our best to keep him sitting down.

The End of an Earring

I remember another memorable fit of corpsing from years ago, appropriately on the set of a Dracula film. It was directed by Peter Sasdy, famous for his Hammer Horrors. A nice enough man but jocularity was not his forte. During the latter stages of shooting, he had a sense-of-humour bypass. The principal cast, assembled on the altar steps, were about to drink the steaming blood of Dracula from the chalice when the whole lot got hysterics. Now, we all know that the more you, or somebody else, tries to repress that reaction, the worse it gets. The only way to deal with it is to let people relax, release it, and then get on with making the show. It served him right if the scene took longer to shoot.

It was thanks to Peter Sasdy, though, that I had been cast in an advertisement that was being filmed in Milan. Not only was that financially welcome and an interesting job in itself, but it turned out to be an annual event after my first advertisement won an award. This meant that for several years I pottered over to Italy, usually by train, which made for an enjoyable jaunt. I had been asked to do one of those adverts that was an ongoing story of a woman's domestic life, similar to Katie in the Oxo ads of the sixties. Now, I don't speak Italian; I had the script written phonetically so that I could mouth the words and an Italian actress could synchronise the dialogue later. After a couple of years of this routine, I was invited by a different director to see a mock-up of the new story on film, prior to shooting the advert myself. Imagine my surprise when I saw an Italian actress, who looked exactly like me, speaking (Italian of course) in a voice that had exactly the same tone as mine. Why on earth were they paying for me to come to Italy, stay at the Grand Hotel in Milan for a week to have a jolly time when they'd already made the film with a home-grown performer? Of course I said nothing.

Advertising was a blooming aspect of our work from the seventies onwards. It was also the training ground for many directors who went on to become major players in the movie industry. In those days, to be in a frequently shown advertisement could be very lucrative, as one was paid repeats every time it was screened. The pinnacle was to get a buy-out, which meant one was paid a handsome sum not to do any other advertisements during the life of that particular one. I worked with someone who had a buy-out with Kit-Kat. The biggest bonus was that it enabled him to carry on working in theatre, which was always more poorly paid compared to film and television. Any advertisements were welcome; they meant we could pay the gas bill at least. One particular advertisement where I was playing one of those much-loved ladies of the road, a traffic warden, caused great hilarity among some of my friends. They would, when they saw the ad on television, chant, 'Pam's advert . . . Pam's advert . . .' a sort of mantra to will frequent repeats for me; amusing to think that two are now successful writers, another an eminent director and the other a well-known actress.

I missed Michael French when he left *EastEnders* to do other work and was so thrilled that he came back to see Pat out. Not only because I wanted to work with him again, but because I felt it was essential for the story. Pat spends most of her last day on earth anticipating David's arrival. As her undeserving but favourite son, it is only dramatically right that she dies in his arms.

Some of the actors playing my onscreen family have been somewhat peripatetic, dropping in and out of the show for heightened dramatic interest; particularly Sid Owen, who plays Ricky, and Patsy Palmer playing Bianca. I love them both, they have a terrific onscreen relationship and have created fantastic, enduring characters and made them so wonderfully their own. They are both naughty little actors, even worse than Michael and me together. There have been moments in the past when I have been sorely tempted to nail them to the set to get them to concentrate. Maybe the end result justifies the means but, occasionally, the end has been hard won! Despite their high spirits, they are both delightful to be with and were integral to the success of *EastEnders* when they were both working on the show. Bless him, Sid called me Mummy . . . and I took my responsibilities very seriously!

Lindsey Coulson joined the cast in 1993, initially for four years, as Carol Jackson, the mother of Bianca and ex-partner of Pat's son David. It later comes to light that David is Bianca's father. The relationship between Carol and Pat is a fiery one. Pat never thought she was good enough for her son, and common to boot. There's an irony, she could almost have been a younger version of Pat! The situation gave us some gritty scenes and earthy dialogue in those early days. Lindsay has an unswerving devotion to work when she is on set but, off the set, is great fun to be with and has a wicked sense of humour. We have had some great weekends with mutual friends, filled with laughter, good food and a lot of good wine.

Tony Caunter is the sweetest gentleman one could hope to share working time with. He is a great film buff and he and Shaun Williamson, who played his son Barry, would spend any free time they had pitting their wits against each other in true *Mastermind* fashion, with film as the specialist subject. I was sometimes invited to join in, probably more from courtesy than competition because I couldn't hold a candle to either of them. So keen were they on their movies that they hatched a plan to nip round to the local cinema to catch up on the latest releases, if they had a long enough break in the afternoon. In order to be on call, in the days before the universal use of vibrating mobiles, they planned to arrange with the cinema to flash up a message on the screen telling them to return to the set. It was doomed to failure. Our schedule was always so uncertain, it was impossible for them to leave the studio for long enough. Tony and I both lived close to the studios during the working week and would meet up quite often after work to chat over Chinese meals or to go to a movie. Despite living a long way apart now, we are still in touch.

It might seem unethical that I was told informally about Tony's departure before it was announced, but it gave me a chance to argue fiercely against it. I didn't want him to go, or the character to be killed off. I felt the programme needed some solidity, which could be gained by an ongoing family unit, when so many others were breaking up. Even though it might mean that we would not always get the dramatic and exciting storylines, we would have provided a pivot around which dramas could unfold. However, the producer at the time thought my character worked best when she was pushed to the edge, left on her own at the bottom of the heap, fighting adversity. Once again, a character was killed off for the sake of a storyline when, with a little bit of thought and imagination, the door could have been left open for a possible future return. Though, as actors, we know that we always were and always will be dispensable.

As for the final adult cast member of my close *EastEnders* family, Charlie Brooks, playing Janine, was an absolute delight to work with. It was no mean feat to create a character that at one level was so evil and yet, at the other, had so much texture and dimension. She seemed to have created an onscreen personality that the audience delighted in. The viewers loved the villainy she portrayed so brilliantly and wanted to see how outrageous her next exploit would be. There was nothing pantomimic in her wickedness, she played it brilliantly, for real, with depth and belief. Off stage, Charlie has an enquiring spirit and a constant quest for knowledge, but still finds time to be a devoted mum to Kiki. The classical actress Margaret Tyzack, playing Janine's grandmother Lydia Simmonds, joined the cast for a brief spell, prior to her untimely death. She once remarked to me not only how much she enjoyed working with Charlie, but how impressed she had been that Charlie, in her free moments, had her nose buried in one of the classics. She was not the first Janine; two youngsters had played her as a child, Rebecca Michael and then Alexia Demetriou. It hardly seemed likely that these two could have had the same parentage, let alone be the same person, they looked so completely different from each other. One being very dark and the other being very fair was really stretching the imagination rather too far.

It was only when I had been in the show a while that I was to find out how fame can beguile some of the audience, who can be attracted to a character being portrayed, rather than to the person the actor really is. Despite the fact that I have never looked like a twenty-two-year-old supermodel, or portrayed one, it amuses me that I have been propositioned by both men and women, in person as well as in fan mail. Although an approach through the post is much easier to deal with! Going from the sublime to the ridiculous, I have had many proposals of marriage on the one hand, and even an offer of a 'threesome' on the other; all of which got the thumbs down! Despite being amazed, I was also somewhat tickled that American *EastEnders* addicts voted Pat Butcher as the 'woman with the most sex appeal in the show', as canvassed by BBC America. Maybe our cousins over the water felt comfortable with my plumpness!

Talking about such things reminds me of one very interesting piece of fan mail I received. During the early days of *EastEnders*, Jillie Sutton, along with other responsibilities, opened our letters to filter out any mad, dangerous or threatening post. I had a call to go and see her. 'I haven't passed this on to you before because I was worried that you might find it offensive but, on second thoughts, I know you are quite capable of dealing with it,' she said as she handed me a sheet of good-quality bond upon which, in the most beautiful copperplate writing, were the words, 'Me, every time you appear in *EastEnders*', signed 'George'. The remainder of this piece of 'art' was taken up with the traced outline of a large member, presumably his, at full mast. It goes without saying that this sort of fan mail does not elicit a response. Anyway, whatever else he had, he didn't have the balls to put an address!

What is very flattering is the other artwork that has been created to 'celebrate' the character of Pat. One student, from Central St Martin's College, submitted several small ceramic busts of Pat Butcher for finals; indeed, one of them graces my dining room. So does a small pastel drawing by the artist Josie McCoy, kindly given to me by the BBC on my leaving the programme. It is a much softer image, gentler, than the very large canvases of four Walford women she was commissioned to do by the BBC many years ago. At the time, Josie offered to do a duplicate for me. So horrified was I at the notion of taking up half a wall with my own image hung upon it, I turned down her kind offer. How foolish and how much I regret that now.

The most bizarre homage is a tattoo of Pat's face on the forearm of a fan who endured the needle for five hours. What dedication to put up with such pain. I only hope she doesn't have cause to regret it eventually; after all a picture you can burn, a ceramic you can break, but an arm – one hopes – is with you for life!

❦

Occasionally, there were not only memorable, but unexpected, moments in the working week. It was one of those bonus days when one is called in to do a little scene and is free for the rest of the day. The favourite thing was to be in work early so that, when you had finished, the rest of the day spread before you like a luxurious carpet; free time for chores, script learning of course, maybe going to the theatre, a movie or even just socialising. On a particular day, in 1995, I was called in for mid-afternoon to do a few lines with Wendy. The scene had been written only a day or so before as an additional one. I assumed it had been added to an episode that was running under the allocated time; especially as it was a piece of nonsense that took place at the far end of the market while we were looking at Hallowe'en decorations. I was struck most forcefully by Wendy's equanimity as she too had been hauled in just to do that scene. Normally, she would have been extremely critical of such a thin piece of work, as well as the parentage of everyone involved. I made my opinion plain enough but I was not getting any encouragement from her. Indeed she seemed to be twinkling and on the verge of laughter. How odd, I thought, a fleeting response that went no further. After the scene was in the can, the first assistant director called everyone over, en masse, to the Queen Vic to announce that filming would resume after a forty-five-minute supper break. That was unusual; we all knew the routine. It was weird, why weren't the cast, supporting artists, crew, costume and make-up dashing off to put their feet up or to have a bite to eat? Suddenly, over my right shoulder I heard a familiar voice say, 'Hello, ladies. Nice day for a stroll through Walford I must say. This isn't an interruption actually, because this scene was created so that I could turn up this evening to say, "*This Is Your Life*".'

I turned to see Michael Aspel and assumed that he was talking to Wendy. I didn't even wonder whether she had been 'caught' before. It became apparent while I was looking at her and smiling inanely that, in fact, the victim was me. The smile became a perplexed rictus as I battled to look cool and not the bumbling idiot I felt. How embarrassing, but I covered that with a quick quip.

Michael must have seen the panic in my eyes that read: Heathrow, Channel Tunnel, anywhere . . . just run! No such luck. It became apparent that a member of the *This Is Your Life* production team would drive me home, stay with me while I chose an outfit and accoutrements, then drive me on to Teddington Studios. Oh Lord, I was under unarmed guard! The tension built up to the point where I was flinging clothes all over the bedroom with my expletives sounding more like the opening scene of *Four Weddings and a Funeral*. They had contacted Aunt Sylvia for background history and to invite her to the recording of the show, but she had made it clear that she didn't want to collude in the invasion of my privacy. My agent and a couple of people at work had been asked for facts about my life and they too were uncertain as to whether I would like to be part of that programme. In the final event, it was a delightful evening and a great honour to be with friends, workmates, college tutors and many people from *EastEnders*. I must have had the odd tincture before going on stage because I seem to remember being completely calm and not overwhelmed by the occasion. Looking back, it was a bit like a waking dream. It seemed so odd, at the party afterwards, to be both guest of honour and host at the same time.

Only those among us who have a weight problem can understand how problematic it is, especially in a time of plenty. Grace Nichols sums it up perfectly with wit in her delightful poem 'The Fat Black Woman Goes Shopping':

> Shopping in London winter
> is a real drag for the fat black woman
> going from store to store
> in search of accommodating clothes
> and de weather so cold
> Look at the frozen thin mannequins
> fixing her with grin
> and de pretty face salesgals
> exchanging slimming glances
> thinking she don't notice
> Lord is aggravating
> Nothing soft and bright and billowing
> to flow like breezy sunlight

The End of an Earring

when she walking
The fat black woman curses in Swahili/Yoruba
and nation language under her breathing
all this journeying and journeying
The fat black woman could only conclude
that when it come to fashion
de choice is lean
Nothing much beyond size 14.

I enjoy eating, drinking and sharing those sensual pleasures. Being overweight isn't always a case of being an out-of-control glutton. Many of us ingest more than our bodies expend in today's lifestyle. My parents were not small. My father was six foot but slim and in her photograph my mother looked comely, but neither carried excess fat. In the days of their youth, between the two world wars, not only was food seasonal but less plentiful. Added to which a day's activity encompassed a considerable amount of incidental exercise; more walking to destinations, less mechanical help in the workplace and home.

Possibly a psychologist would say I ate to compensate, to take into myself something that couldn't be taken away from me, or even ate for comfort, though I have never been aware of that sort of insecurity. There's little point in speculating. All I know is that I was a bonny child, a sturdy athletic girl who grew into a buxom and eventually overweight woman. Oh, like so many of you, I have tried every diet: the High Protein, the Beverly Hills, the Cambridge – they were all fine for a quick-loss fix, fine for a beach holiday or the special occasion, but not for the long term. During the first ten years of my time in *EastEnders*, my weight ballooned. I don't like having my main meal during the working day, which meant that there was a great temptation to indulge, even reward oneself, with a big meal late in the evening; accompanied, of course, with the inevitable few glasses of alcohol, which doesn't help. Maybe I am just too indulgent but I definitely do put on weight and retain it more easily than many people.

As I've said, my weight as a child must have been a concern to the adults because I wasn't allowed Radio Malt. I was having strict school meals along with all the other children but was still plumper than nearly all of them. I had certainly not been fed too many sweets during my youth, because those were rationed. At my primary school, the Red House, we were allowed two sweets after Saturday high tea, probably only a Glacier Mint or a boiled sweet. I even had a thyroid test as a child because of my weight. It was negative.

It was time to take matters in hand, for no other reason than a middle-aged desire to have a last fling with clothes and image. I embarked on a supervised liquid food regime. During the many months it went on I avoided going out for dinner, excusing myself by saying I had a prior commitment or was working late. I would turn up in time for coffee. It was really tough and not sustainable or desirable for this regime to continue for too long. The next move was to go on to a maintenance diet, introducing solid food back, but slowly.

It was fun being skinny – well, as skinny as I will ever be. After about four years I found a good fighting weight which I thought I could maintain, even to the point of throwing out all larger clothes. Fatties out there will know what a mistake that is; we need a range of three sizes in our extra-large wardrobes. Do we come down on the side of nature or nurture? I am sure it is a combination; you can't fight your genes but you can exacerbate a predisposition to something by your behaviour.

The diet had worked for me but, alarmingly, in the early days of it, there were photographs and speculations in the press about my health, even to the point where there was a cancer rumour going around. There was no way I could let that lie because it could have been damaging to my career. After speaking to my agent, we decided that I would do an article in a newspaper to set the record straight. That's what you have to do when you're in the public eye.

Having worked so hard to lose weight some six years before, it has been disheartening to find myself putting on weight once again, this time accelerated by the medication I have to take. Moon face is a well-known side effect of steroids. Lowering the dose was possible by taking methatrexate, which completely cripples any immunity one may have, so every little snuffle can turn into a chest infection and yet more pills in the form of antibiotics. I decided to knock that drug on the head. Polymyalgia is chronic rather than terminal and, once it was under control, life continued pretty much as usual and I went back to work full time.

Lovely as fans are and much as I enjoy my work there are times when you have to take a break from being on show all the time. With actors' demanding schedules, it's essential to find time to relax. Quite apart from the health benefits, for me there's the sheer joy of planning a holiday. One minute I'm going to Antarctica, the next Rome. The choices are endless, and I've covered the globe in my mind before even setting out. The anticipation of a trip heightens the enjoyment – but nothing can surpass the adventure itself.

Zoo Chronicles: with Whipsnade's lemurs.

Chapter Thirteen

A Walk on the Wild Side

What is man without the beasts? If all the beasts were
gone, man would die from a great loneliness of the
spirit. For whatever happens to the beasts, soon
happens to man. All things are connected.

Attributed to the Native American Chief Seattle

Working on *EastEnders*, I might dream about a holiday, but
there was no point actually planning it until I had requested the
time off. This had to be done as much as a year in advance,
which is understandable. The possibility of everyone applying
for a vacation during the same period would leave the storyliner
with a grave problem. Imagine six characters having to hold the
fort for three weeks! But, once the powers-that-be had given
their approval, the holiday was sacrosanct. By and large, two to
three weeks was the time span possible to accommodate a
character's absence, although I was always concerned about
getting back a little earlier to give myself enough time to look at,
and learn, scripts.

My first long trip after joining *EastEnders* was to Kenya. My love of animals, nurtured on Aunt Sylvia's farm in Devon, and further heightened by David Attenborough's incredible and wonderful films, meant that wildlife has often been the driving force behind my choice of destination. I have returned to Africa many times, but there are other countries that attract me also. India is like no other, a riot of colour, noise and chaos with some of the most beautiful women in the world. Despite the Empire, and the commerce that has come about through globalisation, day-to-day living is still wonderfully untouched by the West in so many ways. It reaches your soul. In the twenty-eight years since I joined *EastEnders*, I have visited sixteen countries on seven continents. During those years I realised that travel enabled me to put down the burden of work and, unencumbered by the worries of everyday life, I found myself open to the wonders of the world. Sometimes I travelled with friends (the few who are adventurous travellers), but I was just as happy on my own.

From the golden moving deserts of Namibia to the flat herd plains of Kenya and Tanzania, from Zimbabwe and its wild roaring Zambesi to the land-locked plateau of Zambia, and from the Indian Ocean coast to the *vlei* of Eastern South Africa, I have breathed in the heady animal smell of Africa. My memories take me back to an equatorial sun lighting my skin with its warm glow as it sinks below the horizon, heralding the start of the predators' night-time hunt. Gradually a huge blood-red moon comes up, like a vast Chinese lantern, hanging over the savannah. I listen to the grumbling roar of lions mixed with the chuckling whoop of a hyena.

A Walk on the Wild Side

My relationship with the African bush and its wildlife started in the early 1990s in Kenya's Masai Mara. Maybe every first safari should start there, or in Tanzania's Serengeti. There is nowhere else one will see such vast herds of elephant, gazelle, wildebeest, impala and zebra in such an open space. However, the day I arrived I was ready to fly straight home. I had jumped into a Land Rover and, on that game drive, came upon a pride of lions with golden cubs, furry playful things, without the cold yellow eye of the predator that would develop later. My greatest surprise and shock was the arrival of several other vehicles full of noisy tourists shattering that moment with their own culture, as though they were sitting in front of a television programme, chewing sweets and chatting loudly. I wanted no more to do with such a circus but, coincidentally, that same day, I met Simon King who was shooting one of his *Big Cat Diary* programmes. Seeing that I was in a state of barely controlled fury, he commiserated with me but said, 'If it weren't for the tourists the entire Rift Valley would be a wheat field.' I realised then that the income from tourism was of great benefit to conservation, and I either had to put up with it or leave.

For many years I had wanted to spot a leopard, even to the point of going out on full-day excursions to their known haunts. I was envious when other people, possibly out on their very first game drive, had spotted a spotted cat! Probably the one that had so far eluded me. I was staying in a camp near Sabi Sands in South Africa run by a delightful couple. The husband, who was built like a Springbok player and most inappropriately named Bambi, told me that my leopard, my *ingwe*, was out there

281

and that, when the time was right, I would see it. I was with them for several weeks and, on one particular day, the weather was filthy. It would have been easy to ignore the five-thirty morning call, roll over in bed and miss the game drive. After all, most of the animals would be sheltering from the weather, apart from the stoic little impala, but, somehow, the lure of what could be spurs you on. So, booted and swathed in waterproofs, we headed out. Indeed we saw impala but suddenly they started pronking, a four-legged jump used in joy or alarm, also known as stotting. Clearly something was afoot. We stayed still and watched to see what was spooking them, but try as we might there was no sign of a predator. The grass was thigh-high and, as some of the herd started to edge away, we had a clue as to the direction in which to look. There it was − the tip of two furry ears, almost indistinguishable from the fronds of grass. It was my leopard! We saw her start her hunt, stalking with that catlike-grace towards the antelope, which took off in a dash for survival. There was no way we were going to race after her and influence the outcome of the chase by disturbing either predator or prey. We were visitors in their world. The ranger suggested we return in the late afternoon if the weather cleared. He said, 'If her hunt has been successful she is likely to have stashed her kill and will come back to feed before dusk.' When we returned later we found that she had indeed stored her kill up a tree, intact, but she was nowhere to be seen. We waited quietly, patiently, hoping that she would return. I don't tend to take many photographs on safari because, with a lens between you and the object you are viewing, it somehow interferes with the experience but, this time, I did. Just before dusk she approached the tree and, as she climbed a sloping branch, she turned and looked straight down into my lens with those cold, emotionless killer-eyes. Being face to face with raw nature, I had a fleeting feeling of something walking over my grave. Such a beautiful beast, an opportunistic devious hunter, in the most glorious camouflage coat of tawny colour, dappled with brown rosettes.

In Kenya I was charged by a bull hippo. The outboard engine of the small boat in which we were travelling across Lake Naivasha clogged up with water hyacinth. Water hyacinth may have been taken to Africa as a beautiful exotic plant but its unforeseen effects have been its prolific growth, clogging lakes and rivers and causing a decline in fish and other vegetation. It also provides an ideal breeding ground for mosquitoes and the snail that carries bilharzia. Altogether a most undesirable plant except that, on this occasion, it saved our lives. We were in an inlet very close to a pod of hippos when the engine suddenly spluttered and died. The bull hippo was so enraged by what he deemed to be our proximity that he charged through the water towards us at an amazing speed. To my eternal thanks, the only thing that impeded him somewhat was the thick carpet of periwinkle-blue water hyacinth. It is a terrifying sight to see a hippo exploding out of the water and charging towards you, his huge mouth wide open with water hyacinth hanging from his ferocious jaws, sporting twenty-inch canines. Even as that was happening, the engine coughed and came to life. How we were able to move faster than the hippo was a miracle, because we too were slowed down by the weed. Vegetarian he may be but, as a deeply territorial animal, when his path is crossed and he feels threatened, he will kill. Hippo are responsible for more fatalities in Africa than any other large animal.

When I was staying in a tented camp by a river in Zambia, there was a hippo who visited most nights. He would stand about a foot from where I was sleeping, outside the tent, I hasten to add, and defecate, his stumpy tail wiggling rapidly from side to side, scattering his dung. That splattering noise, and his grunting laugh, make up some of the most memorable sounds of Africa.

❧

In the Laikipia region of northern Kenya lives a tribe called the Samburu, a proud, stately and friendly people who were asked to dance for us one evening, high on a hilltop, overlooking the surrounding plains and distant mountains. The track to the summit passed through a river bed that would normally be dry in that season. However, the rains had been bad that year, causing flooding everywhere. The Samburu told us that they would keep a check on the river bed and, once it had dried out enough to walk on, they would come to fetch us. The day arrived when the river bed was deemed safe enough for the trudge up the hill for sundowners and the dancing date. Knowing that the surface was now dry we set out in high spirits, following the two tall and lean young Samburu warriors. All was going well until I almost disappeared from view. I had sunk up to my thighs in the soft mud lurking under the supposedly hard crust. Humour is universal and the Samburu thought it was terribly funny. It took a few moments before they stopped laughing long enough to fish me out of the squelching morass into which I had sunk. I felt a complete idiot and thought that, because I wasn't a Samburu, I had missed obvious signs of the terrain being weak at that point. It was very reassuring a few minutes later to see one of the young Samburu doing exactly the same thing, causing even more hilarity. Score: one all. Arriving somewhat the worse for wear, we huddled around a welcoming fire. The flames acted like a kiln, firing me like a figure in clay. The sundowners were a welcome sight as was the biltong, that chewy dried meat which some people may equate with shoe leather but, for me, is synonymous with the African bush.

The Samburu (meaning butterfly) are semi-nomadic and seemed to be closely related in culture and language to the Masai. In contrast with our bush wear, they looked magnificent in their *shukka* (red cotton skirt), wearing earrings, bracelets and necklaces made of swathes of colourful beads; their faces painted to emphasise their noble features. The Samburu had no musical instruments, using only their own voices and jangling bracelets to provide the rhythm as they danced. Some of their dances included a standing jump, somewhat reminiscent of a two-legged version of a pronking impala. Fortunately this was not one of the dances we were expected to take part in. However, had I known that the dance in which we were going to be involved was a wedding dance, I would have packed a special outfit to look my best. Somewhere among the Samburu tribe is a gorgeous twenty-six-year-old to whom I am loosely, if not technically, married.

285

The End of an Earring

The next day I moved on to another camp on camel back, which somewhat surprised me because I hadn't seen camels this far south in Africa. Having been warned that elephants can react adversely to camels and to keep vigilant, we stopped at one point to allow a lone ellie to cross our path, some distance away. The journey took a few hours and was one of the most uncomfortable I have ever made. The wooden saddle was agony and it was a few days before I could face straddling a more comfortable leather saddle to go trekking on horseback. Unlike the elephant's reaction to a camel, I did expect once on horseback that zebra and giraffe would be more at ease with something seemingly more familiar. I was amazed to find, therefore, that it was impossible to get as close on a horse as you could in a Land Rover, which by now are so familiar that they are rarely seen as a threat.

Micro-lighting over the bush in Zambia was fantastic; maybe I should be ashamed to say that. After all, I am an animal lover and conservationist and I was disturbing the natural order – but it was great. It is not a regular form of transport, and certainly not for tourism, but used as a speedy way of getting around by the locals, where a light aircraft is impractical. Taking off early in the morning, to avoid the thermal build-up during the heat of the day, I was able to spot game and the dispersal of animals. The panoramic view was incredible, some five hundred to a thousand feet over the South Luangwa River and bushland; high enough not to disturb the animals. Only the crocs slithered from their sandbanks into the barely disturbed water as I banked and came into land.

❧

Namibia is very different from the usual safari. It is an experience of place more than of the creatures that live there. One is not greeted by the smell and the call of the wild but by the Namib itself, a vast sea of sand, blown by the winds into rich patterns of seemingly textured shapes and folds. They are forever changing and re-forming themselves into some of the largest desert sand dunes in the world. As the light changes, so too does the colour of the desert, moving from light gold at dawn, through to orange, and then, as the sun goes down, the red of sunset. You stand under a blazing sun, the heat of the sand almost burning through the soles of your desert boots, wondering what on earth can live here. It is surprising how many mammals and creatures do, particularly the strange little acrobat, the Namib Desert beetle, commonly known as the fog beetle but referred to locally as the handstand beetle; probably because it stands on its forelegs to collect droplets of moisture created by the morning fogs on its undercarriage. These fogs blow in from the Atlantic coast and are the life blood of all living things in the Namib. Not surprisingly, the desert elephants travel from river gully to river gully in search of water, grasses and roots. Most of the time the rivers are dry and it is a difficult and time-consuming task to dig for water and sustenance below the sandy bed. No wonder they are smaller and seem more cranky than elephants elsewhere.

In 1998, we flew from our first base in a small light aircraft across the endless sands and over an old shipwreck, one of a number along the Skeleton Coast. The name is no coincidence;

many a ship has foundered on this dangerous coast with its treacherous crosscurrents, made worse by the dense fog. The meeting of the cold Benguela current with the warm Hadley Cell provide perfect conditions for fog. Partially buried in the sand, the rusty wreck lay a great distance from the water line. Legend has it that the vessel was used as a brothel for the miners many years ago!

It was that very fog that sent us racing back inland as it rolled towards us without warning. One minute the sky was clear, the next, a bank of dense cloud came at us like a charging animal; causing us to make a slight detour en route to Swakopmund, thence to Walvis Bay. We arrived as the fast and unpredictable fog was slowly dispersing; a little late, but still in time to meet up with a local fisherman who was taking us out to spot sea life. The Atlantic is a formidable ocean at the best of times but the temperature of the Benguela current makes it a fertile feeding ground. The sea is a dark, dark blue, mysterious with an almost frightening density. You feel as if almost anything could loom out of those waters. The first company we had on our trip was a large pod of Heaviside's dolphins. They are such sociable creatures and, amazingly, seem to enjoy human company. There is something about their playful antics that lifts the spirits. A monster from the deep did land in the boat, giving us all a hell of a shock. It was a Cape fur seal on the look out for fish. Often the fishermen have difficulty keeping the opportunistic seals out of their vessels – after all, it is so much easier to jump onboard and grab a ready-made take-away than hunt for it yourself. Slowly, like 'Curtain Up', the last remnants of fog lifted to reveal a small pod of southern right whales moving sedately through the water. What a scene. I was longing for one of them to breach, but those gentle giants decided not to perform that day. It was some years later, while climbing down a clifftop south of Walker Bay in South Africa, that I saw my first breach. No sight can quite compare with such an enormous sea mammal flipping itself out of the water, then over and . . . splat back into the sea. Strange that nobody appears to know the reason for this behaviour.

⚜

There were no turtles visible in the dark waters off the Namibian coast but, a few years later, I was privileged to help out on a marine leatherback turtle conservation project on the KwaZulu-Natal coast, in Maputaland. Turtles can hang on to their eggs if the weather is inclement but, when I was there, the weather was ideal for laying. I spent some nights on the beach with those prehistoric-looking creatures. Each stately turtle made her way slowly from the shoreline to well above the tideline. This was followed by a methodical digging with her front flippers to make a deep, safe hollow. Then, with her back flippers, she gouged out the egg cavity, which was the length of her outstretched back flipper. During the early part of this process it was essential not to disturb her, no bright torchlight or noise. When she started laying, the turtle went into something akin to a trance and it was possible, at that point, to approach her in torchlight to tag her for monitoring purposes. In the dim light surrounded by a curtain of night we watched a magical theatre of birth.

It was a long process, slow as everything is with these creatures on land. From the moment she covered the soft-shelled eggs with a three-foot layer of protective sand and left them to go back to the sea, they were threatened. There is nothing that a monitor lizard, a genet or a mongoose likes better than a turtle egg for breakfast. When the baby turtles hatch, they make a dash for the sea, many of the hatchlings being picked off by hordes of waiting ghost crabs. Braving further danger from the sky, in the form of frigate birds and other raptors, the survivors reach the ocean. No wonder each turtle's clutch is sufficient in number to allow for this loss.

It was while in this area, close to the Mozambique border in Ndumo, that I went on a birdwatching walk with a ranger through the deciduous forests and wetlands. It transpired that he had been a poacher, capturing wild birds for the exotic pet market, but had some sort of Damascene experience. A true tale of poacher turned gamekeeper. Realising that he had an affinity with the feathered creatures he had been luring into his nets by mimicking their songs, he decided to train as a ranger. A post that would allow him to work with birds which in the long run would help in their conservation. He was like the Pied Piper of Hamelin; he could call any bird to him. It was magical hearing him sing the song of a female Natal robin, and watch the male fan out his tail feathers on a nearby tree as he sang a response.

Many creatures make me smile, but the sound of a couple of them make me laugh, however many times I hear them. One is the Australian kookaburra whose laughter you have to share; the other, the persistent howl of the aptly named howler monkey greeting the Costa Rican dawn. This Central American isthmus is a place where there are earth tremors most days; I felt them. Landslides are a common occurrence; I saw them. Despite its size, it is home to the largest variety of birds and other living species, due to its many different eco-systems which form an amazing biodiversity. Ecosystems range from warm humid rainforests, deciduous forest, the fertile soil of the volcanic central area where coffee is grown and agriculture flourishes, to mountain ranges and cloud forests, some 12,500 feet high. In the hot humid rainforests, one's travel journal and Costa Rica bird-guide curl up in the humidity, binoculars steam up and clothes are permanently damp. These luscious forests, patterned with wondrous textures of vegetation, are suddenly lit up with flashes of turquoise, scarlet, yellow, bright blues and greens as birds and butterflies flit through the foliage. As for the multi-coloured toucans and frogs . . . well, if you gave a class of children their outline and asked each one to colour them in, you would get almost the same result as creation has given those creatures. Howler monkeys are brilliant alarm clocks; without fail they start their howls at four-thirty each morning. I would get up willingly, stand on my balcony and look out over the rainforest with the mists rising and the sound of those bizarre howls reverberating across the valley. No wonder I found myself starting each day with a big smile on my face.

Clambering down through the rainforest towards the shore I almost missed a sloth. It could have been mistaken for a large piece of moss hanging from a branch, except that it had this strange, slightly creepy, undefined sort of face. It was a bonus to see one because they are not that easy to spot. Unattractive as they might be, they do have rather genteel habits. Despite their name, they stir themselves once a week to come down to earth, to urinate and defecate in their own midden. It seems incongruous that their midden has a dual function in that it also serves as a sort of dating agency – it's where sloths meet a mate. Killing two birds with one stone is hardly surprising when one considers that they hang upside-down, in solitary state, clinging to the branch of a tree for the rest of the week, spending a lot of that time asleep! The sloth seemed remarkably unperturbed by spider monkeys swinging, spider-like, through the trees on their disproportionately long limbs and long prehensile tails, creating mayhem, especially when they met another troupe of monkeys. I hadn't yet seen a white-headed capuchin and, as though they had read my thoughts, I suddenly found myself being bombarded with the occasional coconut. Looking up, I saw some very pretty capuchins, with wicked little faces, hellbent on murdering me. Pretty they may have been, with their white fur, black skull caps and black gloves, looking for all the world like priests, but they did have evil, rather than good, in their eyes. I had to get out of their line of fire, but this proved quite difficult . . . not only did they move like greased lightning but their trajectory was alarmingly accurate. The only course of action, to avoid being killed by those murderous priests, was to get away from the trees fast and head back along the beach, avoiding their territory.

A Walk on the Wild Side

Now, I am not paranoid about snakes but wouldn't welcome an unexpected encounter with an aggressive species. By and large, snakes are shy and avoid human contact unless they feel trapped or threatened. The Costa Rican fer-de-lance, a member of the viper family, is deadly; its poison fatal. The death toll from them in Costa Rica is relatively high. Thank goodness the one I came upon was very sleepy and showed no inclination to take a stab at me. I was close enough to see the detail and beauty of his skin: black, light brown and terracotta, forming a symmetrical pattern, similar to a leopard's pelt. His skin could have been woven from tribal fabrics, the colours of Africa, rather than Central America. The only other close encounter I have had with a snake was picking up a rock python, fortunately not venomous, in the African bush. It was basking in the sunshine on a track in front of our vehicle and showed no inclination to get out of the way. The ranger I was with suggested that we lift it off the path, which we did. It was six feet or so of solid cylindrical muscle and, consequently, very heavy. The ranger took its head and I grabbed the lower part, conscious that I needed to let go if it showed any signs of wrapping itself around my arms and giving me a fatal hug, as a python is wont to do. All went well; we lowered it to the ground and it slithered slowly away into the bush as we drove on.

From Costa Rica's coastal rainforest I made my way up to the cloud forest in search of the elusive and exotic resplendent quetzal, a member of the trogan family. We drove along a road that had been badly damaged by a recent landslide, making driving very hazardous. The highway ran quite close to the

Cerro de la Muerte (Mountain of Death), one of the highest points of the Talamanca Range. Glancing frequently at the rosary swinging from the driver's mirror, my unspoken prayers were answered. I arrived in one piece at a delightful rustic eco-lodge set in the hillside, overlooking what could have been Alpine lowland. The slow drive enabled one to adjust a little to the altitude, which was about 9,000 feet. Pathetically, I didn't adjust completely, even after a week. The thin air made every climb an effort, causing a slight headache and nausea all the time. Strangely, this was immediately alleviated by going 1,500 feet down the mountain in search of the quetzal, although the miraculous cure might have been the sheer joy of seeing this glorious bird feeding on avocados in the cloud forest. The quetzal is a shy bird living in the canopy of the forest and, consequently, difficult to spot. However hard I try to describe him, I can't do him justice. He has a bright yellow beak and his breast is bright red with a shimmering emerald-green back and wings. His head is topped off with a feathery punk-like spiky-green crest and he sports a magnificent pair of iridescent tail feathers, about four feet long, which end in a crossed fork. Indeed, in flight, this extraordinary bird's tail feathers glisten and spiral around each other, in serpent-like fashion. There is a theory that the resplendent quetzal was the inspiration for Quetzalcoatl, the feathered serpent god of Mayan and Aztec mythology.

I returned to my eyrie in the clouds, back once again to my Shangri-la with its fast-flowing river and grassy glades. Everywhere, tiny humming birds with iridescent feathers like shot silk hovered bee-like over flowers, their long beaks seeking the nectar within.

❧

As a member of the *EastEnders* cast, I was asked by a women's magazine to do an article about my interest in exotic animals. This was something that often surprised people when I was interviewed about my involvement in wildlife charities. After all, the only wildlife that Pat was interested in took the form of animal-print clothing and her hall wallpaper! Whipsnade Wild Animal Park provided the ideal backdrop for some photos that would accompany the article. At the same time, unbeknown to me, a producer and director from a company commissioned to do a series about Whipsnade were on site doing a recce for the programme. Meanwhile, I was driving around the park's some 240 hectares with a photographer and a member of staff from the Whipsnade public-relations department, choosing suitable areas in which to take shots. A herd of stripes in the distance caught my eye. 'I didn't know you had Grévy's zebra here,' I said. She looked at me in amazement, as though I had grown stripes myself, and before I knew it, I was being introduced to the producer and the director of the planned Whipsnade series. After a long chat they alluded to the possibility of my presenting a thirteen-part series on Whipsnade for Anglia Television, later named *Zoo Chronicles* when screened on Animal Planet. The opportunity of marrying my profession to my passion was a dream come true. There was a minor hurdle to jump. I was a regular in *EastEnders* at that time, so it seemed nigh on impossible

295

to contemplate being involved in another job. How could I fit anything more into an already very demanding schedule? Meeting the Anglia producer at a later stage, she said it would be possible, within a three-month filming period, to work around my hours. Despite her offer of flexibility, I knew that it would be difficult to get permission from the BBC to do a programme for another channel, outside my contractual commitment to them. It was something I badly wanted to do, but I needed to convince the Beeb. It was thrilling when they agreed, on the strict proviso that it wouldn't interfere with my work commitment to them. Our arrangement was that at the end of each week I would let the Anglia team know what hours I was needed for 'Enders and they would work around them.

Thus, in 2000, I started a summer of dashing up and down the M1. Once I had finished work at Elstree, I'd change into jeans and wellies and reach Dunstable in about twenty-five minutes. I arrived to find a schedule waiting for me with a breakdown of activities: script for pieces to camera, a timetable of any interviews with the keepers et cetera. If I was lucky, one of the activities would be with Edmund, the vet. I was even happy to be woken at night for such exciting events as emergencies or births . . . my idea of heaven! Early in the filming, the vet realised that I wasn't going to be fearful of hands-on work but would take it in my stride. As a consequence, I had my first close and enormous encounter with a massive Indian one-horned rhino called Rupa. She had dermatitis under her armour plating (layers of hard skin) caused by damp and cold climatic conditions. The keepers, who were absolutely amazing with the animals, had trained her to be calm and still, even to lie down so that they could rub ointment on her bad patches. All went well if she was distracted by someone stroking her head and giving her carrots, and I was asked to do this part. She was sweet-tempered and gentle but, at nearly three tons, one had to be aware that something could go wrong and be prepared to jump through the bars of her enclosure, large enough for us to go through but not large enough for her. Having made sure I could fit happily through the bars, I was mighty pleased I didn't have to put this to the test.

The days on which anaesthetics (knockdowns) were admini- stered, were both tense and exciting. With the big cats there was no option but to put them out for even routine treatment. On one occasion a male cheetah needed to be checked. He had been on a course of antibiotics for an abscess, probably a fighting-wound infection, which we know well with our domestic cats. Food lured him into the indoor housing area, while a small team of us remained behind wire fencing. The vet loaded the dart gun with a light anaesthetic and, lifting it, fired a dart through the fencing, piercing that beautiful patterned fur. The cheetah became temporarily agitated but then the drug quickly took effect, and he staggered and sank down. Galvanised into action, with only about ten minutes to complete the task, we dashed to our prearranged positions and duties. I had to kneel at the cheetah's head to monitor the breathing and eye move- ment that would give us a sign of returning consciousness, allowing us a few minutes to get to safety; not that cheetahs are the most savage of the big cats but you wouldn't want to be at close quarters once he was up and running. Like all animals that have had an anaesthetic, they are a sad sight as they come round. Disorientated, they are unable to get their balance, but that passes very quickly.

The atmosphere was far more tense on days when a zebra or giraffe needed anaesthetising. Zebra, like horses, can develop rigor-like symptoms when coming round from an anaesthetic, which can lead to complications and even death. Fortunately, the only zebra knockdown I assisted with was crisis-free, but nevertheless still tense. A giraffe knockdown is in a category of its own and has a high injury and mortality rate due to their anatomy and physiology. It is, therefore, a major event when it happens. Not only does a giraffe fall from a great height on delicate legs, but its very long neck can easily be damaged in the descent. Veterinary surgeons from the Zoological Society of London and other vets specialising in exotic species were there to assist. An entire high-roofed barn was padded out with bales of straw to protect the giraffe's fragile frame and to enable the animal's neck to rest at a higher level than the body. The excitement and tension at such a rare event was palpable. I was so lucky; I had a perfect view looking down on the entire proceedings perched on the edge of the hayloft, next to the cameraman. A prone and unconscious giraffe is an awesome sight.

One particularly gloomy day, when even the penguins huddled together for comfort near their pool at the top of the Dunstable Downs, it was another bird that was the centre of attention. A vulture, a member of the display team flown for the entertainment of visitors and, more importantly, for exercise and stimulus, decided to do a runner during that afternoon's rehearsal. By the evening the bird still hadn't been found and, as darkness descended, the search was abandoned. In the gloom of the following morning, in a village in the valley, a churchwarden was walking through the churchyard. To his horror, through the early morning mist, he saw the errant vulture perching on a gravestone, staring sombrely at him! Getting over his initial shock and suspecting that the vulture must be an escapee from Whipsnade, rather than part of a Hammer House of Horror movie, he telephoned the zoo and the miscreant was recaptured.

The black rhino is an endangered species and, consequently, forms part of Whipsnade's conservation programme. They were hoping to mate a young male rhino, a recent addition to the park, with one of their established females. These two were put together at the appropriate time and left to get on with it. However, the youth was not in the least bit interested in her. He didn't even get close, viewing her from as far away as he could as he careered around the perimeter of the field, running wild as boys are wont to do. The two animals were separated for a while before a second attempt was made to tie the knot, but the same thing happened. In the absence of any action we decided to shoot some footage explaining to viewers what had been happening, or rather not happening. I was sent off to visit the recalcitrant rhinos for the first time, and while recording the piece to camera, I was aware that something was causing the keepers and cameraman some hilarity. Apparently, the young rhino, upon spotting me, had at long last developed some amorous intent, mounting the female with vigour. Clearly, his *Playboy*-like image of the perfect female being manifest in my rhino-like form!

Oh, the dangers of presenting. There was an occasion when I was interviewing the sexton of Fairford Church for a holiday programme. At the time, the American Air Force was flying bomber aircraft in the area. Now, Fairford Church has beautiful and much-admired medieval stained-glass windows. The church authorities were concerned that the vibration from the aircraft taking off and coming into land might shatter the windows. However, the sexton told me on camera that the findings concluded there was probably no more vibration from the aircraft in question than there was from the church organ. What was my response? 'You must have a very large organ!' Only as the cameraman's shoulders started to shake, along with his camera, did the horror of what I had said dawn on me. Mortified lest I had embarrassed the elderly church member (oh Lord, I've done it again), I struggled on, trying to subdue my mirth, all thoughts of churches and windows having long since vanished. It will not surprise you to learn that my one and only effort at news reportage was edited out.

Zoo Chronicles had been an incredible and enjoyable learning curve with hands-on experience, in an open environment committed to the welfare and conservation of its animals. Consequently I was thrilled to be asked to do a second series the following year, which led to me being involved in more animal programmes, and further afield. In 2001 I was in Madagascar, the island distinguished for its many unique species and lack of predators. I was on a lemur quest to be transmitted by Animal Planet. Not starting as the tourists do, with the most accessible lemur, the ringtail, I was going in search of the bamboo lemur, one of the most endangered of the species. So called because of his diet and habitat, this is probably the shyest and most elusive of them all; hence his other name, the gentle lemur. Working with animals is unpredictable and time-consuming. They don't have a copy of the script, they don't know their exits and their entrances, or what is expected of them. So filming in the wild is a matter of patience and endurance, with a dash of optimism.

We took a light aircraft, which could only just cope with our ruck-sacks and camera equipment, to Ambatondrazaka, where we stayed in a very basic and filthy hostel with no apparent tourist trade, hardly surprising as we were soon to learn. It was in fact the same place in which the great naturalist Gerald Durrell had stayed, and in which lemur stowaways he had rescued were hidden. On our first morning, we bundled into an old jeep and made for Lac Alaotra, which was the haunt of our little lemur. One of the crew spent the entire journey scratching and fidgeting; in fact he just couldn't keep still. When asked if he was all right he said he certainly wasn't, because he was infested with fleas. His condition was made worse in that most of them seemed to be attracted to his underpants. We all pitched in, offering words of solace, but it was not long before we had all had night visitors of one sort or another. We were under attack from mosquitoes and cockroaches as well as fleas, although the latter had seemingly migrated mostly to him and his undies, for which we were very grateful. Undeterred, we pressed on to the lake to meet the headman of the Malagasy village. We were there to plant reeds about fifty metres from the water's edge, as a barrier to prevent the heavy rains washing all the nutrients from their fields into the lake. It was also a symbolic commitment to raising the profile of the endangered bamboo lemur. Bamboo was the mainstay of the village economy as well as the mainstay of the lemurs' diet – both needed bamboo to survive. The problem was that all too easily lemur could be an item on the local menu, were it not for a little encouragement from the Durrell Wildlife Conservation Trust project, in the form of my guide Hassina, who looked like a gentle little lemur himself. Thanks to this dedicated man's work, a large section of marshland around the lake had been donated to the project, to ensure the future for the lemur. After the planting, the village had a celebratory dance in which we all joined. We were invited to the headman's concrete shack where we all made speeches, helped somewhat by the local brew (their version of rum) which was quite foul and probably pure alcohol. The alcohol helped as we stood around listening to an unintelligible speech from the headman. Malagasy is a difficult language to understand at any time but as we were half-pissed, his forty-minute diatribe passed by in a haze until we managed to escape and stagger out to look for our little lemur. This involved me and Hassina climbing into a hollowed-out tree trunk and taking off across the lake, both paddling like fury and heading for the first clump of bamboo.

Behind us came the film team in the luxury of a battered old rowing boat with an outboard motor while we were having to sit in our dug-out on the water hoping to spot the podgy, rodent-like lemur. For three days we went through the same routine, but nothing was sighted on the lake.

By now I was almost on speaking terms with my cockroaches and the sound man had made peace with his fleas, thanks to the wonders of Flit. We were due to leave but, undeterred, decided to give the lake one more shot at dawn. Expectant, like Mole and Ratty in Kenneth Grahame's *The Wind in the Willows*, we sat quietly in the light of the rising sun. We almost fell out of the tiny craft in our excitement at suddenly seeing a greeny-grey lemur clinging, beautifully camouflaged, to the bamboo. Nobody knows how this little creature digests and copes with the high concentration of cyanide contained in the bamboo, any more than we know how this rotund little fellow can swim.

❧

Having achieved what we came for, we packed up and left for the next location. Somewhat worryingly the local fixer was concerned that the light aircraft they had found for us wasn't suitable for carrying heavy camera equipment as well as passengers. When we drove up to the airstrip there was what can only be described as an ex-pop group's plane, waiting for us. A small battered-looking eight-seater jet sat on the airstrip. Inside, there were grubby velour curtains at the windows and faded walnut veneer with lustreless and tarnished gilt decoration.

Most of the seat belts were unusable but, what the hell, as long as it flew we were happy. After all, we were on a wildlife shoot and getting used to the conditions. The men suggested that I had a seat with my back to the engine, a gentlemanly gesture for which I was eternally grateful. I could see the sound man's face as we were taking off along the runway; he had virtually stopped breathing. When we were airborne he turned to me and said, 'Just as well you couldn't see that – we barely made the tree line as we took off.' It was a somewhat hair-raising flight as we bumped over the mountains. We could see the scarred hillsides below, looking for all the world as though they were bleeding; the result of the damaging and irreversible policy of slash and burn. Luckily we landed safely at Tamatave and lived to fight another day.

Parc Ivoloina, a rainforest reserve, was our next filming destination. The reserve abounded with many species of lemur, including the strange nocturnal aye-aye. His long middle digit is used for digging out delicious beetles, insects and other morsels from the holes he makes in the trunks and branches of trees. But it was the monogamous indri, rarely seen, whose shrieking wails almost raised the hair from my head. This mournful sound was more than made up for by seeing them sitting facing the sunrise, eyes half-closed, in an almost lotus position with palms upturned as though meditating.

From here it was overland to the dry deciduous Andajavy forest in the north-west of the island. I spent several days under canvas in a minuscule tent on the sandy forest floor, beneath trees through which Verreaux's sifaka, that delightful black, cream, gold and grey lemur, swung. From time to time they plopped down on to the additional canopy hung over the tent top, a sort of safety net for lemurs and the odd rodent. Down on the ground the sifaka became a dainty dancer, prancing balletically sideways, in a sort of *jêté* with his front legs mirroring his back legs. These are my favourite lemurs; I could watch them all day. Their extraordinary name comes from the sound of their cry, 'shif-auk'. I walked through the forest during the day accompanied by a ranger, who then suggested going out at night to see some of the nocturnal creatures. When we did, I think he was almost more surprised than I was to see a fossa, a small, dog-like creature, which climbs trees and predates on lemurs; known as The Villain in that factually misguided film cartoon for children, *Madagascar*.

It was time for a little comfort: sun, sand and sea. A small speedboat bore me, as I balanced uncomfortably on a seat of rice bags labelled 'Produce of Pakistan'. Madagascar, once self-sufficient in rice, has paddy fields but, due its slash-and-burn policy for farming and logging, now imports rice mainly from Pakistan. My destination was a couple of hours from the mainland: the island of Nosy Iranja. Plunging through the waves of the Mozambique Channel, the occasional dorsal fin appeared from time to time. I clung on to my rice bags for dear life, fearing that, at any moment, I might join the shark, all thoughts of my paradise island and Man Friday consigned for ever to the depths.

The End of an Earring

There was no jetty; we just jumped off the boat into the surf, making our way up the beach on a glorious tiny spit of sand, joined by a sandbar, a third of a mile long, to its sister-island Nosy Iranja Kelly. The latter, a small community, provided us with vegetables and chicken's eggs. It was a breeding ground for the hawksbill turtle, which weren't laying at the time. Despite that, it was a glorious few days. I swam, snorkelled and played in the surf. I did find my Man Friday, with whom I braved the teeming ocean to visit a nearby island. He was handsome and gentle, a wonderful mixture of the different races who would have visited Madagascar on the trading routes – Arabs, Africans, Indians, Malay and so many others. We hand-fed fish in the ocean, we made a fire on the beach and cooked fresh fish. I felt young and without a care on earth. That is what travel does for you.

All too soon, the real world of work called. Madagascar is served by two airlines, Madagascar Air, known as Mad Air, and Air France, sometimes referred to as Air Chance; neither names inspiring confidence. Once airborne, imagine my surprise at seeing a passenger lift a bag from the floor, place it on her knee and pull out a dog, like a rabbit out of a hat! It transpired that dogs are welcome on Air France, even long haul. Not in the hold as with other carriers, where Fifi can do her pee-pee or run riot without upsetting her fellow passengers. But then the French are a law unto themselves and much more animal-doting than we are animal-loving.

So, back I went to Walford. After all, those globe-trotting interludes were a bonus, albeit refreshing and stimulating and essential to my well-being, but it was also essential to answer Walford's call; to return once more to those familiar streets – streets that were just as potentially hazardous in their own way as the wild places I'd visited.

My last photo shoot as Pat.

Chapter Fourteen

The Bells of St Clements

Oranges and lemons, say the bells of St Clement's.
You owe me five farthings, say the bells of St Martin's.
When will you pay me? say the bells of Old Bailey.
When I grow rich, say the bells of Shoreditch.
When will that be? say the bells of Stepney.
I do not know, says the great bell of Bow . . .

Traditional English nursery rhyme

I've sometimes found myself amused by people's misconceptions about backstage life on the drama side of the entertainment industry. Sorry to disillusion those of you who think we have pampered luxurious conditions – we don't. How lovely it would be to have that, perhaps mythical, Hollywood environment, with hairdressers, beauticians and masseuses on hand. How divine to have a health club with a swimming pool on site . . . but the fact is that we are there to do a job of work and that's that. Like theatre dressing rooms the world over, the studio ones are small and fairly inhospitable. They are Portakabins, boiling in the summer and cold in the winter, but it's home for us most of the time. Indeed, I was in awe of the actors who made comfortable living areas out of them, with a few cushions and a throw.

As you would have gathered by now, working life on set has its own routine. After make-up I would go up to my dressing room to find my dressers had put the appropriate costume on the rail for my first scene. I couldn't have managed without those 'frock girls', overworked and underpaid, but always on hand to help, making the day so much easier. We invariably jumped about in episode and scene order, so could have several changes during the course of the day. Costumes were hung in running order on the rail, each one labelled. As a safeguard, I used to keep my own continuity notes for my earrings, written on my script. In due course there were probably a hundred or so pairs in my collection. They were kept in a series of small toolbox drawers fixed to my dressing room wall, each colour-coded. Another group of boxes was for specific occasions such as funerals, Christmases and weddings. I would say that a large percentage of them over the years were sent in by the viewers, to whom I owe a large debt of gratitude. This was marvellous because they were not readily available in shops. As the notes accompanying them described, they came from a variety of sources – attics, boot-fairs, second-hand shops, closing-down sales, some even from overseas and others that were hand-crafted especially for the character.

By and large Pat was sartorially colourful, always colour-coordinated in her own 'slightly off' way. This, of course, included the ear adornments. When the action was downbeat and depression was in the air, I would choose a more sombre coloured earring, a bronze, or an amber; then choose a sober outfit to go with them. For a costume that required a bit of pizzazz, diamanté was the order of the day. I must confess here that some of the diamanté earrings, made by the jeweller John Wain, I coveted and wore occasionally off-screen. I have a weakness for diamanté in the absence of diamonds! So, my faithful fans, you played a much greater part in the series than you perhaps realise. Cynics might say I got the earrings to do the acting for me. Sometimes the earrings did in fact have a starring role, such as the one that gets lost when Pat goes to bed with Frank in Spain. In her haste to dress before Peggy returns to the villa, Pat leaves an earring behind in their bedroom. Later, when Peggy has changed for dinner and is putting a shawl around her shoulders, Frank spots the errant earring stuck in the threads of her shawl and spends the next few minutes in various embraces, endeavouring to extract the telltale piece of jewellery. He succeeds and peace is restored – for the moment. People have often asked me how my ear lobes were able to support such heavy earrings. In fact most of them were quite light; the real killer was the clips. I'm tickled to think I might have had a hand in making large earrings more popular when they became retro-fashion items in the early 2000s. With regard to retro-fashion I never imagined in a million years that Pat's style would one day be mentioned in *Vogue* – but it was, much to my amusement and delight.

Getting me dressed in character was a collaborative effort. A few days before starting a new episode I would trot down to the costume department, where the wardrobe supervisor and I would choose an outfit to suit the situation and mood. If there was a big event like a wedding coming up, I would confer with the supervisor even earlier because, at such times, Pat was allowed to splash out on something decent. The costume designer or assistant would go out and buy a choice of outfits for me. These had to be right, not only for the character, but they couldn't clash with or be similar to that of any of the other characters' costumes on set. These purchases were brought back on 'appro' for me to try on. It was a credit to their ability that the outfits they brought back fitted perfectly. Pat was big in every way, so her wedding hats had to be big and showy, much to Peggy's chagrin! Standing for much of the day means that shoes can be a problem. Although my heels were never that high, even in the early days, it was uncomfortable to be in character shoes for the entire day's shoot. I was not the only one who slipped into trainers or Ugg boots on the lot, or in the studio, getting quickly back into character shoes when we were going for a take. Those days when one had a lot of scenes sitting at a table in the Queen Vic were divine – you could even wear slippers!

❧

Canteen food held no temptation. Looking at me this may surprise you. In the early days, meals were produced by cooks employed and subsidised by the Beeb, so at least it was home-cooked. However, the management, presumably to cut costs, decided that it was not their brief to subsidise their workers' food, and put the canteen contract out to tender. Initially, maybe because the new caterers had something to prove, the food was good but, over the years, it has declined considerably in quality. In a way, it is a self-fulfilling prophecy: the food gets worse so people boycott the canteen and, because of more wastage, less is on offer . . . how true is the old adage, 'speculate to accumulate'.

After the imposition of the smoking ban, most of the socialising between scenes and during meal breaks was done in the foyer. This meant that the smokers could pop out of the front door when they wanted a fag. Unlike Pat, I had stopped smoking by then. When I first devised the character, I was in a non-smoking phase, using herbal cigarettes instead. They made my throat extremely dry, rendering me practically speechless, probably because they were made of something quite foul, similar to a rolled-up lettuce leaf. Not only that, but people would come on to the set, sniff the air, and enquire which one of us was smoking wacky baccy! Tired of defending these hideous herbals, I once again took up Sir Walter Raleigh's leaf on set, I hadn't smoked for many years and didn't intend to pick it up again. When it was necessary for Pat to smoke in a scene, I would merely light a cigarette, just hold it or stub one out – whatever would give the illusion of smoking. Thank goodness I was never an addictive smoker.

The rush to fulfil work commitments in the shortest possible time sometimes led to problems. We had a situation during a freezing spell a few winters ago, when we were due to film funeral sequences a distance away from the studio. The BBC take risk assessment seriously and an assessment would have been made. The conditions were treacherous and it was potentially unsafe to work in such icy conditions. We later discovered from BBC TV Centre that an additional evaluation was undertaken by a senior member of staff who was unhappy about the planned shoot, suggesting postponement. These concerns were, I believe, disregarded by a manager and you have to wonder if that was because one eye was on the budget. What a day that was. The daytime temperature didn't rise above minus five and there was filming outside as well as in the chapel. Our only saving grace was some mobile cabins, which had been provided for us to thaw out in. It is unusual for a manager to go on location but I think I would have gone if I had made that decision and felt responsible for it. The ground was covered in sheet ice that was hastily sprinkled, on our arrival, with bags of cat litter to prevent us from slipping. Actors were supporting each other to save themselves from falling over – what an expensive accident that would have turned out to be. It is interesting to contemplate the possible outcome if the coach in which we were all travelling had crashed on the way. Where does that famous duo 'Elf and Safety' stand when a risk assessment is disregarded? As it happens, we all got on with the job with a good grace and nothing did happen . . . that time! Little did we know until lunchtime that the catering company was also having a nightmare. By all accounts the milk froze and some disaster happened to the Calor gas used for cooking lunch, resulting in our being served an inedible plate of some-thing akin to dog food – which was not the caterer's fault.

Adam Woodyatt was so horrified that he photographed the meal and put it out on Facebook or something similar, and got severely reprimanded for letting the side down!

All the risk assessment in the world, though, couldn't allow for totally unexpected danger, like the time we were filming Ricky and Bianca's wedding. This was in 1997, on location in a housing estate. The church, surrounded by its own railings, stood in the centre of a square, around which were narrow streets with two-storey maisonettes, some having good views of the church. It didn't take long before locals were renting out their first-floor rooms to paparazzi so that they could take photos of the cast drinking coffee, learning lines, having a fag. In other words, any number of uninteresting things that would eventually lead to the pay-off, the one shot of the bride and groom; the picture that would hit the press in advance of the episode.

It was a school day but, by lunchtime, word had gone round and the kids were bunking off classes, coming home in the hope of seeing people they knew off the telly. By early evening we were delayed, shooting having been interrupted by the noise of the crowd outside. It had penetrated the solid church walls and was being picked up on the soundtrack. It was dark by the time we completed the final scene, but the crowds were still outside waiting for us to emerge from the church. Understandably, it had probably been deemed unnecessary and costly to have a security company at what seemed like a secluded location. So, given this completely unexpected situation, nobody seemed to know quite what to do. We just sat in the church wondering if we were ever going to get home. It seemed perfectly obvious to the cast that the Old Bill was needed. I'm not sure if there was a reluctance to call the police, but as the situation showed no signs of abating someone eventually did. However, there were further delays while negotiations were made over the cost of an escort, and then only two members of the police force were actually sent . . . obviously all we could afford! When at last we came out of the church, it was bedlam. The police themselves were clearly surprised and shocked by the gravity of the situation, by now becoming something akin to a demonstration. They had difficulty preventing the pushing, grabbing, screaming horde of teenagers from reaching us. One by one we were filtered on to the coach to find the driver equally unnerved. Who could blame him, when youngsters were running all around the vehicle, banging on windows, despite his moving forwards slowly. In a moment which took us all by surprise, possibly in order to get away from the madness, he put his foot down and accelerated fast, just as a girl jumped in front of the coach. We screamed, shouted a warning and he swerved. It was a miracle she wasn't run over.

A number of us were angry that events had been allowed to develop in this way, culminating in nearly injuring a child. We felt that senior management should hear the facts in order to draw up some guidelines for future location shoots. Lindsey Coulson had some free time the next day and said she would act on behalf of those of us who were concerned. She spoke to the executive producer, someone we thought of as sensible and intelligent who, despite not having been on location with us, assured Lindsey that there was never any danger or cause for alarm. No discussion about the events would sway her as she replied, 'I was in Vietnam; I knew what danger was, filming in 'Nam.' Lindsey was furious. But when she came back her sense of humour won through as she reported: ''Nam? The only Nam she's ever been to is Cheltenam!'

Mind you, potential danger on the road happened quite frequently, with fans waiting at the front gates of Elstree Studios, who would dash out in front of departing actors' cars to obtain autographs. Their enthusiasm was touching but the vision of a press headline reading '*EastEnders* actress mows down teenage fan' was not. Apropos the press, they were regular, uninvited, attendees of funeral scenes at our local cemetery, a vast, open, public place almost like a park. To our amusement, in the middle of proceedings, a lens or two would be spotted poking out from bushes some hundred yards away. Members of the crew would then place themselves strategically to obstruct the view that would give away a vital clue as to who was in the coffin. Of course, the relationship between the programme and the press is a delicate balance of giving something, but not everything, away. It is akin to serving the starter but keeping the main dish as a surprise. It's necessary in order to keep the press onside, but I am not sure the balance is ever achieved that well. The bottom line is: who needs who the most?

I often worry about high-profile young actors these days who can easily be manipulated by the media, or someone who wants to exploit them. It can lead to damaging stories at a time when they are still finding out about life, themselves and how to cope with the responsibility celebrity brings. Up to a point one needs to be allowed to make mistakes when one is growing up. As for 'kiss and tell', it must be all too easy to fall into the trap of thinking that someone loves you or that you are wanted for who you are, only to find that you are the victim of a set-up merely to create a headline. Being exposed to all and sundry, when well known, is a far cry from how most of us start, poor jobbing actors longing to elevate their work profile. Not to be famous, just praying for the phone to ring with an offer of exciting work. Often we don't feel alive unless we are acting or have work in the pipeline. Feast or famine; each carries its own burden.

It surprises me that there weren't more frequent spats. That isn't to say that, with the changing mix of cast, there weren't undercurrents of competitiveness; there were. These usually came from those actors wishing to establish their place in the hierarchy. There were, of course, those who didn't play that game and focused their energy and attention on their performance. It amazes me and makes me rather proud to have been part of a production that has, over the years, engendered so much loyalty and trust from the diverse departments that contribute to it. Each one, in its own way, endeavouring to make a smooth-running working environment. It is, therefore, additionally noticeable when you get someone whose interests are not primarily concerned with the quality of the work and the happiness of the workers involved in the series. Indeed such people are company creatures looking for their own advancement. When you get a manager with an agenda of their own, who is rowing in the opposite direction, attempting to annihilate those staff seen as a threat as they row steadily upwards, it is deeply unsettling. We had such a member of staff, and I can only imagine the unhappiness caused by her bullying behaviour towards other members of staff, efficient in their work and with good communication skills. What a bitter potion is envy.

By and large the big bosses back at TV Centre, while grateful for the end result, do not always understand the loyalties to the show, the pride in the work and the effort that goes on behind the scenes, beyond the call of duty. At a time of financial austerity, that loyalty is being taxed in the extreme. Actors are also having to take a cut in salary, but it is the people who are working on the programmes, rather than appearing in them, who are most affected. They are the very ones who are needed to make good-quality programmes to keep the BBC afloat and maintain its good name. At the same time, they are asked to tighten their belts, take cuts in wages and work additional hours and, for the few who are still on the staff of the BBC, to take early redundancy. All this is in sharp contrast to a well-paid top management who, a few years ago, seemed more interested in protecting their own financial security and pension pot. Let's hope the year-on-year budget cuts don't mean a lowering of standards. Not that it needs luxurious budgets to make good productions, but goodwill can only stretch so far.

There was talk of *EastEnders* being part of the BBC move to Media City in Salford. It would have been ridiculous for an ongoing London-based series to be next door to *Coronation Street*, indeed on its very territory. Fortunately that idea was scotched. In my opinion, the whole move was a nonsense. The public broadcasting flagship should be in the capital city.

Unlike the early days of the programme's schedule, there was no longer a hard-and-fast timetable for us, and so our hours could vary from day to day; the only prerequisite being that the day was no longer than twelve hours. The twelve hours did not include learning and working on scripts, however. At least the actors were likely to have the occasional scene off. I did once have a day when I had thirty-two scenes, which was pretty tough, but long hours were even tougher on the crew. Some actors were very good at having a snooze in their dressing rooms. What a wonderful thing to be able to do, but I never could, except in extreme circumstances such as feeling below par. When I needed an energy boost I meditated; not something I do on a regular basis but I found it a most useful tool after my first visit to India. I developed this further in England, with a Krishna tutor from Bhaktivedanta Manor. The manor had been bought by George Harrison as a centre for the Hare Krishna movement, and was located close to where I was living.

EastEnders is, on average, filmed six weeks ahead of transmission. This can be problematic as the seasons change. The hours of filming in daylight, especially during the winter, are somewhat limited if there are many outside scenes to be shot. The reverse applies in the summer when it doesn't get dark until 9.45-ish. I was never aware that the scriptwriters wrote with that in mind. What I mean is that, in a six-week period, daylight can vary enormously at certain times of the year, especially when the clocks go backwards or forwards. Thus, scheduling scenes could be problematic for many reasons.

Wendy and I were once due to do a scene in which we were having a heart-to-heart about our men. Due to time constraints, the scene couldn't be done and had to be slotted in on another day. On the allotted day, the set for which it had been written was no longer available. We ended up shooting it in the playground, on the swings, in the rain. What the scene gained was poignancy, through a serious subject being discussed alongside the absurdity of two grown women doing a childlike thing. Drama, in writing and performance, is often at its best when it has counterpoint; the tears behind the laughter, the comedy that can creep into tragedy.

These conflicting emotions would be very much part of me during my final year on the show: the sorrow of the approaching loss and the excitement of a freedom to come. There would be little counterpoint in Pat's story at the very end. The final chapter of her life is, most importantly, about redemption – and what more could one hope for at the end?

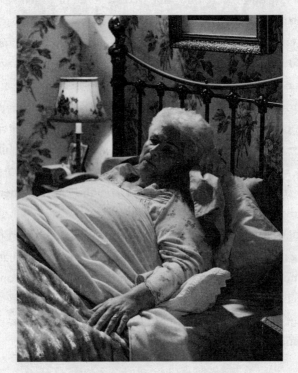
Waiting for David, to say goodbye.

Chapter Fifteen

Farewell, Dear Earrings

In this short Life
That only lasts an hour
How much – how little – is
Within our power

Emily Dickinson, 'In This Short Life'

The force with which Pat entered The Square some quarter of a century before is now a thing of the past, its energy spent. She is an ageing and, as we discover, sick woman. The issues with her son David and her stepdaughter Janine are unresolved, and the day of reckoning is approaching.

Looking hard at myself made me remember that I too was ageing alongside Pat and, like her, needed some kind of resolution, in the form of a break; leaving to find renewed energy in the hope that I might return from time to time. Without this, intuition was telling me that I might come to resent the very job I loved doing, and the gilded cage in which I was doing it. The resolution for Pat, as we know, was to lay her to rest for ever. That secret somehow stayed secret until a press release some weeks before we shot the final scenes. Of course, all storylines are secret, or supposed to be, but it felt so underhand, keeping my going from friends and colleagues. Despite my misery, though, it was important to remember that I was not the only player in this drama. Many people would be involved, but the story was the starting point and the writer the one drawing all the strands together.

The most difficult thing for a writer, who has not created a particular character in a drama series, must be to write dialogue for that individual. Sometimes a character is born of a writer's own psyche. This was never more obvious than in the writer Tony Jordan's creation of Alfie Moon, that cheeky chappie behind the bar of the Queen Vic, played by Shane Richie. Alfie is the mirror image of his creator, even down to the leather coat.

The writer Simon Ashdown is completely different. His stories are very dramatic, though often the effect is more in the breadth of the drama rather than the impact of the drama on the day-to-day nuances of each character's inner life. Although Simon had written for me in the past, I had often felt that he didn't like my character; he had never written as though he had understood Pat's soul. However, my final episodes written by him were probably the most challenging I have ever had to tackle. They were a fine tribute to the character, despite not being the ending I had hoped for.

The structure worried me. Pat has to spend the entire episode in a state of near death but be *compos mentis* enough to fulfil a dramatic role and to be reasonably active vocally. This was something I had to find a way round. Pat is dying, she is on morphine and probably unable to sustain a long conversation. Because of this, it was necessary to allow for dramatic licence. Thankfully, Simon was open to talking about ways in which we could make it work before embarking on filming. I was grateful because writers can be quite precious about their words, even suspicious of an actor's motive in wanting to tamper with them. The leap from page to stage was fulfilled by our director, Jennie Darnell, a joy to work with. She is one of that rare breed of television directors with theatre experience, whose priority is the drama unfolding between the characters. Thus, the audience is drawn into the action rather than beaten over the head by action shots.

It was necessary to have some help in portraying the last hours of someone's life. Research notes were helpful, but I felt it was essential to have a medical professional on hand for guidance. It was important to get it right. The Macmillan nurse who was on set was brilliant – encouraging but never intrusive, just giving me simple notes in a gentle way. Having been assured that the medication could be self-administered on demand at this stage, I could at last see a way to play the often long scenes. After Pat is reconciled with her stepdaughter Janine, Janine lays her head on Pat's chest. The nurse said quietly, 'Don't forget, even though you are happy to be reconciled, the weight of her head would hurt you.'

The incongruity of wearing earrings on your deathbed, as was written in the script, had me in a bit of a lather. I worried that it would look as ridiculous as Jack Nicholson's nose plaster in the film *Chinatown*, and certainly didn't want to encourage comedy. When Ricky puts the earrings on Pat, as she says, 'Your dad got me these before we got married,' I think it worked. It was a moment Sid played beautifully, both awkward and sorrowful.

One scene with Dot (played by June Brown), a farewell really, incorporated our past history with a rather bald reconciliation. June didn't like it and, due to time constraints, didn't have a chance to chat to me about changes that she had okayed with the script department and the director. I was greeted in the studio with a new scene that she had rewritten but, being an experienced actress, she had left my lines intact, I just had different cues. I must admit the scene we finally shot was well constructed and more subtle, drawn from the years of knowing our characters' relationship and the changes within it. So the acknowledgement of that often difficult relationship between Dot and Pat was in the performance, rather than in the words. June is an actress who is a stickler for perfection, which always made working with her a demanding but welcome challenge.

The last time Pat sees Mo is in the hospital before she goes home to die. Mo toddles into the ward, diffidently, asserting that she's visiting some old slapper she used to know. Their following exchange has the usual banter and backbiting. It ends with a somewhat chastened Mo saying, 'Keep yer chin up . . . all three of them.' What our characters were not able to say, we obviously felt as actors. We were sorry to part.

Throughout the episode the family and others parade into the bedroom where Pat lies dying, to make their farewells. Now, we were all feeling a little frayed to say the least. It was my farewell and Pat's farewell but I couldn't indulge in any emotion that wasn't one hundred per cent Pat's. If I had, I would have lost it completely. So, in a little cocoon of her own making, Pam protected herself while Pat suffered.

Of course the culmination of the episode has to be the arrival of Pat's son David, the one she has been longing for. Far from reconciliation, she throws recrimination after recrimination at him. Unsurprisingly he has arrived, not to make his peace but in an atmosphere of dutiful distance, harbouring his ever-present resentment of her. Even Pat telling him how much he means to her does not soften David's attitude, he's going to have his say. He's going to punish her. Inevitably he walks out, he can't cope.

The final scene, in which David returns after the ever-attentive Ricky tells the assembled family that Pat is dying, is a bittersweet reconciliation. David, at last, tells Pat he is sorry for everything, that he loves her and forgives her. He holds Pat, promising her that she isn't going to die – but she does. David, true to form, even at the last has made a promise he cannot keep.

Pat's Dying Thoughts

In the following pages I have tried to envisage Pat's final moments as her memories flit in and out of consciousness. Memories of a colourful life – wishes not yet fulfilled, chances lost, and yet interleaved with glimmers of happiness.

PATRICIA LOUISE EVANS
(BUTCHER, WICKS, BEALE NÉE HARRIS)

28 December 1942 — 1 January 2012
R. I. P.

I know I'm dying . . . I won't be having a knees-up this New Year . . .

Not like 1960 after my eighteenth birthday, when I stayed up all night seeing the New Year in at a club in the West End, with Jonnie, Vi, Dell, Ronnie and Tosh. Vi was a looker, but she couldn't compete with me that night. I was on fire. Moving like the dance floor was too hot for me to be still for a second. The boys were sweaty and fumbling, trying to be the one I would give in to. But I was enjoying being the life and soul, the main attraction. I knew I looked good – me skirt flaring out and nearly showing me all. Earrings swinging and bangles glittering in the light of the mirror-ball. Hair up in a beehive and eyelashes like two spiders on me lids. Trouble is, I wanted to be with you that night, Frank. I always did . . .

I soon will be, won't I?

The only thing helping me bear this is that I'll be seeing you again soon . . .

Oh Frank! You've got no idea how much grief you've caused me over the years when I couldn't have you for me own. The booze to blank out me pain and the men in the darkness I tried to imagine were you . . .

Look, I've got your earrings on . . . the ones you bought me before we got married . . .

I never stopped loving you . . . not for a minute . . .

Cor, you was a good lover. I wonder if they allow it in heaven . . . well, if we're still up to it, that is . . . hope so. As long as it ain't as cold as the day you come round my back door bollock-naked . . . just a spinning bow tie and a big grin. Your Old Man was so shrivelled up I couldn't hardly see it . . . Larf? I nearly wet meself!

It was awful when you died and left me . . . like part of me went with you.

Peggy was really kind. She didn't have to be. Gawd, the arguments we'd had over you, but she weren't right for you . . .

Blimey, she didn't arf give me a whack round the chops that night we was going to run off together. I would've done it, Frank, but why didn't you get it planned like you said you would . . . We wasn't kids. You can't just take off to never-never land without a home or a job, with nothing, at our age . . . You great doughnut . . . all mouth and no trousers . . . you always was.

If you could see what good mates Peggy and me have become, you wouldn't arf crack up . . .

I wouldn't want her to see me like this, weak . . . not able to give her back as good as what I got, not only when we was fighting . . . but when we was laughing.

You'd never've believed your eyes seeing us two old birds in an ice-cream van getting pissed on vodka and guzzling sweets . . . dunno what was in them sweets 'cos I can take me booze, as you know . . . just as well the Old Bill didn't turn up, we'd have been had up for being drunk in charge of an ice-cream cone . . .

Funny, I've had more real laughs as I've got older. S'pose being like a kid is easier when you don't mind so much about what people think . . .

I was so desperate to grab fun when I was a girl – couldn't get enough of it. Didn't know what I wanted, did I? Thought I had to please all the blokes around me, thought they would love me if I came across for 'em . . . or was I trying to find another you. I don't know, Frank, but all I know is it hurt me boys. Well . . . at least I kept a roof over their heads . . . we never had to go on the Social.

. . . all them boys at school buzzing round me like flies, Den and Pete was in the front of the queue . . . though Den always fancied Angie . . . even when he knew he could have a fumble with me behind the bike sheds. Ange was a great girl, she deserved a better deal than what Den gave her . . . bastard!

How the hell did I end up with Pete . . . what a pain in the arse. Sleeping with him was about as exciting as a wet Sunday fishing down the canal. Your fault that, Frank, 'cos nobody could ever compare with you . . .

What about that day at the holiday camp, when I was crowned Miss Butlin's 1958 . . . I could see your eyes, like X-rays they was, looking at me from the crowd . . . Chalet 204, where I did it with you for the first time . . . Oh yeah, I can still remember the number . . . couldn't get enough of you; never did. But you was engaged to June. S'pose I should be proud of you that you did your duty and stayed with her when she got pregnant, but when you took her up the aisle, I could have scratched her eyes out . . . if I'd been allowed anywhere near.

You and her had some good kids, though . . .

I didn't know Clare well but she seemed a nice enough girl. Diane was the fighter . . . all that trouble she had when she was young, running away . . . going to France . . . us going off to find her pregnant. Then, after all that, living with a woman! What the hell, she sorted her life out. More than Ricky's ever done, bless him . . . he's too like you, good heart but no drive. He's lovely, but not always the full ticket about life. He lets people walk all over him . . . not that you ever did . . .

It makes me sad when Ricky and Bianca ain't together. Your boy and my granddaughter, as it should be.

Janine was the bad apple . . . but you didn't help. Thought you could buy her love and not give of yourself . . . listen to me talking, as if I'd been the perfect mum. I've tried with her, Frank, but when she told me she'd killed Barry, oh . . . I know I didn't have much time for him, but murder and so proud of it. What a fool you was, sitting in that courthouse waiting for her with a teddy bear, as if she was a little girl. I loved you for your pain but hated you for trying to use me and . . . d'you know what? All I ever wanted was a daughter.

You'll be glad I've made me peace with Janine after all them years of fighting and hate. Pity it had to take me dying to do it . . . could've sworn she'd come in to gloat. All right . . . I know I can be a silly old cow . . .

No . . . not yet . . . I can't . . . I gotta hang on for David . . . there's things I need to say.

I dunno why it matters so much after the way he's treated me . . . I know I wasn't the best mum in the world but I loved me boys . . .

David's still got his life ahead of him . . . he's gotta forget the past . . . stop blaming me . . . he don't stick at nothing . . . yeah, but I didn't neither . . .

Can't think why he's me favourite boy. P'r'aps 'cos I see meself in him. He can't go on messing up his life, blaming everything on me. Not that I don't deserve a bit of bad-mouthing but he's making everything what happened to him when he was a kid, an excuse for everything now. Why does he have to try and destroy everyone around him . . .

Janine was the same and she weren't even mine . . .

He won't come . . . that's how he can punish me . . .

I wanna tell him how much I love me beautiful boy . . . he's ruining his life and hisself . . . always running and destroying . . . destroying . . . never healing . . . he's like a jealous little kid . . . not wanting anyone else to have what he ain't got. Smashing his own brother's relationship like a toy train, then walking away . . .

You men are all like babies . . . yeah, yeah, you can flex your muscles, carry hods, fight, mend cars. But you're blooming useless at mending hearts, or even understanding 'em.

Jimmy . . . Oh Jimmy, I can feel you're here and all . . . you was the loveliest brother anyone could have had . . . why didn't you get in touch with me when you was ill . . . when you got the cancer . . . I could've told you how much you meant to me . . . all them lost years.

What a picture you and Frank'll make . . . waiting for me at the Pearly Gates . . . two Pearly Kings waiting for their Pearly Queen.

David, you came . . .

Seven minutes later she dies in his arms.

Epilogue

Time for Myself

I am as young as the most beautiful wish in my heart
– and as old as all the unfulfilled longings in my life . . .

Attributed to an elderly Bushman of the Kalahari

Not to put too fine a point on it, I was drained after we had finished shooting but, by the time we got to the farewell party the next day, the post-performance adrenaline had kicked in and I felt the exhilaration that comes after doing one's best. Not that in the cold light of day that was the case, because even now I think, Why didn't I play a certain line differently?

Too late. The performance can't be changed, any more than one's life history.

There is life after *EastEnders* but it has changed a lot since that death, the death of a character I inhabited for over a quarter of a century. It was sometimes easy to resent being reminded constantly, in public, of Pat when I was creating and living with her all the time at work. It was as though she was taking over areas of my life that were not hers to have. Pam was almost being sidelined. In fairness, some of this could be due to the similarity of the names Pat and Pam and consequent confusion. Whatever the reason, I don't feel that pressure now and can think of her objectively, even fondly. More so because of the wonderful response I still receive, even now, from people who say how much they miss her. I can't thank them enough.

I had deliberately avoided returning to the place that my character inhabited and in which I had worked, despite invitations and requests to do so. I feared being the spectre at the feast, the person who has gone but won't stay away. Of course, I am still in touch with those I worked with and whom I consider to be close friends. On one occasion I was meeting a friend for lunch in Elstree. Without my knowledge, she had mentioned to the executive producer that she was meeting me. His immediate response was to get her to make sure that I went to the studios to meet up with him; rescheduling his meetings for that afternoon. I obeyed the summons with some trepidation but was made so welcome that I didn't feel alien with the passing of time, as I had expected. I was not a stranger; it was like returning to a place in which one has lived happily, to find it hasn't changed and, despite the passage of time, doesn't reject you as a thing of the past. How often in life one anticipates events, dreads them even, only to find that the feeling is unfounded and it's nothing in the doing. I popped over to Stage 1, the home of the Queen Vic, as well as the make-up and costume departments. While I was having a chat and a cuppa with the frock girls, one of Pat's earrings was produced from a drawer. Strangely, it was waiting to be mended for some unaccountable reason. A collection of the better-known ear adornments is in an archive box, under the guardianship of the costume department. It's almost as though they were are awaiting a call to be exhibited in an *EastEnders* section of a future media museum.

The greater the distance from my Elstree years, the more I realise how much I have to thank the people with whom I worked. In hindsight, it is a miracle that, at its best, we were a team all pulling together in a creative environment. At its worst, it could be chaotic, stressful and, on rare occasions even divided but, whatever else, we were like a family.

A major change has been taking control of my life again. I vowed when I left *'Enders* that I wouldn't commit myself immediately to work that tied me down long term and dictated my daily timetable. I still wanted to work, I was on a high but, to be completely honest, I don't think I realised quite how deeply those years had drained me physically. With a little sense I should have had a complete break somewhere warm, somewhere stimulating and yet relaxing, for a few months. Well, I certainly went somewhere warm when I was asked to appear in a BBC series for youngsters called *Leonardo*. It was to be filmed in South Africa. It is rare that a portly, soft-featured actress is cast as a villain; that was a temptation too far. Off I went, to be clothed in fifteenth-century robes, with dreadlocks, blackened teeth and a somewhat demure gypsy hoop in one ear – you never had one of those, Mrs Butcher!

Before going off to play a baddy in *Leonardo*, I joined the team at *This Morning* as a regular to do the animal advice slot *Pam's Problem Pets*. What a joy that was, working with such a super team as well as with animals. It also opened up the opportunity to do other items on the programme.

Between periods of travel I was popping into *Loose Women*, and taking in that *Antiques Road Trip* with Rudolph Walker. It was great fun being with Rudy again, and so was the red kite item I did for *The One Show*. I flew in a tiny helicopter over the Chilterns while we swooped and rode the same thermals as the birds. To add to new and informative experiences, I made a film for Hearing Dogs for Deaf People, one of my special charities, in which I was deaf for a day. With the aid of ear moulds, implanted by an ear specialist, I tried functioning in everyday life. What a learning curve that was. It affects everything. Most people take their senses for granted but lose one and you easily lose confidence. I didn't know how to pitch my own voice, whether I was shouting or speaking too quietly. I couldn't hear anything people said and tried to lip read. Crossing the road was a nightmare, as was walking down the street because I had lost all sense of spatial relationships; I couldn't hear where people were in relation to me. It was a very isolating experience but, because of my long-term work with the charity, I know that the dogs not only become a deaf person's constant companion, they stimulate social interaction and give a deaf person confidence by alerting them to various dangers.

It is as though, throughout my working life, not a day would pass when I didn't feel a need to be in work; theatre, television or film. If I wasn't acting, clothing myself in the role of another, I didn't feel complete. Now, suddenly, I am delighted when performing roles are offered but don't live every day with an all-consuming need to be someone else, much as I welcome any interesting roles that may be round the corner.

Having a less demanding work schedule has meant that I have more time for the charities, both animal and human, to whom I have a long-standing commitment. In 2014, with the anniversary of the start of the First World War and the D-Day Landings, it was particularly rewarding to be an active supporter of several forces charities.

⁂

I had no intention of writing an autobiography but, after several approaches and words of encouragement, I started it in the calm atmosphere of Forest Mere health resort. Ironically, and quite coincidentally, I found myself back there writing these last few lines. It is an ideal place for quiet and introspection, with only oneself to think about and I owe them a debt of gratitude. Writing this book has been a time of reflection. Strangely it has not been unduly cathartic but more of an analysis of what seemed to be random and disordered elements that made up my past. Once these were laid before me, I could see them for what they were, no longer random once they were sewn together to form the patchwork of my life. It has more than anything left me with a great sense of thankfulness for a good life that has outweighed a potentially bad one.

I now live in the countryside where early morning visitors are likely to be deer, not always very welcome in the garden where they happily nibble my flowers, as do the rabbits. The cock pheasant announces his presence very loudly, hoping for a handful of grain, and then troops across the lawn with two or three of his wives. The catlike cries of the buzzards overhead and the bleat of lambs in spring remind me of Dartmoor. The birdsong from the woods is my summer symphony and so the nature lover in me is constantly being stimulated. Like the Seven Ages of Man, the wheel is coming full circle for me in the autumn of my life.

Acknowledgements

My gratitude and thanks to everyone who has made my life a journey of delight, particularly to Sylvia and Molly and to all those I love, especially the young who keep me from becoming a grumpy old woman: Rona, James, Birdy, Rosie and Florence.

A big thank you to all those I have worked with over the years and, most particularly, to all those at *EastEnders* with whom I have spent so much of my life.

Also thanks to Julie and Verran for all their help and encouragement; to Stephen and Dorothy Purdew for their kindness; and Emma Tait, who has been a pleasure to work with.

Index

Index

Index

Index